TURNING JAPANESE

TURNING

JAPANESE

Memoirs of a Sansei

DAVID MURA

Atlantic Monthly Press

Published simultaneously in Canada
Printed in the United States of America
First edition

Library of Congress
Cataloging-in-Publication Data

Mura, David.
Turning Japanese : memoirs of a sansei
/ David Mura.—1st ed.

1. Mura, David—Journeys—Japan.
2. Japanese Americans—Travel—
Japan.   3. Japan—Description and
travel—1945–   4. Japanese
Americans—Biography.   I. Title.
E184.J3M784   1991
915.204'48—dc20   90-49529

The Atlantic Monthly Press
19 Union Square West
New York, NY 10003

First printing

For my parents
with love and gratitude

TURNING JAPANESE

PART ONE

I

"Coming home at last
At the end of the year
I wept to find
My old umbilical cord."
　　　　　—Matsuo Bashō

"And we have the feeling that the hero lived all the
details of this particular night as annunciations, as
promises, or even that he lived only those details that
were promises, blind and deaf to everything that didn't
belong to his adventure. We forget that the future was
not yet there; the man took his walk in a night empty
of premonitions, a night that offered him its monoto-
nous riches indiscriminately, and he did not choose
among them."

　　　　　—Jean-Paul Sartre,
　　　　　Nausea

1

For more than a week after I came back from Japan, I would find myself collapsing several times a day. The heat had lingered into September, and the house of our friend Kathleen wasn't air-conditioned. But this weakness wasn't due to the heat. It was as if the muscles inside my limbs were turning to jelly, as if soporific drugs were slowing the blood flow to my brain to a trickle, my thoughts to the haze of unconsciousness. I'd try to make it to the bedroom. The bedspread and walls were white, a Vermeer reproduction hung on the wall, the curtains were lace. And the room seemed foreign and familiar, like a tomb, like the women you sleep with in dreams. The bed oddly far away, like a mirage.

Jet lag? Perhaps. But the vertigo I felt seemed to come not just from the spinning of the earth but from a sense of hovering above the earth, from the very unreality of the country I had thought was my home.

I sat on the deck with a book on my lap, opened my eyes an hour later to the same page, a fly buzzing at my wrist. The sunlight off the lawn was blinding, the spaces between the houses immense, the sky an unbelievably wide expanse of blue. Where were the crowds, the small, cramped spaces of Tokyo? Susie, my wife, called from St. Paul to say she'd found a lead for an apartment. Her voice seemed to come from the depths of the ocean. The static on the line seemed the roar of the waves. I put on a tape, the score for Kurosawa's *Ran*. The *Noh* flute calmed me, then made me edgy, as if I'd forgotten something. I saw some figure, some body, move near the window. Kathleen was at work, the house was empty. Her children had grown up and moved away. She was our surrogate mother. We'd returned like wayward children.

I pulled out the things I'd brought home from Japan. Journal entries, letters, a few poems. Programs, magazines. Photos. I mooned over them, wondered what the people in the photos were doing, worried about what would become of the pages, whether I'd ever be able to shape them into a coherent whole. The novel looked ragged and unfinished, like the hull of a ship rotting on the beach.

Once, I made the mistake of going to a shopping mall. It was the middle of the week, the walks were almost empty. A few baby strollers, the mothers pale, the clothes white and casual, loose around their bodies, their infants with bonnets or bare fuzzy heads. The stores were like warehouses, a stage set waiting for actors. I stopped in the chain bookstore. There was nothing there to read. I found a novel by Mishima—*The Sailor Who Fell from Grace with the Sea.*

I pulled out the *sumie* brush and ink, set them on the Formica kitchen table, spread the tissue-thin paper. I could not quite recall how the waterfalls were made. I thought briefly of practicing my standing meditation, but the idea of getting to my feet seemed a mythical task. The heat had hit ninety-five. I could feel the Japanese words slipping like droplets of sweat from my brow.

"I know," said Susie. "It was hard for me too when I got back. But it's not that bad now. You'll get over it."

The thing was, I did not want to get over it. This disequilibrium was like a cold you caught from a brief affair, the only proof of your passion.

2

I am a *Sansei,* a third-generation Japanese-American. In 1984, through luck and through some skills as a poet, I traveled to Japan. My reasons for going were not very clear.

At the time, I'd been working as an arts administrator in the Writers-in-the-Schools program, sending other writers to grade schools and high schools throughout Minnesota. It wasn't taxing, but it didn't provide the long stretches needed to plunge into my own work. I had applied for a U.S./Japan Creative Artist Exchange Fellowship mainly because I wanted time to write.

Japan? That was where my grandparents came from, it didn't have much to do with my present life.

But then Japan had never seemed that important to me, even in childhood. On holidays when we would get together with relatives, I didn't notice that the faces around me looked different from most of the faces at school. I didn't notice that my grandfathers were in Japan, my grandmothers dead. No one spoke about them, just as no one spoke about Japan. We were American. It was the Fourth of July, Labor Day, Christmas. All I noticed was that the food we ate—*futomaki, mazegohan, teriyaki, kamaboko*—was different from what I liked best—McDonald's, pizza, hot dogs, tuna-fish salad.

For me Japan was cheap baseballs, Godzilla, weird sci-fi movies like *Star Man,* where you could see the strings that pulled him above his enemies, flying in front of a backdrop so poorly made even I, at eight, was conscious of the fakery. Then there were the endless hordes storming G.I.'s in war movies. Sometimes the Japanese hordes got mixed up in my mind with the Koreans, tiny Asians with squinty eyes mowed down in row after row by the steady shots of John Wayne or Richard Widmark. Before the television set, wearing my ever-present Cubs cap, I crouched near the sofa, saw the enemy surrounding me. I shouted to my men, hurled a grenade. I fired my gun. And the Japanese soldiers fell before me, one by one.

Of course, by the eighties, I was aware, as everyone else was, of Japan's burgeoning power, its changing image—Toyota, Nissan, Sony, Toshiba, the economic, electronic, automotive miracle. Rather than savage barbarism the Japanese were now characterized by a frightening efficiency and a tireless energy. Japan was a monster of industrialization, of huge, world-hungry corporations. Unfair trade practices, the trade imbalance. Robot people.

But none of this had much to do with me. After all, I was a poet.

So, when I did win the fellowship, I felt I was going not

as an ardent pilgrim, longing to return to the land of his grandparents, but more like a contestant on a quiz show who finds himself winning a trip to Bali or the Bahamas. Of course, I was pleased about the stipend, the plane fare for me and my wife, and the payments for Japanese lessons, both before the trip and during my stay. I was also excited that I had beat out several hundred candidates in literature and other fields for one of the six spots. But part of me wished the prize was Paris, not Tokyo. I would have preferred French bread and Brie over *sashimi* and rice, Baudelaire and Proust over Bashō and Kawabata, structuralism and Barthes over Zen and D. T. Suzuki. At least I had studied French in high school. And having grown up next door to Skokie, Illinois—the land of perpetual spring, a Rosenbloom on every corner—I knew more Yiddish than Japanese.

I had always been terrified of travel. In college it took me till my senior year to move to a new dorm. I'd lived in Minneapolis since then. My only other trip outside the country had been two weeks on an island off Cancun; my reaction to that trip was an astonished "I spent two weeks out of the country and did not die." I feared places where ordering a meal would be a chore. I liked knowing directions and streets, not having to refer to a map wherever I went. I loved my friends; with strangers I was always uneasy and quiet, almost rude. A true landlocked Midwesterner, I wanted to read about the world. But go there? Never.

This contradiction remained. Much of my life I had insisted on my Americanness, had shunned most connections with Japan and felt proud I knew no Japanese; yet I *was* going to Japan as a poet, and my Japanese ancestry was there in my poems—my grandfather, the relocation camps, the *hibakusha* (victims of the atomic bomb), a picnic of *Nisei* (second-generation Japanese-Americans), my uncle who fought in the 442nd. True, the poems were written in blank verse, rather than *haiku, tanka,* or *haibun.* But perhaps it's a bit disingenuous to say I had no longing to go to Japan; it was obvious my imagination had been traveling there for years, unconsciously swimming the Pacific, against the tide of my family's emigration, my parents' desire, after the internment camps, to forget the past.

Susie had none of my misgivings about our trip. After two

years of a pediatrics residency, after weeks when she'd sometimes work two days straight on two hours' sleep, she was eager for a break. Her father was a world expert on public health and had been one of the first American medical officials to visit Russia after the war, to visit the People's Republic of China; he had taken her family on trips through Europe and imparted to his daughter a love of foreign places and exotic foods. For years, she had found my reluctance to travel stifling; just as she had converted me from a diet of pizza and hamburger to a range of the world's cuisines, she kept hoping she could inject some nomadic impulse into my rooted Midwestern bones. Perhaps the trip to Japan would accomplish that.

And so she read eagerly through the travel books, notching the pages, making lists of places we would visit. She talked of the temples in Kyoto, of various festivals, of how she might take up tea ceremony, study *shiatsu* (acupressure), learn about the Japanese medical system. She left book after book on Japan by our bedside—all of which I ignored. While I was in New York studying Japanese at Columbia, she sent me articles on Japan, and after she joined me in the city, we argued when I wanted to see a film by Fassbinder or jazz in the Village rather than go to the Asian Cultural Society or to see *Kabuki* at the Met. It was she who arranged our tickets, she who dragged me shopping for the huge canvas hockey bags we were to use as luggage, she who had packed up our tiny bohemian apartment in the university section of Minneapolis.

This tension between us lasted until we left. After three days visiting my brother in L.A., having stayed up late the previous night talking, I packed at the last minute and planned on sleeping most of the flight. On the plane, Susie was nervous, excited. She wanted to go to the World's Fair at Tsukuba immediately after we arrived. I said maybe, annoyed at her tendency to make plans. Maybe we'll be too tired to do anything, I said. We argued briefly. Then I nodded off. My nervousness and excitement had gone inward, into somnolence. Over the next few hours, I dreamed of Mozart, Salieri, the images of *Amadeus* that flickered on the screen when I opened my eyes. I forgot where I was going. I was reading a book on Sartre, sentences about the lack of plot in *Nausea,* a new conception of action and event, dialogues stemming from the French Resistance. And by the end of the fourteen-hour plane ride, as we tumbled out into the terminal at Narita, I was exhausted and exhilarated. Frightened. Astonished that all the faces at customs looked like mine.

II

"Anthropology conquers the estranging function of the intellect by institutionalizing it. For the anthropologist the world is professionally divided into 'home' and 'out there,' the domestic and the exotic.... The anthropologist is not simply a neutral observer. He is a man in control of, and even consciously exploiting, his own intellectual alienation ... a 'critic at home' but a 'conformist elsewhere.'"

—Susan Sontag

"Everyone I see on the street is tall and good-looking. That, first of all, intimidates me, embarrasses me. Sometimes I see an unusually short man, but he is still two inches taller than I am, as I compare his height with mine when we pass each other. Then I see a dwarf coming, a man with an unpleasant complexion—and he happens to be my own reflection in the shop window. I don't know how many times I have laughed at my own ugly appearance right in front of myself. Sometimes, I even watched my reflection that laughed as I laughed. And every time that happened, I was impressed by the appropriateness of the term 'yellow race.'"

—Natsume Soseki,
from his London
diaries, circa 1902

1

It was the beginning of autumn, the season of rains. We descended from International House, a club for businessmen and scholars from abroad, to the Roppongi streets and found ourselves wading through a sea of umbrellas. Gaggles of shop and "office girls" giggled past, their umbrellas by Givenchy, their skirts by Miyake; others with gray suits, white blouses, jet black hair. *Sarariman* (businessmen) in blue suits, carrying briefcases. The schoolboys wore navy-blue uniforms and caps, the girls navy-blue jumpers and white blouses. A city of cool, dark colors, of groups gathered by dress.

We were dazzled by the foreign, by the familiar. Though the faces looked different from those in America, they still looked like mine. The clothes were like those in the States but darker and more formal. *Kanji* (characters) were everywhere, but so were Roman letters—McDonald's, Mister Donut, Seibu, Hana Mori, Häagen-Dazs, the Playboy Club, Antonio's, Kinokuniya, Colonel Sanders' Kentucky Fried Chicken.

On the main streets of Roppongi were dozens of restaurants, a barrage of neon. Each building's entrance advertised half a dozen bars and restaurants, stacked one above the other. The spaces inside were cramped, windowless. A city of interiors, a hive of honeycombs. None of the buildings was much taller than six stories; with the threat of earthquakes, skyscrapers are expensive.

Moving at a snail's pace, the cars and taxis were shiny and new, without scratches or rust. Rain splattered off the hoods, reflecting the streetlights and neon. At the subway entrance, beneath the pink neon of the Almond Coffee Shop, people scanned the crowd for their friends. As we descended the stairs, umbrellas folded around us, shoulders, elbows closed in; space grew tiny. Everyone accepted the closeness and jostling with no hint of violence or frustration. The density was simply part of the atmosphere.

Down below, lines of people were putting coins in the machines, pulling out tickets. Thank God, I thought, the yen signs are in Roman numerals. We found a small map with the names of the stations written in Roman letters, but we couldn't figure out how to buy our tickets. I felt a touch of panic. My aunts had warned me about this, had said the system was quite confusing.

"Let's ask someone for help," said Susie.

"Just a second. I can figure it out," I said.

A young man in a business suit saw our plight and told us in English how to calculate our fares and where to deposit our coins. We were off.

The first day we hit the Ginza, one of the shopping centers located along the Yamanote-sen, the train line that rings the heart of the city (other lines run out from the center, a huge endless megalopolis fanning across the great Kando plain: this was where the majority of commuters lived). Tokyo seemed to be one immense shop: everywhere there were billboards, neon signs, shop windows, crowds of shoppers clutching bags from My City, Seibu, or Isetan, or the other major *depato* (department stores). The doors opened automatically. Mechanical and human voices greeted you, singing *"Irasshaimase"* (welcome), then accompanied you on elevators and escalators, announcing sales. Video screens, sometimes even a wall of them, displayed fashion shows, the models implacable, pale, beautiful.

The basement of Seibu was like an outdoor market. We passed counter after counter filled with food: teriyaki, *tempura,* slabs of sashimi—beefy slabs of tuna, thin white folds of squid, the puckered tentacles of octopus, medallions of scallops, tiny beads of red roe. There were vegetable bins with long, fat legs of *daikon* (radish) root, knobs of ginger, cabbage, and spinach for *sukiyaki;* then tins and boxes of pickles—cucumbers, yellow slices of *tsukemono* (pickles), red-peppered leaves of *kim chi* (pickled cabbage), greasy black slivers of roots. When we got to the tea section, with its various blends, a cloud of scent arose, like fields of mowed hay: rich, smoky, subtly pungent. Shoppers crowded by, plastic bags in their fists; they chattered with shopwomen in blue uniforms with kerchiefs around their heads.

Susie was delighted. Some people know the world through their eyes, some through their ears, she does it through her sense of taste: "It's a whole new world of foods, a brand-new heaven!"

In other departments, the interiors were strikingly sparse. The object—a kimono, a suit, a dress, a tea set—was suspended in space, surrounded by blankness that conferred on it a matteness, an absence of history. The displays made me think of the famous rock garden of Ryoanji, great expanses of white rippling pebbles dotted here and there with the darkness of larger, ragged stones. How easily the Zen sensibility camouflaged its advertisement, presented each item in a realm apart, pure, peaceful, timeless.

In the vast depato everything could be bought. They contained restaurants, movie theaters, food shops; on the top floors were art galleries, performing spaces. The stores were cities in miniature, mazes to wander through. They attested to the Japanese fascination with newness, with forever-evolving codes of how to belong to the group. The Japanese are aesthetes, connoisseurs, do not equate beauty with frivolity. Here the consumer's desire centered on a cult of beauty and nationalism and less on the need for individuation.

Surprisingly, amid this commercial mecca, I felt less need to buy. I did not share their fears and hungers, the compulsions of those around me. The commercials on the TV screens, the ads in the magazines, on the billboards, were not designed for my desires or my American ego. I felt somehow disburdened; a small sense of contentment set in.

Leaving Isetan at evening, we were greeted by the neon signs of the Ginza. In the settling dark, the blue neon of Nissan, the angled, flashing red of Mitsubishi. A light sprayed like a comet across the Parco building; the squares of the four-story Neco sign shifted like a tumbling kaleidoscope from checks to stripes to diagonals, from kanji to Roman letters. The colors pulsed against the eye, left an image burning there long afterward.

With the rain trickling down, at the huge intersection I looked from the neon to the faces around me and felt proud: my genes linked me not to the poverty of the Third World but to a country as modern as, even more modern than, America. It was a dizzying sensation.

2

My fellowship was administered by the people at International House. Hasegawa-san, our contact, was a woman in her late twenties. Her dress was understated, her demeanor distant and proper; she wore the wire-rim glasses of an accountant. Though she listened to my inquiries about making contact with other writers, she was hardly encouraging. They were often busy, she would have to look into it.

I had the feeling that we were mainly on our own devices, and I worried how we would manage to meet people. Though we'd expected that the fellowship administrators would help us find a place, Hasegawa-san said we would have to contact real-estate agents ourselves. It was difficult for me to calculate just what my stipend in yen would allow us. Hasegawa-san said it would be hard to find a place along the loop of the Yamanote line. We would have to pay not only a deposit but key money, the equivalent of one or two months' rent, just for the privilege of renting an apartment. Half or more of my first month's stipend might go to housing. I'd probably have to dip into our savings back home.

Hasegawa-san informed me that grant protocol required that I meet with Shimon Miura, the head of the Bunkacho, the Cultural Affairs Department of the Japanese government. Miura was a novelist, fairly well known; his wife was even more famous and appeared on television talk shows.

At the Bunkacho building the next day, we were led into a large office, with a few tiny cubicles marked off by file cabinets.

Under the fluorescent lights, everything looked crowded and a bit dingy, in sharp contrast to the slick decor and displays of the department stores. The drab institutional quality of Japanese offices and hospitals revealed the Spartan-like, penny-pinching, peasant aspect of the Japanese character; it was the flip side of the highly aesthetic, aristocratic sensibility displayed in restaurants, shops, temples, and places of entertainment.

We were greeted by a couple of assistants. Susie and I bowed. They held out their hands. Realizing the mix-up too late, already bent over, I lifted my hand to shake theirs. Time out, I felt like saying, let's start again.

An "office girl" was ordered to bring us some tea. No qualms here about secretaries as hostesses or maids. We later learned that most young women enter the work force only for a few years, long enough to find a husband. Few have any chance of moving up the corporate ladder, no matter whether they've graduated from Tokyo University, the Harvard of Japan, or a small women's school. In the Japanese work world, women are props, gofers. This attitude would become increasingly difficult for Susie as the year progressed.

Miura's office was both private and enormous by Japanese standards. The president of Honda, for example, has no private office; his desk is out in the open along with those of other employees. Miura was handsome, sophisticated, with silver hair and a sharp gray suit, a burgundy tie. About fifty, he had aged well, his body trim and solid, more imposing than his slight, crow-like, bespectacled assistants. He spoke English fluently. We were relieved. After my one year of lessons, my Japanese was still rudimentary; Susie had been studying just a few weeks.

I asked about his work.

"Well, I have less time for writing now. I get up every day at five and work for three hours before I come here."

Japanese authors are known for their prodigious production. The collected works of Mishima, who died in his forties, spans several shelves and dozens of volumes. Japanese authors make less of a fuss than American authors about the distinction between literature and hack work. Mishima wrote soft porn and potboilers as well as *Confessions of a Mask.* Twenty years after his death, the standard complaint now is that all that Japanese authors write is soft porn; the same goes for movies, where memories of the great directors like Ozu or Mizoguchi are just that and Kurosawa, the aging lion, seems the last of an extinct species.

"I see you want to go to Hiroshima and Nagasaki. I don't know if it's a good thing for you to visit there," said Miura.

I suddenly grew attentive. Having written poems about hibakusha, the atomic bomb victims, I had cited a desire to go to those cities in my grant proposal. Perhaps naïvely, I felt I might somehow capture the Japanese perception of the event, but with an American eye. Still, I worried about seeming like a vulture, scraping away at the remains of the dead. Was Miura picking up on this?

"It's best you forget about such things. We have gone on from there. This is the new Japan. We have forgotten such things."

I nodded feebly. What did he mean by "We have forgotten such things"?

"There's so much else to see. I've read you're interested in visiting your grandfather's hometown. Where is that?"

Smiling and maintaining a polite demeanor, I felt my usual self-righteous voice of protest grow silent. I was a guest here, this man was my sponsor. Even though he was condescending, taking the tack of the elder and wiser writer and dismissing my interest as youthful misguidance, was that a reason to instantly loathe his presence?

It was a posture I was to take often in Japan: the smiling, simple, and assenting American, polite and silent, without protest.

3

The next day, after looking for apartments without much luck, we had lunch in a *soba* (noodle) restaurant with Shauna, a playwright and another U.S./Japan fellow, and her husband, Hal. They had already been in Japan for six months, with their eight-year-old son. Shauna wore her hair in a Jewish Afro; she had on a loose-fitting, almost late-hippie dress. Hal was tall, academic, and imperious, with silver wire-rim glasses, khaki pants, a button-down shirt. A literary couple, they were committed New Yorkers and lived on the Upper West Side. Both agreed vehemently on Japan and the Japanese: they hated them.

Even before we ordered our bowls of soba, Shauna and Hal started in. Their list of complaints was endless. First was the heat: Tokyo summers are infamous for their heat, and the past summer had been the hottest on record for fifty years. They found the constant crowds not only annoying and claustrophobic but dangerous. The Japanese rail lines use pushers at rush hour to pack the cars, and once, after Shauna had been squashed in, her hand got caught in the door and she broke her wrist. In a country built for those under six feet, Hal, who was six-four, was always bumping his head in doorways.

Not having studied Japanese beforehand, they hadn't been able to communicate with many people, and hadn't really made any Japanese friends, except for a few women in Shauna's cooking class. Shauna had hoped to work with a theater troupe, but the best she had been able to manage was to watch one troupe's rehearsals. Our Japanese sponsors at International House were useless and had provided her only a few contacts, she said. It was impossible to find a decent, cheap apartment in Tokyo. They were looking again for a new place. It turned out that we had just looked at and refused the same apartment they had, but we had been offered it for 150,000 yen, about $900 at the time, while they had been offered it for 250,000 yen, about $1,500. This only reinforced their opinion that the Japanese were unfriendly and unhelpful and possessed all the honesty of a herd of used-car salesmen.

"Besides," said Hal, "I'm not really interested in Japanese culture. All this emphasis in the culture on the aesthetics of surface, on outside appearances. I'm interested in people's psychology. But the Japanese have this unwillingness or inability to even consider the psychological. They keep maintaining that they're different from us, but I don't believe them . . ."

He took a sip of Kirin beer. The waitress passed behind him, her wooden clogs knocking on the bare floor. Her features were soft, cushioned by flesh, and reminded me of my cousin Debby.

"I gave this talk at a meeting of Japanese English professors in Tokyo," said Hal. "In part because I knew the reaction I would get, I decided to talk about young women poets in America. After all, they're writing the most interesting poetry. After my talk, the first question I got was, 'Well, that was nice, but what about the men poets?' "

"You can't believe how chauvinist this society is," said Shauna. "It's going to get to you, Susie. You just met with Shimon Miura, right? . . . Do you know what he said a few months ago when he was asked about physical fitness? He said that Japanese men should keep themselves in good enough shape so that they could rape a woman if it was necessary . . ."

I felt my anxiety rise. Shauna and Hal's vehement distaste for Japan, their inability to make friends, seemed to portend a long visit of frustration and hassles. Did Hal's feelings arise in part because he wasn't a fellow and was bridling under his status as adjunct? Would Susie feel the same?

I started to dislike Shauna and Hal, as one often does with bearers of bad tidings. I felt irritated that they had taken us to a soba restaurant. They were both into natural foods, which I abhorred, and I had always disliked Japanese noodles.

In part their complaints were not unreasonable. I had known that Japanese society was going to be chauvinist, but the response of the Japanese professors went far beyond chauvinism. I agreed with Hal: many of the best young American poets are women, and the Japanese ought to know about them. Someone had lied to Shauna and Hal about the rent for an apartment. Perhaps it was hard trying to live here as a foreigner with a child.

So why did I want to defend the Japanese?

I looked down again at my noodles, the flecks of green *wasabi* mustard.

I'm going to enjoy this, I said to myself, I'm going to eat it all.

* * *

Perhaps it was simply our fears about the future, our worries about finding friends, finding an apartment, perhaps it was our annoyance at Shauna and Hal, perhaps it was simply the tensions and strains of having just arrived in a foreign country, perhaps it was my stupidity and neuroticism—well, more than perhaps—but halfway through the train ride, Susie and I started to argue.

At first, our disagreement wouldn't have been obvious to anyone. We had passed a station, Akihabara, and Susie asked me how to pronounce it. I whispered the answer.

"What?" she asked.

I whispered my answer again.

"Why are you whispering? I can't hear you."

"I'll tell you later. I'm reading now."

The book I was reading was so important I can't remember what it was. What I do remember is feeling self-conscious about speaking English on the train. Crunched in among the Japanese, I liked the way I could blend in if I remained silent. I was telling myself that things would be different for me than for Shauna and Hal. They were *hakujin* (white people). They didn't have the sensitivity or flexibility to deal with Japanese culture; they came here with too many preconceptions. "Why can't they do things this way . . ." Shauna seemed to say throughout her conversation. I wanted no part of it. To speak English on the train created an island, separated me from the people around us. I didn't want this to happen.

A few minutes later we stood at a stoplight in Roppongi, the crowd perched on the curb around us, the ever-present rain dripping down. I turned to see a young woman, sitting in a coffee shop, brush back a long swath of black hair and blow out a stream of cigarette smoke. She was waiting for her girl friend, a sarariman, the ruffled first moment of a blind date. I saw my face reflected in the glare of the window. Small tears all over my face. I blended in with the crowd.

As we turned the corner, away from the bustling intersection, Susie leaned over to me in a familiar gesture. "Let's have a kiss," she said.

"No, not here."

She frowned, gave a shake of disgust. I recalled how often in the past she had resisted public physical gestures, their hint of impropriety. I was relishing now how the tables had been turned.

"What is your problem?" she said.

"I'm pissed," I said, spacing the words evenly, emphatically.

Silence.

As we walked, I looked down the hill, at rooftop after rooftop where clotheslines were strung out. No dryers in this country, despite all its electric marvels; no need to save on women's work.

The long street to the hotel was empty except for two schoolgirls in jumpers beneath an umbrella. As we passed under a pine that jutted out over a wall, I tried to explain about decorum, about Japanese manners, about not wanting to display physical affection in public here.

Susie stopped, pointed toward me. "You, you act as if you know everything about politeness. I read as much as you, even more, about this country before we came. Back home, I'm always running into your rudeness, easing it over. You're the most self-absorbed man I know . . ."

I knew I was being supercilious. Less consciously, I sensed I was angry at the white world and unable to separate her from the ghost of a million others. I was probably unconscious of just how much trouble I was having distinguishing between slights to my race and those criticisms of my own imperfections, my own neuroses. I wanted to blame everything on her, all the tension of the past few days looking for an apartment, worrying about rent costs, trying to order meals in broken Japanese, listening to Shauna and Hal kvetch about the Japanese. Perhaps I remembered that when we were back home and I was writing, I could not be disturbed, would not come out to greet the guests, wash dishes or clothes, cook or answer the phone, would not say hello or good night, would not cuddle or kiss, would not remember the time or pick her up from work, but instead kept myself closed, inside a shell, a life of words. What I could not see was that I was doing this again in Japan, in a whole new way.

The rain had stopped. I closed the umbrella, droplets springing. Susie turned, waited.

"In fact, there are situations where I know more about what's happening than you. It doesn't matter that you know more language than I do. Who made you Mr. Politeness?"

Mr. Politeness. Mr. Coffee, Mr. Fix-It. I was beginning to feel like a character out of a Raymond Carver story.

She grabbed the umbrella and pointed. "And another thing. I hate these slugs on the walk. And I hate all this polite bowing. And the fair at Tsukuba and the stupid childish exhibit I'd waited a year to see and how we had to wait in line there for three hours. And when we met Shimon Miura, I was just an adjunct, someone to fetch tea. And I hate how you never say how you hate any of this, even the endless rain."

Then there was the squish of the end of her umbrella meeting a slug. I thought: That was meant for me. The squish of anger; the squish of *uni* (sea urchin) that slips down your throat, the raw moistness of hunger, the sea, the endless rain. The squish of sexual fulfillment, bodies sliding with sweat.

Suddenly we were laughing. It was all too dramatic. Simply absurd.

One morning at our hotel I was surprised by a phone call. In broken English the woman explained that her name was Reiko, that she had received my letter, and that she would come the next day to pick me up.

Before I left the States for Japan, I had sent a few letters to possible contacts. I had received Reiko's name from Adam Weinburg of the Walker Art Center, who had recently visited Japan and had met there this "marvelous woman" who knew about everything in the Tokyo avant-garde art scene. "She's a riot. She knows all the tiny clubs and out-of-the way performance spaces," said Adam. "And she drinks like a fish."

Of all the letters I sent, only one really worked out. I was lucky Reiko was the one.

The next morning, in front of our hotel, a taxi opened and wearing a dark loose turtleneck and slacks, out stepped a Mama Cass–sized woman. Reiko wore her hair in bangs and had thin, smiling eyes; a nose like a fist; and a leathery, pocked complexion. Despite her appearance, I was immediately taken by her. Her whole demeanor seemed open and friendly and quite unlike that of the Japanese bureaucrats at the International House and the Ministry of Culture.

At our introduction, though, I felt a bit awkward and tongue-tied. I couldn't conduct any real conversation in Japanese, and I was reluctant to speak in English, as if I were in someone's house and should be behaving according to their rules. I felt ashamed at being so *heta* (unskilled). I hadn't worked hard enough in my studies, and I thought I was expected to know Japanese simply because of my genetic makeup.

Though Reiko didn't speak English very well, none of this mattered to her. She took us to her cramped, paper-jammed office, where she published her magazine, *Danceworks.* Her secretary translated for her and told us we would first be going to lunch, then to a studio for Buyo (traditional Japanese dance), then to a teacher of the *shamisen* (a traditional stringed instrument), then back to the office to see some videos of Japanese dance. I asked the secretary why Reiko was being so kind.

"You are in her country, you are her guests."

"But we're total strangers," I said.

"It doesn't matter. She is very kind."

At lunch, as we ate soba (I was beginning to actually like the stuff, despite its blandness; the stinging shots of wasabi mustard helped), Reiko, Susie, and I played a game we were to play often on first meeting people in Japan. It consists simply of names and nods of recognition or shakes of the head.

Reiko started first. "Simone Forte." We shake our heads. Susie and I know little about modern dance, which is Reiko's specialty. "Trisha Brown." A mild assent. Apparently, Reiko has interviewed Trisha Brown for *Danceworks.* "Bob Rauschenberg." Reiko gives a garbled explanation of how Trisha and Rauschenberg worked together on a piece. "Merce Cunningham . . ."

I went through my meager list. "Oe . . . Mishima . . . Kawabata . . . Susan Sontag . . . Kurosawa . . . Oshima . . ." Here and there Reiko would give a *suki* (like) or *kirai* (dislike).

By the end of the lunch, I felt a bit like a cultural idiot, but Reiko didn't seem to care that my knowledge of dance was infinitesimal.

A half hour later, after a short cab ride through the winding and narrow streets of Tokyo, we were sitting on cushions in a Buyo dance studio with the *sensei* (teacher) of Reiko's daughter. The room was light and open, the wood floor bare. The sensei asked my grandfather's name.

"Jinnosuke," I said.

"Ah, a *samurai* name."

I felt proud that he didn't have a commoner's name. I was also relieved that the sensei hadn't asked me my other grandfather's name, because I didn't even know it. How would I be able to explain such a lack of filial piety? I thought of my plan to visit my grandparents' hometown, my vague interest in the past my family had forgotten.

After Reiko arranged for me to attend a Buyo class, we were off again. She sometimes seemed to me like a fullback barreling through a crowd of tacklers, a flurry of activity that left us gasping after her.

A few minutes later, after a short taxi ride, I was sitting before her shamisen teacher in a room of *tatami* mats. Or rather, I found myself kneeling, my buttocks placed on my calves, and already sensing the twinges of sheering pain that come from a position that many modern Japanese, much less Westerners, are no longer used to sitting in. Reiko, clearly trying to keep some degree of decorum before her teacher, couldn't help but burst into giggles at my discomfort. Her manner with her teachers was much more formal than with us; she seemed to switch modes with startling agility.

Across my lap was a shamisen, a three-stringed traditional Japanese instrument. Reiko's shamisen teacher was plucking and singing in a quavering voice, *"Sa-ku-ra"*—cherry blossoms—and I was fumbling along, very very badly, trying to follow, my voice somewhere between those of a sick cow and a love-sick mongoose. What little guitar I had played as a teenager seemed no use to me now, and I realized that I was going to have to find some way of refusing to take lessons on the shamisen without being impolite; I was still insisting to myself that I was interested only in the Japanese avant-garde.

My predicament was one in which foreigners in Japan often find themselves: the Japanese are very concerned about treating their guests properly, but it often happens that what foreigners are offered in the way of services or gifts is not what they want. An awkward situation arises, as it had in my case: would my refusal offend Reiko or, worse, her teacher?

At first I feigned incomprehension at the offer of lessons, then insisted it was too much trouble, though I don't know how much of this Reiko understood. Her teacher, thank God, understood none of it. Somehow the drift of my wishes got through and the lessons were presented as an option. I only had to call up Reiko and they would be arranged. I breathed a sigh of relief.

It was at Reiko's office, viewing dance videos at the end of the afternoon, that I found the first thing I truly wanted to study. Reiko started with a video of Kazuo Ono, the eighty-year-old co-founder of Butoh. The video was startling: Ono, in whiteface and full drag as an aging chanteuse, cavorted across the stage in short, mincing steps to a piece by Mozart. With the pathos of camp, he addressed a bouquet of flowers, put them in his hair. His face was exaggerated, arresting in its sadness. Some gestures—like the cupping of an ear, the primping of his hair—reminded me of mime. He was Blanche DuBois, Ophelia, a hag in the forest; he fell to the floor the way one imagines Daisy in *The Great Gatsby* falling on a bed full of Gatsby's shirts. He was awkward, pathetic, stumbling backward, his arm and hand crooked limply. He found a sheet on the ground, picked it up, bit it, threw it over his shoulder, continued prancing. He stopped, looked at his hands, and began to weep. All of this was done with a studied slowness, as in Noh drama, as if under water or in a dream.

I had known that there was a long tradition of men playing women in Japanese theater, but this combination of parody and empathy, this revealing of the woman inside a man, seemed at once more stylized than Kabuki and more honest about its masquerade. Yet it was entirely without the hilarity that inevitably comes with drag shows in the West.

Afterward, Reiko told me she could arrange for me to attend Ono's training sessions. I'd be delighted, I told her. I suddenly realized that with my stumbling Japanese, perhaps the only way to break the barrier of language was to enter the culture through my body, through sight.

I told Reiko I had never danced before.

5

After a couple of days of looking, we finally found our apartment. It was part of a small two-story complex owned by a retired professor. Opening onto an alley-size street, the front door was flanked by a jade plant and a translucent screen that covered the one main window. The apartment was small by American standards, roughly the size of a large American living room; we learned later that a Japanese family of four might live in such an apartment. There were two main rooms, each about ten-by-ten, one of which was a tatami room, where we would sleep; there was also a kitchen about twelve-by-ten, and a bathroom. Other than the front window, whose view was blocked by the screen, there were no clear windows, just two sets of smoked-glass panes. It was clean, cheaper than other apartments we'd seen, and located in Mejiro, a stop along the Yamanote-sen. We were a fifteen-minute walk and a fifteen-minute train ride from Shinjuku, one of the main shopping centers; some Tokyo commutes are two hours. The rent was a bit more than a fourth of my stipend, but we had to pay key money for only one month, so we wouldn't have to dip as far into our savings as we had anticipated. We felt lucky, relieved.

The streets of most Tokyo neighborhoods are the size of alleys and wind back and forth with maze-like intricacy. Everywhere concrete blocks wall off space, and the walls and tightness of the streets make them seem quiet and protected in comparison to the noise and bustle of the commercial main streets. As we climbed to the top of our apartment building to see the view, our realtor, Okubo, told us that this was the neighborhood where the former prime minister Tanaka lived.

"Everyone calls him the scandal man."

"Is that bad?"

"Not so bad. He's very rich."

Okubo was a lively, elderly man, though his age, as with the case of many Japanese, was hard to guess ("We age well," I had always told Susie). His body was wiry, his cheeks hollow, and his skin flecked with age spots, but he possessed a vibrant, outgoing energy, and little of the quiet formality of the other real-estate agents we had met. He wore a straw fedora with a bright yellow band, a gray suit, and a raincoat.

"This raincoat is my favorite," he said. "It's like the TV detective Corumbo."

Unlike the other realtors, he seemed at ease with our foreignness. We trusted him.

"I will always be grateful to America. After the war, we were starving, we thought the Americans would come and kill us. And the G.I.'s came and started handing out chocolate to the children. We were all so surprised." Since he had fought in the army against the Americans, Okubo was even more surprised. "I owe everything to MacArthur. When the Americans came, I got a job with them. I translated and helped distribute food. MacArthur saved my life."

I didn't know what to say. Influenced by thoughts of MacArthur and Korea, by the stereotypes of *Teahouse of the August*

Moon, by the relocation camps and the West Coast wartime hysteria, I didn't completely share this positive attitude toward postwar Japanese and American relations; still, I was glad Okubo seemed to like Americans so much.

"I tell all this to my sons, but they don't care. They don't remember the war. How bad it was when we lost. It's all in the past, they say . . . All the young people are like that now."

He looked out over the skyline of Tokyo, the towers of Shinjuku, Shibuya, and Ginza, spires in the distance spread around the circle of the Yamanote train line, the miracle of a city built from rubble and ash, from starvation and exhaustion.

"I will always be grateful to America," Okubo repeated.

I could not say the same.

III

"Philosophy is really homesickness, it is the urge to be at home everywhere."

— Novalis

BROWN ARTISANS STEAL BRAINS OF WHITES

JAPANESE A MENACE TO AMERICAN WOMEN

THE YELLOW PERIL—HOW JAPANESE CROWD
OUT THE WHITE RACE

— *San Francisco
Chronicle* headlines
(circa 1920)

1

Going to Japan brought me right up against the idea of home.
Home, in one sense, is a limit. It restricts by categorizing: he was
born in the country of ———, the city of ———, in the home
of ———. The Japanese, those insular, rooted, island people, are
highly conscious of where they come from, their *kuni.* In contrast,
I was pleased when my Japanese teacher told me that Kobo Abe,
the Japanese novelist, once remarked, "I have no kuni." A compatriot, I thought, another of the homeless.

Long ago, for my ancestors, the village of my name was
the center of the world, and the mountains or the seashore the edge
of that world. Sure of their kuni, their gods, their values, those
ancestors knew what lay beyond was the realm of unreality, the
country of the dead, the dwelling of phantoms and nothingness.
Generations removed from those ancestors, I suffered from a lack
of center, a fixed point from which to chart the stream. Instead, I
was constantly sinking into the foam of formlessness, a dissolving
identity—What God do I believe in? Who are my people? What
language do I speak? What are my customs? How shall I raise my
children? Where will I be a year from now, ten years, on my
deathbed? What is my history, the stories of my family, the myths
of my people?

The man who emigrated—my grandfather—carried
within him the memory of home, the former world, the place where
he was once "real." It tore at him, that memory, and yet it kept him
anchored: he knew where his home was, knew that he had lost it.
The son of that man—my father—believed he could make the new
place his home. The task was probably impossible, but it kept him

occupied. The son of that man—myself—realizes what? That the new home—in my case, a Jewish suburb—is no home; is, in fact, for me, an absurdity, a sham, and that the old home is lost in unreality.

At the time I went to Japan, I saw my sense of homelessness and my defiance of limits as intimately related to my reaction to stereotypes. If American culture wanted to see me solely as Mr. Moto or the bucktoothed gardener, I wanted to outplay, to leap beyond the bounds of, other people's conceptions of me. I would not choose, would not settle; I would keep my options open. I countered with the illusion that I could be anything. One day, Yeats said, the poet will wear all masks. Perhaps that was the reason it took me so long to return to the lost center, my grandparents' kuni.

2

As September swept on, the days were still wet, slippery with mist and fog. We learned to take our umbrellas every time we left our apartment and began the short, winding walk to the Mejiro-*dorii,* the main street. One rare clear morning, the windows of a two-story white house we passed every day were open and we could see the racks of dresses, the women bent over their sewing machines—a small dress factory. We turned the corner at the sweet shop, with traditional Japanese desserts made of rice, like the *mochi* I shunned as a child. Across the street was a chocolate store. The Japanese, we learned later, love sweets and give gifts every time they visit someone. Behind us, a woman with her child on a bicycle sounded her bell; probably she was on her way to the Pikokku (Peacock), the local grocery store.

We still had more basic things to buy than groceries, and we stopped in a little hardware shop. The building was wooden, with a green plastic awning; the shop had none of the sheen of the recently built stores along the street. The owner, a woman in her

sixties, was tiny and wrinkled. She wore a loose-fitting kimono and
a kerchief. I didn't know the word for mop, and as I tried to explain
what we needed, she kept shaking her head. Finally, Susie got down
on her knees and began to rub the floor, then she got up and began
to push an imaginary mop or broom, stopping from time to time
to point to the imaginary object in her hand. In this way, we got
our cleaning supplies, and Susie, pleased at being a local customer
now recognized by the shop owner, always tried to shop at the store
for at least our household items, even if they were cheaper at
Pikokku. She developed the same relationship with the local *sushi*
shop, the cleaners, the tea merchant.

   After the hardware shop, we went home to drop off our
supplies, and went out again armed with a dictionary. But when I
tried to use my Japanese at the local furniture store, I failed again,
even with the aid of the dictionary. Susie pulled the dictionary from
my hands, held it out, and simply pointed. The woman laughed.
"Rezoku . . . soo desu ka?" and showed us a number of refrigerators.
For some reason she hadn't understood my pronunciation. After
some more struggles with the language, we understood that the
store would deliver it within an hour. We were just beginning to
learn about Japanese service. Later, when the refrigerator broke,
we called the store and a repairman arrived a couple of hours later.
There was no charge.

   Things went like this for several days as we bought a *futon,*
tables, chairs, and other items for the apartment. Susie, less self-
conscious, more open to new people, and, as a hakujin, more of an
anomaly, seemed to make friends more easily. When problems
arose, she was apt to do the sensible thing—ask for help. I, on the
other hand, was too embarrassed to do so. I felt I should somehow
know things intuitively, through blood.

   One day we took the train to Shinjuku, one of the giant
shopping centers along the Yamanote-sen line. Walking through
Shinjuku station—where two and a half million people pass daily—
into the street we saw thousands of impeccably and innovatively
dressed young people. And yet, despite all the innovation, there
were a limited number of combinations. I counted about five basic
sets of uniforms for women and men. I also saw that what seemed

innovative was merely variations on the traditional. There were, for instance, the loose-flowing, baggy lines, cuts that seemed to come from some futuristic, sci-fi sense of garb, or the part of punk ballooned from cartoons, like David Byrne's oversized suit in *Stop Making Sense*. Such lines were merely a basic reworking of the fundamentals of the kimono. It was clothing cut for people who once spent much of their time sitting cross-legged or kneeling, who live in a climate that is often insufferably humid and requires that clothes have room to breathe, people whose garb was first designed for work in the fields, the unconstrained stooping and squatting of a rice farmer.

I loved the way Japanese design was not linear and vertical as in the West and did not depend on symmetry of the left and right. Instead, Japanese design was horizontal, asymmetrical, round, formed in layers. Take the typical Tokyo collegiate uniform worn by many of the young people who passed us: the paisley shirt with a solid or striped cardigan pulled over it and the bottom of the shirt sticking out of the cardigan, spilling over baggy, oversized, sometimes striped or checkered pants, often with the pant legs rolled up. This looseness of form and clash of patterns, while in one sense reminiscent of punk, seemed totally appropriate to a Japanese sensibility. The unisexual quality of such outfits was in keeping with the less obvious sexual demarcations of the kimono.

Surrounded by this grand display of beautiful young men and women whose every detail of appearance seemed calculated, cool, colorful, and correct, I felt surprised by the city's sense of wealth. Though it lacked the extreme forms of luxury which appear in New York, Tokyo overwhelmed New York by the sheer numbers of its fashionably dressed. Given the limited housing space, perhaps this was what people chose to spend their money on. Young unmarried women in Tokyo spend half their income on clothes, which they are able to do because most of them live at home. And of course, the Japanese place far more value on surface, on beauty and appearance, than the depth-seeking, psychologically and morally conscious Americans. Like the French, the Japanese do not view fashion as trivial or immoral.

A small confession: In high school I was voted not the

most intellectual or the most likely to succeed, much less the most athletic, but the best dressed. Later, in the Lutheran plainness of the Twin Cities, I had often felt a bit overdressed compared to the natives. As I walked amid the crowds in Tokyo, it was not just my skin color that helped me blend in but also my love of fashion.

I was beginning to see my situation as a Japanese-American in a new light. In America, I had been told that I could be American, and yet I had never quite felt a hundred percent American; too many of the images on the TV and movie screens of my childhood had only white faces, too much of the history I had learned never mentioned us. On the other hand, I had come to Japan not expecting to fit in. Any time I felt I did, it seemed a pleasant surprise, an unexpected bonus.

Still, I sensed another meaning in the vast vocabulary that crowded the streets: Miyake and Kenzo, Grass Men's and Men's Melrose, Galamond and Linea Fresca, the solid, luminescent reds, purples, and greens of Jun Saito, the "bad guy" look of Koichi Nagata, or the robe-like layers of Masayuki Abe. All these were more than names and images to spray across the pages of a magazine, more than a simple evidence of the Japanese cult of beauty. On arrival in Tokyo, Americans may suddenly feel that their countrymen are too casually dressed, are, in comparison, slobs. The fashions of Tokyo revealed not just a change in couture consciousness but a change in political power, a shifting of the economic ground; the rise of one country, Japan, and the decline of the other, America.

I was pleased by this conclusion. And surprised. It was as if I were cheering for the other side.

As we walked through Shinjuku, Susie and I talked about all this. "Of course, you love it here." She laughed. "And yes, it's superficial. But that's the reason I married you. You're just a fashion bimbo."

The great zipping neon of Parco ripped like lightning across the building's white façade. We were standing amid the crowds pouring out of the station, right in front of the dozen or so shoe-shine stands set up on the walk. Across the street, on the giant Alta video screen, danced a thirty-foot-tall Madonna.

"Let's go see a movie," Susie suggested. We bought *The Tokyo Journal,* a magazine in English, and looked in it for the movies. Among the listings was a picture of a man in a Western suit talking with a woman in a kimono. The caption read, *Hito Hara no Yuki.* "Something about snow or snowflakes," I said.

The movie was in Japanese, no subtitles. Language practice, we told ourselves. The colors were rich, delicate. A woman slipping off her kimono, the sound of silk. She opened a *shoji,* a man slid up behind her, cherry blossoms were falling. Then the man was in an airport slipping change from a leather pouch, calling her at home. She ran down the bare wooden stairs, stepped onto the tatami. Sometimes it was difficult to understand what was happening. At one point, Susie leaned over and whispered, "Is he having sex with his daughter?" I burst out laughing. She'd missed the entire plot. The man and woman were having an affair, and now her daughter was trying to seduce him. It was mid-afternoon; there was no one in the theater.

That night, on the way home from the station, we decided to poke our heads through the banners in front of one of the small little bars along the avenue. A dozen stools before a counter; in the back, wooden tables. Two men in suits sat on the center stools; at one end were men in work clothes. We were nervous, uncertain. We sat on the stools next to the door, as if we wanted to make a quick getaway. We looked at the menu on the wall. It was mostly in kanji, though some names of sushi were in phonetic characters which I could read. One of the men behind the bar, tall for a Japanese, and thin, asked in English if we needed help. I explained we didn't read Japanese, so he translated the menu and ordered for us. *Karei karaage, yakitori, nasu, ika, onigiri*—fried fish, teriyaki chicken on a skewer, eggplant, slices of squid, rice balls: a working-man's fare.

"I'm from Taiwan," Yoo-san said. He knew what it was like to be a foreigner. "I'm studying engineering at a technical college. Then I'll go back home."

With exaggerated lavish gestures, he soon began laying food down on our small square porcelain plates. Susie was radiant, excited, eager for dish after dish. After a while, the men began to flirt with her; they would say something to Yoo-san, laugh, and cast glances her way.

"What did they say?" Susie asked.

"Oh, they just wanted to buy you a drink." I felt flattered, not threatened. I thought I recognized in their glances my American privilege, possessing what they could not.

The next morning, Susie went to Roppongi to meet a friend of her father's from the States. I stayed home to write. Near noon, the doorbell rang. I opened the door to find an elderly woman dressed in polyester pants and a flower print blouse. Though she was dressed like one of the neighborhood housewives, the packages she carried made it obvious she was some sort of saleswoman. After our greetings, when it had become obvious I wasn't a native—a condition which will send many Tokyo shop clerks scrambling through the store for the one English speaker—I expected her to desist. Instead, I was surprised, pleased, and annoyed to find her persisting.

"*Basu kontororu,*" she said.

I had an urge to go running for my dictionary, but this was merely panic. It seemed obvious from the syllables that this was an English word which had been converted to Japanese pronounciation.

"*Basu kontororu?*" I repeated, as if this would do some good. She in turn repeated the words. All the while my brain was whirring: I could tell that the second word was "control," only the first word sounded like "bus"—the Japanese would pronounce bus *ba-su*—but "bus control" didn't make any sense. Perhaps she meant pest control.

"*Mushi? Mushi ga inai,*" I said, telling her we didn't have any bugs.

She shook her head, "*Ie, ie, ie,*" and asked me to let her show me. I nodded. As she pulled out what was obviously a condom, I began to laugh and repeat, "Ah, *basu kontororu . . .*" A determined saleswoman, she took one out of the wrapper and held it up, asking me to feel it. At this point I was afraid that she was going to ask me to try it on, so I told her that we actually wanted to have babies. My white lie prompted her blessings of good luck, and after she asked about Susie, the saleswoman observed that since my wife was a hakujin our babies would be very beautiful.

As I watched her walk down our narrow, alley-like street, past the small firs and jade trees in front of the houses, I surmised that there might be something at least a little different between American and Japanese attitudes toward sex. I wondered when we would be ready to have a child, if ever. There was too much for me to do now, I didn't want to be tied down.

When I later asked a Japanese friend about this incident, he said that these salesladies go through the various apartment complexes around the city hawking their wares. "I imagine," he said, "there must be some exaggeration if the men answer the door. You know, 'Well, you'll be back in two weeks? I guess I'll need at least two dozen.' "

3

In October, the skies cleared, the umbrellas vanished. Susie came home with flowers, placed them in a pot on my desk. We discovered a place down the road that served scones and whipped cream, a real find. The coffee was thick, bitter, meant for long hours of talk. I read in the booths, Oe, Enchi, Lévi-Strauss, Barthes. College kids passed by in sweaters of all colors. The girls' hair was long, straight; the boys' in cuts from the twenties, clean, blunt, weighted to one side.

We went to museums, galleries, Kabuki, watched Tomasaburo, the great *onnagata* (portrayer of women) dance as a court lady, flirt with a samurai, and then, in a marvelous, exaggerated swoon, surrender to grief at the samurai's death. On the stage were huge painted mountains, a giant cedar, a meandering stream. The plucked twang of a shamisen, held a moment too long. And then came the calls from the audience, thunderous applause.

At night the neon signs and the lights at the station were

muted and diffuse. Susie and I grew accustomed to the rhythm of
the trains, to waiting on the platform late at night, watching
drunken sarariman stumble past, bursting with song or with a
laughter that seemed to threaten their destruction, it was so uncon-
trolled. Once in a while, one would bend over the platform or fall
to his knees, spilling himself, his night. We turned away, moved
farther down. It was late, we had no obligations, no job, no children. We felt giddy as runaways.

We were on an adventure, anything could happen. It
would never happen again. We ate in restaurant after restaurant.
Walked home at night through deserted streets. We found a washing machine, a TV, dumped out with the trash; we dragged them
home, waving at the policemen standing in the doorway of their
tiny hut. No one in the country wanted secondhand goods. We did.
It was as if some gift had dropped from the skies. A motorcycle
skittered down the alley. We passed the circular-shaped house
owned by an architect; a pine that was like a painting, perfectly
shaped. At home, before rolling out the futon, we soaked in the
shoulder-deep bath, the steam drifting upward, sweat dripping
from our foreheads. We were exhausted. We never wanted to go
home.

At night I talked a bit about the Japanese women, then
veered away. It was something to be mentioned, not dwelt on. I had
had an affair years earlier with a Vietnamese student. That was part
of it. Once there had been a list of women. They were behind us
now. We had reached high ground.

Susie spoke of being restless, wanting to do something
with the year. She had planned to take up crocheting, flower arranging, to interview Japanese pediatricians, study shiatsu, to go over
papers on new research, the latest techniques in pediatric oncology.
She didn't know how to begin. After two intense years of residency,
of working eighty-, ninety-hour weeks, she had trouble adjusting
to not working. Suddenly I was the one who required more time
for my work, who wasn't always available. I couldn't, absolutely
couldn't be disturbed when writing. Our apartment was cramped.
There was no room for her. I felt she needed to break out, stop
following me around.

Susie said that I'd fallen in love with so many things about Japan, had tried so hard to fit in, that I'd even become a Japanese workaholic.

I did seem to require more and more time for my writing; I was recording a multitude of impressions, glimpses of street scenes, descriptions of performances, reflections on our adjustment. I had begun taking notes immediately after we arrived. I was prompted in part by my brief meeting with Donald Richie, the critic of Japanese movies. Sitting in the lobby of International House, where we stayed after we first arrived, Richie remarked: "Keep a diary; things will be changing so fast for you, all your impressions might be lost."

I didn't want to be a mere tourist. Unable to find a clear emotional or familial tie to the country—our family had had no contact with any relatives—I concentrated at first on the intellectual idea of Japan. And, out of a wish to shun *geisha* and floating-world stereotypes, I was more interested in what was happening in contemporary art in Japan than in the traditional arts. I intended to go after the post-modern Japan, not the Muromachi or Edo or even the Meiji Japan my grandparents knew. Certainly, I didn't want to go to Japan simply as a sightseer or an information gatherer, making the humanist assumption that human beings are all alike beneath the skin, all desire the same things, all think in the same basic ways. Because of my background, I saw myself as someone with an ability to look at Japan without the blinders of prejudice and ideology that hampered many of the accounts I had read. I did not realize that my sense of being able to write without the blinders of prejudice and ideology was chimerical. Instead, Japan was to help me understand more fully my own blinders.

October 12, 1985—What do I find here? Thousands of faces that look like mine, that day by day rush past me like a rain storm, my eyes registering the movement, trying to adjust my body to avoid collision, never having a moment to stare into any face, to observe its features. Then we are there on the platform, craning our heads down the track, or lost in a book or newspaper, or quietly talking, or blankly staring, and the train comes, and we push inside, crushed together, a wave of muscles and dead weight

*colliding, tugging, shoving, crunching tighter. In our own tiny space we
stand and look down, away from each other, but sneaking these looks, I see
the infinite variety of the faces, the ones that look Indian or Mexican or
Black or Chinese or Korean; that look like my aunts, my mother, my brother,
my cousin, my sister; that look like the women in the ads plastered across
the subway, the posters in the stations. I note the pale powdered faces, the
lavender eye shadow, the cool, placid surface, the perfection of a mask, a
beautiful Japanese mask, or the fresh-faced schoolgirls or boys, slight pimples
breaking their complexion, or else the complexion whole and smooth, dark,
rich, without a single splotch or blemish, and perhaps, like me, a tiny
teardrop dimple just below the eye. Or the sarariman, in their glasses and
slicked-back hair, their crewcuts, their suits not cut like those of younger men
in baggy, Japanese-dandy splendor, all paisley and bright colors, or impassive and cool black, but in blue pinstripes, with lines out of a Sears, Roebuck
catalogue . . . And I love it all, the sea of faces, the uncanny resemblances,
the hints of foreign genes in the cheekbones or lips or kink of the hair, and
yet the singular stamp of Japanese in each face, and I feel a wave of
happiness coming over me, a calm and combustive joy, a stamping of the feet
in my soul, a smile and a voice that says, You are unnoticeable here, you
have melded in, you can stand not uttering a word and be one of this crowd,
and in each job in this country, there is someone who looks like you, from
the Emperor to the rock singers, from Nakasone to Kazuo Ono, the great
Butoh dancer, from the newscaster to the hottest new fashion designer, from
the farmer to the man who adjusts robots in the Mitsubishi factory, from
the conductor to the schoolteacher, from Oe, the novelist, to Takemitsu, the
composer, from the onnagata to Oh, the former home-run king, all the
mothers and fathers and children—they look like you, and you are no longer
budgeted by your color, parceled out into certain jobs, certain places of
non-power, certain ghettos of the aesthetically backward and unappealing,
of the dull and downtrodden, of the inarticulate and the invisible.*

*Of course, this is all an illusion. I am American by birth and
tongue and cultural manners, and I will never be a true nihonjin, I will
always be outside, but even that seems okay—no one told me I should belong
here; in fact, everyone said I wouldn't, that I would come to love America
here, that I would realize how American I am, how deeply rock and roll
and football and Whitman and Huck Finn reside within me.*

Instead, the mirror has shifted. When I see hakujin on the train

*or in crowds or walking down the street, I think how out of place they look,
how awkward, how ungainly and even ugly, how pasty their skin looks,
how splotchy; how loud, how coarse, how unfashionable, how "uncool,"
how un-Japanese they are. And yes, they complain of this, of what they do
not understand of the manners here, the distance of the people, the lack of
center and depth, the absence of psychology, and I feel like saying, "The
power here does not reside in faces like your own, in language like your own,
in clothes and food like your own, in metaphysical and religious assumptions
like your own, and if there is no sin here and Christ is a funny little man
who has decided to grow skinny, and if you worship the nails in his flesh,
well, that's your masochistic trip. How does it feel to be incomprehensible,
to face the incomprehensible, your own ignorance, your own displacement
from the center of the world? . . ."*

As I talked about my writing, Susie listened patiently, with
energy she had never had as a resident, when she was drained by
working thirty-six-hour shifts. I sensed at times her uneasiness at the
anger that sometimes cropped up in my writing, but I didn't want
to stop. Our talk spun on to Rilke, Cortázar, Hemingway in Paris,
expatriates, memoirs, notebooks. Her patients, their deaths, their
recoveries seemed far off, though they hovered in her dreams. One
night she woke sobbing.

"Are you okay?"

A slit of blue light slid through the shoji. She rose up,
stared ahead. "It was a code," she said. "I was running down the
hall, but I could never get there. I kept hearing my name being
paged over and over. Then we were eating soba in a restaurant.
And I realized I'd forgotten my beeper. This panic came over me."

"It's over now, you're awake."

"I'm not so sure."

Her long brown hair slipped across her face, faint in the
shadows. She looked as she looked our first night together, she
looked nothing like that at all. She turned toward me and slipped
beneath the covers. A life, through dreams, calling her back. I
touched her face.

"Good night, hon."

"Good night."

4

Those first few weeks in Japan in many ways involved becoming like a child again. No, even the youngest Japanese schoolchildren knew more than we did. After all, they could speak the language.

A year before I left for Japan, I began studying Japanese, first at the University of Minnesota, then in New York at a summer session at Columbia. Japanese is, for a Westerner, an immensely difficult language. Unlike French or Spanish, Japanese requires that an English speaker forget everything he or she knows about English. No common roots, a totally different syntax. I'm not very good at languages, and even as I started to understand the basic grammar, even as I mastered my first kanji, I also felt a weariness and panic. I will never learn it. I will be totally unprepared.

These feelings were reconfirmed even before my summer class at Columbia began. Columbia wouldn't take my first-year credits at the University of Minnesota on faith, but they told me the entrance exam to the second-year course would be easy, I was almost assured of passing. Two days after I arrived in New York, on the morning of the test, I found myself in a room with only one other student, a rather studious-looking young girl with tortoise-shell glasses. The secretary handed out the test. I panicked. Many of the grammatical structures were unfamiliar, as was much of the vocabulary. Halfway through the period, the studious-looking girl stood up and handed in her test. I was still scribbling when the period ended.

When the results were posted that afternoon, I looked for my name. Something inside me plummeted like a gun-shot duck. I'd failed, I wasn't going to get in the class. My trip to Japan was over even before it had begun.

Immediately I went to talk to the instructor, Professor Ogawa. Opening the door to his office, I saw a small Japanese man bent over a book which was no farther than two inches from his nose. He seemed almost to be eating it, rather than looking at it. He looked up, squinted, his hair shaggy and straw-like. I knew this was going to be a struggle. He was adamant: I had failed to make the cut (a grade of B) by five points, there was nothing he could do. I should go back to the basics, do the first year over again. Regulations, rules. Nothing about my situation, about my having traveled a thousand miles and relocated in another city, about the conditions of my grant, which wouldn't pay for my repeating the first-year class, seemed to sway him. I was doomed.

And even though he finally let me in the class, even though I studied twelve hours a day, in the end, he was right. I wasn't prepared, I didn't work hard enough, I kept falling behind. The longer the class went on, the more impenetrable the language became, and my self-esteem fell as my grades became a steady stream of mediocrity. Or worse. Other students in the class also suffered the sensei's mockery when they misread kanji—*"Kakeru?"* he'd shout, as if the student had come to class without a stitch of clothes—but I seemed to get more of his criticism. I wondered if all Japanese were going to be like this. I thought about the joke circulating college campuses: If you go into class the first day and the majority of students are Asians, drop the class, the curve will be too high. Yet here I was, studying the language of my grandparents, and the hakujin in class were beating me, as were the Chinese grad students from Hong Kong. Was it because I was lazy (read: mentally deficient), a third-generation Americanized Asian? What would the Japanese say about such an obviously non-Japanese Japanese?

I quit after the first summer session, admitted my failure. It was not a very auspicious start.

5

"Ohaiyo gozaimusu!"

We blinked into the sunlight at our open door and, after a beat of hesitation, replied, *"Ohaiyo gozaimusu!"*

Hired by the Japanese sponsors of my grant, Mrs. Hayashi, our Japanese teacher, appeared promptly at ten o'clock one morning a few weeks after we arrived in Tokyo. On that first morning, there seemed something fierce and orderly about her, like the stereotype I had of a strict Japanese sensei. She was dressed in a gray suit, her hair in a neatly coiffed wave. We guessed she was probably in her middle forties and later learned she had two college-aged children. She immediately took the role of an older sister. After greeting us in Japanese, she pointed to the shoes in the *genkan* (entryway) and informed us first in Japanese and then in English that we should never leave our shoes out like that; we should put them in the shoe cabinet on the wall beside the doorway. She looked around for slippers to wear. "You need to buy slippers for your guests." Later, when she asked to use the washroom, she informed us that we needed to provide different slippers for the water closet. When we escorted her into the tatami-matted bedroom, she inquired if we had a table to work on and pillows. She mentioned some things about punctuality in Japanese society, as if putting us on guard never to wake up late. And certainly, after this litany of lessons—we would later refer to her fondly as Ms. Manners—we were definitely on guard. Immediately after the lesson we went out to purchase the proper slippers, a table, pillows, and tea and cakes to serve at the next lesson; we never left our shoes in the genkan again. As we expected, she was never late; we lived in fear of oversleeping after some late-night carousing in a Shinjuku bar. We saw ourselves stumbling out of bed to find her waiting in what we imagined as Japanese disapproval of the slovenly, untimely Americans. And yet, when this actually did happen, she quickly answered that she had forgotten to get something at a nearby store and handled our bad manners with remarkably gracious aplomb.

Although she would speak in English as a last resort, the whole session was conducted in Japanese almost from the start. Both Susie and I fumbled around the first few lessons; it was especially difficult for Susie, since she hadn't studied Japanese. From that first day, Mrs. Hayashi intended to teach us the culture as much as the language, and we began to see that her seemingly demanding demeanor was motivated by friendliness and concern. She wanted to let us know what was proper and improper in Japanese society.

She was solid and reliable, and her adherence to Japanese manners didn't seem stiff but instead came from a genuine regard for the other person and the necessity of civility in human relations. She never seemed to notice our mistakes, or corrected them so gently, so quietly, that we gradually overcame our self-consciousness and embarrassment. We were amazed at how rapidly we progressed, how soon we were conducting long, involved conversations in Japanese, though stopping quite frequently to ask her for vocabulary. I began to feel as if I would actually be able to use the language.

Often we found ourselves discussing things that had little to do with the lessons in our books. During the second lesson, Susie asked what to do about the men who pinched her on the crowded trains; every time she turned, all the heads were facing away and it was too crowded to decide who the culprit was. Mrs. Hayashi taught her the word for pervert—*henshitsu*—and told her she should simply yell it out. She couldn't help but add with a smile: "Usually, Susan-san, that happens to people after they've been here a long time, not just two weeks . . ."

During our lessons, odd little facts about the Japanese would come up and I would pounce on them as minor epiphanies of identity. One morning, as the three of us were drinking tea, Mrs. Hayashi remarked that Japanese don't like to drink a lot of liquid with their meals—except for the times when everyone gets plastered on *sake*—because they have small bladders. Immediately I heaved an enormous psychic sigh of relief, for as far back as I could remember, I was always embarrassed when I went into public washrooms and noticed how Caucasians would stand at the urinal for what looked like hours. I seemed to be instantaneously shaking myself dry and zipping up; oftentimes, just to keep up appearances, I would stand at the urinal long after my bladder had run its course. Look up at the ceiling, David, I told myself, count to twenty. At movies, Susie would always kid me about how I could never make it through a whole film without having to get up; once during medical school, she even wondered whether my frequent urination meant I had contracted diabetes. Listening to Mrs. Hayashi, I realized I wasn't a freak; I was simply Japanese.

During one early lesson, Mrs. Hayashi asked if my parents

had spoken much Japanese at home. No, I answered, and told her
this story: Once, when I was in college and we were at a Japanese
restaurant, my father said a couple of words in Japanese to the
waitress, and she began showering him with Japanese. He started
waving his hands in embarrassment, saying he didn't understand.
Just a few fragments remained in his memory.

When they were children, I explained to Mrs. Hayashi,
my parents spoke Japanese to their parents, English to their siblings.
I don't recall ever hearing them speak Japanese when I was a child,
though they must have spoken some to my grandparents. One
grandmother had died before I was born, another when I was four;
both grandfathers then went back to Japan, where they remarried
and eventually died. Of all of them, I felt closest to my father's
father, but this had nothing to do with our actual contact. I was too
young when he left the States.

Mrs. Hayashi asked about my name, which seemed
strange to her. She said that Mura, which means town, wouldn't
ordinarily appear alone. It always had a prefix—Nishimura (north
town), Nakamura (inside town), and so on.

Our original family name was Uyemura, I told her, but
my father, at the time a reporter for International News Services,
shortened it to Mura when I was six. People couldn't pronounce
Uyemura, he said. Up until I started studying Japanese, I too
couldn't remember exactly how to pronounce it. Besides, he believed he would get more bylines with the shorter name.

I didn't know what my grandfather thought of this
change. By then he was living in Japan; probably he had long ago
relinquished his offspring to America. The change of name simply
affirmed what had already happened.

What about the rest of your family? she asked.

My mother's family retained their Japanese names.
Miwako, Sachiko, Tadao, Yukimi, Yoshiko. But these were often
shortened to more American-sounding forms: Miwa or Mimi, Tad,
Yo. I've used my mother's name, Teruko, in a poem on a hibakusha. Members of my father's family changed their names to Ruth,
Ruby, and Ken. Born Katsuji, my father tried out Roy, Bob, and
several other monickers before settling on Tom. For a while it was

Thomas Katsuji Uyemura. Then Tom Katsuji Mura. Today it's Tom K. Mura. His children are David, Susan, John, and Linda. His wife is Terry.

Mrs. Hayashi laughed at this last litany. At the same time, I could tell she was intrigued. I was, for her, an odd version of a Japanese.

On the day Mrs. Hayashi taught me the character for *Uye*—it means plant—I felt a sudden sense of connection with the language and with my grandfather, with my ancestors and the farming village from which my name, Uyemura, derived. I wished I had known my grandparents, wished they were alive so I could talk to them in Japanese. I wanted to ask questions; there was no one to answer. And my frustration at this increased my resolve to return to my grandfather's native village. If I couldn't talk to him in person, perhaps I could talk to his ghost. I meant this as a figure of speech. I had no idea how often, in my journey of return, I would feel myself traversing the lines between the substantial and the insubstantial, the body and the spirit, the living and the dead.

Shortly after this talk with Mrs. Hayashi, I began to think about writing a novel about my grandfather. Only by having come to Japan, I realized, could I even begin to attempt such a novel. Previously I was able to know only the American side of him, and that only through the sketchy stories told by my aunt. His Japanese side was beyond my experience. I was just beginning to understand how much about him I didn't know.

In my clearest memory, my grandfather stands in the hall-way of our apartment, talking to my grandmother about the film *Rodan.* He's wearing a sleeveless undershirt, wire-rim glasses; his silver hair's somewhat long for an old man. His body is slightly bent. I'm sure it's the talk of the movie and the giant pterodactyl that destroys Tokyo that sustains this memory, rather than anything about him. I can't recall whether their talk was translated for me or if they spoke English.

While my father never talked of his father, my aunt Ruth always seemed willing to talk about him. It's through her stories that I've constructed an affinity between his sensibility and mine. I

know, for instance, that my grandfather arrived in America around
the beginning of the century, fleeing the draft and the Russo-
Japanese wars. At that time, almost all the *Issei,* or first generation,
were men, and they often sent back to Japan for brides. Sometimes
the pictures the men sent were fakes, and the brides would step
from the ships and find some dwarfish gnome, with crooked teeth
and a nose gnarled as a ginger root. Aunt Ruth took great pleasure
in telling me that my grandfather was so handsome he went back
to Shingu in person to find a bride. She would tell me about his love
of clothes, his gambling that lost him a pool hall, his bartending
days at a hotel in L.A., where Tom Mix and other stars hung out.
In these tales there was something extravagant and profligate about
my grandfather, something to contrast with the rigidness and busi-
nesslike attitude of my father, the Republican ways that I argued
against so much of my youth. It was my grandfather whom I wrote
poems about, a dashing, invented character who probably had more
to do with the gamblers in Westerns and my yearning for a romantic past than anything Japanese. I never really envisioned learning
that language, entering its otherness. And my father, in his second-
generation eagerness to prove his Americanness, in his own Oedi-
pal rebellion, gave me no encouragement in this direction.

In Japan, as my interest in my family background awakened, I began to read more about the first Japanese immigrants.
When my grandfather came to America in 1903, the ratio of Japanese men to Japanese women was about 10 to 1. Although during
the 1880s and early 1890s, most of the trickle of Japanese immigrants were students who intended to study the ways of the West,
by the time my grandfather arrived in the States the greater bulk
of immigrants were laborers. My grandfather, a draft dodger, was
fairly well educated, but his status was more like that of the laborers
than the students. Often second sons without property, these laborers hoped to make enough money in America to return to Japan and
buy land. It was not a new world they were seeking but a route back
to the old one. And so they brought no women, no family, with
them. All that would come later, a reward in the future.

Still, there were needs, and in various places along the
West Coast where the immigrants settled, there were Japanese
restaurants, bathhouses, hotels, and brothels with Japanese prosti-

tutes. Of course, the Japanese men were forbidden by law and custom to marry Caucasian women; intermarriage was as unthinkable as nuclear physics. My grandfather, like his fellow immigrants, must have frequented these brothels, which I imagine as dismal places, filled with sad men and even sadder women, all overcome by *natsukashii* (homesickness).

Near the turn of the century, various representatives of the Japanese government wrote letters to their superiors back in Japan deploring both the lowly status of many of the immigrants and the connections these lowlifes maintained with brothels and gambling houses. Japan at that time was in the midst of a big push toward Westernization and was desperately attempting to right the power balance between itself and the West and to avoid the Western imperialistic thrusts which had taken over much of Asia. The Japanese authorities were aware that the negative popular image of the Chinese laborers, the "coolies," had not only brought about exclusionary immigration laws but also had damaged the prestige of China and its government in Western eyes.

The distinction the Japanese government wished to make between the student immigrants and the laborers was also based on the strong Japanese sense of hierarchy brought about by centuries of feudal practices. Many of the laborers who came over were of the class which had no family names; family names were a privilege reserved for the samurai class. My paternal grandfather came from one of those whose family had only recently acquired a name.

The few mental images of him I possess start with his return to Japan about ten years later to find a bride. I constantly forget his first decade spent trying to earn enough money for the trip back home, the dreams of being able to buy a plot of land sufficient to live on. I know that something must have changed inside him in that period, that gradually the center of his world must have shifted, or rather, the concept of Japan as home somehow began to disappear. For when he returned to Japan, it was to get a bride to bring back to America; he was not going to raise his children in the tiny fishing and logging village of Shingu, with its mountains and semitropical forests, but in Los Angeles, amid the fields reclaimed from the desert, among the whites.

Who did not want him. When the Japanese immigrants

first arrived on the West Coast, most whites viewed them with the same scorn with which they viewed the Chinese, the "coolies" who had come to work on the railroads or in the logging industry. The Japanese and Chinese were undesirables, necessary for cheap labor but to be discarded as soon as possible.

Like my grandfather, the first Japanese immigrants were determined to raise themselves above their laborer status. Many began to acquire or rent property, to start up their own farms. Almost immediately protests began among the whites: it wasn't only that the Japanese were taking American land, they were taking it unfairly, working impossibly long hours, setting up their own distribution systems, living under housing conditions that the whites found intolerable. The Japanese did not send their goods to market at the same time everyone else did but speeded up their harvests or slowed them down so that their crops came at a time when the market price was higher.

The current charges of unfair Japanese business practices go back a long way. Ironically, the many barriers that the whites on the West Coast put up against the Japanese immigrants probably helped ensure that those immigrants became permanent. If the immigrants had been able to make their bundle quickly, they would simply have returned home. Instead, over the years, they began to cut their psychological and emotional ties to Japan just as my grandfather did.

As for his grandson, eighty years later, I was simply a student come to study his grandfather's homeland. I wasn't going to stay, to become uprooted.

IV

"The Japanese. A delightful people, fond of light wine and dancing."

—Ernest Hemingway,
A Farewell to Arms

"In the Antilles . . . in the magazines, the Wolf, the Devil, the Evil Spirit, the Bad Man, the Savage are always symbolized by Negroes or Indians; since there is always identification with the victor, the little Negro, quite as easily as the little white boy, becomes an explorer, an adventurer, a missionary 'who faces the danger of being eaten by the wicked Negroes.' . . . The black school boy in the Antilles, who in his lessons is forever talking about 'our ancestors, the Gauls,' identifies himself with the explorer, the bringer of civilization, the white man who carries truth to savages—an all-white truth. There is identification—that is, the young Negro subjectively adopts a white man's attitude. He invests the hero, who is white, with all his own aggression—at that age closely linked to sacrificial dedication, a sacrificial dedication permeated with sadism."

—Frantz Fanon, *Black Skin, White Masks*

1

A few weeks after I arrived in Japan, Reiko took me to my first performance of Butoh. Plan B, the concrete basement space where members of the Maijuku group perform, is located a long train ride away from the center sections of Tokyo, amid the endless miles of urban sprawl. Although the troupe and the space were in one sense world-famous—I noticed a cartoon autographed with a greeting by Susan Sontag—I doubt if I would have been able to find the place without Reiko's help. At one point, even she had to ask a policeman for directions. The neighborhood seemed a little more run down than Mejiro, more patches of rusting corrugated panels, fewer glitzy new shops with gleaming white tiles. We had passed several warehouses, gray and bulky as barns.

As we settled in our seats, I remarked to Reiko that I was surprised at how ramshackle, crude, and tiny the space was. She smiled wryly, as if to say, "What else would you expect?"

The night's performance was given by a European who had come to study with Min Tanaka, the head of the Maijuku. The piece took place among tires piled on top of each other. Fish were wedged in between the tires. At first, after the initial blackout, the space was so dimly lit I could barely see the dancer shoving a tire back and forth to the sound of water pumping, as if he were working in some dark, dank boiler room on a tramp steamer. Gradually I saw he was wearing a loincloth, and his body and face were whitened. His movements were strong and muscular, very jerky, much quicker than in the riveting performance of Sankai Juku I had seen on public television. There the dancers, also in whiteface, slithered with infinitesimal slowness in and out of giant industrial

ducts, their faces eerily placid, betraying no emotion; their movements—primordial and subhuman—suggesting the tediousness and
sluggish energy of larvae or worms.

Now marching music started up, and the dancer was suddenly in front of me, caressing a fish, slapping it against his body,
his face twisting into the mock sadness of Stan Laurel, a thin, gaunt
caricature of the tragic mask; he rubbed his nose against the fish,
tore it across his face, the blood smearing. Now he was on all fours,
but upside down, walking like a crab, the fish resting on his belly.
Groans. The smell of his body; sweat like rain dripping down his
face and limbs; spittle drooling from his mouth, no effort to hide
it. Now he was sitting on the floor, hiding his face, curling his body
into a fetal position over the fish, rocking back and forth with the
movements of an infant.

As we sat afterward with members of the troupe and the
audience, drinking tea in a small room plastered with posters of
Butoh dancers, dance magazines piled everywhere, I didn't know
what to think. I found the performance visceral, affecting. I was also
struck by the fact that dancers from all over the world—Greece,
France, Belgium, the Netherlands, America—had come to study
with Min Tanaka. The voices in that small room echoed the multi-
plicity of Babel. Everyone seemed at ease and animated. The dress
was universal bohemian—dark pants or jeans, dark sweaters,
leather jackets, berets and boots, the ever-present cigarette
propped on the crooked arm. I never got over how many of the
Japanese dancers smoked: no difference here between them and the
tobacco junkie sarariman.

Karyn, one of the members of the troupe, turned out to
be the daughter of an American poet; she was pleased and surprised
when I said that I knew his work. I was curious about what it was
like to grow up as the daughter of a poet.

"Oh, I don't know. It's not that different."

I'd always worried that if we did have children, having a
father who was a poet would be a bit strange for them. I felt oddly
disappointed by her unromantic reply.

Karyn said she worked as a hostess in a bar. It was a
horrible job, but the pay was okay. The sarariman liked Caucasian

hostesses. They would get drunk and then, accompanied by a taped back-up without vocals, sing into a microphone. Sometimes they wanted her to sing.

"It's always 'My Way,' or sometimes 'Yesterday,' " she said. "They have such corny taste . . . But the worst is when they start grabbing you under the table."

Still, she loved working with Min Tanaka's troupe. The training sessions were strenuous and exhausting, pushed her to new limits. She was sorry to be going home in a month, and yet it was time to leave. She wanted to get back to the States.

I wondered when or if I would come to feel that way.

There were dance magazines on the bookshelves against the wall. I went over to look at them and found a copy of Reiko's magazine. When I pointed this out to her, Reiko began telling me about other Butoh troupes and dancers. Although when we first met our conversations had been somewhat stunted, her English seemed to be improving fairly quickly, as if the vocabulary was there all along but had been impeded by self-consciousness and a lack of continuous practice. We did reach an impasse at one point when she tried to describe a dance that Hijikata Tatsume did to the Beatles' "I Am the Walrus." Finally she took out a pen and drew a thin man with a huge erection. This, of course, only made things more confusing, and it took me a couple of minutes to figure out that Hijikata was not doing a strip show but had been wearing a dildo strapped to his groin. Not, of course, that this made much difference. I told Reiko I could hardly imagine myself doing *that*. She laughed and gave me another of her smiles. We'll see, it said. We'll just have to see.

Later that night, I wrote in my diary:

More than a month into our stay here, the days go by quicker, and though routine hasn't begun to set in—my schedule is still quite chaotic—not everything has the same intense quality that things did initially. Now, when I walk down the street, I'm not bowled over by all the faces that look like me, a wide grin doesn't always automatically cross my face at the mass of pedestrians in the blocked-off streets of Shinjuku (the effect there is as if they had closed off Times Square and the streets were filled with

*people, sort of like New Year's Eve). I don't notice how alien the omnipres-
ent kanji seem, I'm not surprised at the abundance of katakana (the
alphabet they use for foreign words) advertising everything from the expected
Macudonarudo (McDonald's) to the Pikokku grocery to the clothes shop,
Sumarto Man. Although going into a drugstore or a yakitori shop is often
still an exercise in fear and stupidity, in mime and blank looks, a sense of
shame at not being* joozu *(proficient), more and more we achieve that sense
of grand accomplishment when we walk out with what we wanted or
something reasonably approaching what we wanted. Riding on the trains,
I no longer have to look at the maps to find the cost of where I'm going, I
no longer ride anxiously craning my head backward at each stop, feverishly
trying to read the* hiragana *(the phonetic alphabet for Japanese words) to
see if we're at the right station; instead, I read, study my Japanese vocabulary, barely aware of my surroundings, packed in with the crowds, hardly
noticing the foreign language being giggled next to me by schoolgirls or two
drunken sarariman. I have the stops memorized; I understand what station
the conductor is announcing.*

*We no longer enter a restaurant wondering if we're even going
to be able to get fed, dreading the check, hoping the cash register will show
the cost in Roman numerals and that I won't have to decipher the prices
from what the waitress tells me. And the food is no longer a marvelous array
of things I've never seen in America, incredibly cheap and convenient.
Instead, there are the basics of tonkatsu (pork cutlets), sushi/sashimi,
tempura, soba, yakitori,* cha han *(Chinese fried rice), and gyoza (dump-
lings), with occasional forays into Western food, such as paella or an
occasional Big Mac, but mainly Japanese food, since the Japanese diet makes
any other food seem bulky, bloated, too buttery.*

*So, if what Susie says is true, if I've fallen in love with this
country and the first few weeks here have been the first throes of an affair,
that initial high is ending. And the pummeling, dazzling intensity of each
new day relents a bit, and things begin losing some of their alien quality;
slowly it sinks in: we're actually living here, this place is becoming home,
time has passed—I no longer hear the crickets as I write this; if I stepped
outside my door, my breath would cloud the air.*

*A few days ago, all this combined to bring back some of my old
neuroses, neuroses I hadn't experienced for almost a month and which I had
come to believe I might almost lose here. I began to wonder if what I was*

doing with my time was the right thing, if what I was writing about was interesting or important, if what would come of it would reach those perverse standards my neuroses keep conjuring up. Or will it all simply remain a formless experience, a year when I should have been doing this or that, perhaps writing more poetry, but didn't? These questions search for hard, fast answers when there are none, refuse process and uncertainty, and cling to standards, ambition, predictions of the future.

The next day I decided there is simply too much here to do; my experiences are so varied and odd that I don't have time to worry. I need to have a bit of faith. V. S. Naipaul has remarked that traveling for a writer is a gamble; something interesting may pop up, some crucial incident or revelation, and then again, nothing may happen. Fortunately, given my racial background, my stay here in Japan isn't really a gamble: the dice are rigged.

For one thing, unlike Hal, who complained and disavowed the Japanese eschewal of psychology, I've come to find that the surface of Japan, the seeming distance of the social relations, the absence of psychology, often seems a relief to me. I've gone through therapy and an enormous amount of work to be able to be more open and affectionate, and in America I am constantly hugging people goodbye. And yet I often use such hugs as a barometer of the way people feel about me, and if I am not hugged, I take this as a sign of a loss of love or affection, a personal judgment. Coming into a culture where people do not hug in public takes away a certain amount of worry or neurotic need.

In my family, we did not touch each other, we did not hug, and I wonder whether that was a carryover from Japanese culture. In what ways have I had to make cross-cultural adjustments without even knowing that I was doing so? . . .

After I finished this entry, I sat back, listening to Toru Takemitsu's score to Kurosawa's *Ran.* A Noh flute zagged its way up a scale, amid a flurry of strings. I slipped off the earphones, took a sip of green tea. The room was cool. We would have to get an electric heater soon. Behind me, the sliding doors were closed. Susie had already rolled out the futon and was asleep. I thought of the images of the Butoh dancer, of the smoke-filled reception afterward. I was tired, ready for a scalding Japanese bath.

2

I am going to my first Butoh *keiko* (training). On the train I read
V. S. Naipaul's *The Crocodiles of Yamoussoukro,* about his travels
through the Ivory Coast, a trip to the President's palace, where the
crocodiles, in an afternoon ritual, are fed a live chicken. Stations
pass, their names unknown to me, sounding almost African—Shin-
okubo, Toteneki, Nakano. Since none of them is my destination,
each creates a further uncertainty: I've boarded the wrong train,
will be stranded at some station with no one to call, no way home.
Reiko was unable to accompany me on this first trip, and I am,
despite my worries, grateful for this. I feel I already owe her so
much, without her taking the two-hour trip to Ono's studio. Still,
en route to Ono's house in Yokohama, beyond the familiar confines
of Tokyo, I find my newfound confidence ebbing. Again, I feel
beset by the fears of a foreigner, an illiterate, a peasant in the city,
a primitive man.

   As the train rumbles on, Naipaul is talking to a professor
of African drummologie. "The world of the white men is real," says
the professor. "But, but. We black Africans, we have all they have,
we have all of that in the world of the night, the world of darkness."
And so, says Naipaul, the talk turns away from the modern African
city of hotels and golf courses, the Mercedes and its chauffeur, the
overextended French restaurants with their shoddy service. It turns
away and moves into the night, the other world. It is the world of
djinns and doubles, of travel where the body stays, sitting placidly
while the spirit travels to another continent, to the world of the
dead, seeking a father, a mother, a son.

   We arrive at my stop. I get off under the eye of the video
camera, which shows me on a screen with the crowd erupting from
the train, moving down the platform. As I enter the station, I don't
know where I am. All around are the ever-present crowds, the faces

of strangers, the faces of my ancestors. My next train is leaving. But I don't know where the platform is. And I enter, as I have so many times these first few weeks in Japan, a state of panic. I'm lost. I'm late. I'll never arrive. As I scramble through the giant Yokohama station, frantically asking directions, the image of Ono's dance pops into my head and I think, What in the world am I doing? Why do I want to study with this man?

An hour later, I enter a room, a long gray hall with dark wooden floors. On one wall, there's an abstract etching, like the Nazca lines, and then a color drawing of Ono; beneath, lined against the wall, are women's shoes, including a silver pair of high heels. A snare drum and cymbal behind the old battered couch. Last month's calendar next to a cabinet with vases and artificial flowers on top, a book of pictures of Mishima, porcelain horses, a horn, a Japanese doll. Surrounded by the couch and a couple of old chairs, there's a coffee table cluttered with papers, bottles of Creap creamer, a bottle of Brim. Twisted roots of ginger from Korea, bottled in honey. Kleenex, tea bags, sugar, fruit in a basket, sweet *simbei* (rice crackers).

Ono goes to his house next door. I introduce myself to a man in gray sweat pants with the body of a gymnast or a soldier, his torso naked, muscular, lean, his biceps pronounced. His head is closely cropped, a crew cut; his face is shaved, but the stubble is dark; his eyebrows are thick, close, his eyes deep-set. His face reminds me of the great Japanese author Yukio Mishima; so does his body. It implies strength, a taut wire, the hint of cruelty. I stumble through my Japanese, letting him know where I'm from. (Later I learn that Hideshima has been studying with Ono-san for twelve years. The other students call him "the first student.")

He sits down in a chair as I go to the back to change to my sweats. I pass a table with a makeup mirror, flowers, capes. I suddenly begin sweating and feel incredibly awkward.

The other students, all fairly young, in their late twenties or early thirties, arrive. In comparison to Hideshima, they are smaller, slighter, their bodies less obviously those of dancers. I hand out my newly printed *meishi* (business cards), as I've been instructed, a Japanese ritual. Yet I feel like an impostor, afraid of being discovered, my lack of Japanese exposed. I try to nod appropriately, to smile when the others smile. The others don't seem to notice I'm faking. They are talking to each other. I feel self-conscious writing down notes in English. The man next to me notices.

Ono hands a book of poems to Hideshima, then gives a slighter, smaller man a different book. Another dancer, her face hidden by bangs, her body lost in gray baggy sweats, looks at a magazine with pictures of Ono in a black dress cavorting on an English lawn, while his son, in white makeup and shaved head, stands behind him attentively, like a butler. Long moments of silence as the other six students, now in dark, unmatching sweats, T-shirts, or long underwear, lounge about and look at the books.

Ono is wearing a gray, prison-striped, Mexican-style shirt with a long pointed collar, and blue cotton pants. Barefoot, he squats in the chair, knees settling his lower legs in a V. Not the posture of a European but of a man used to sitting on floors.

Without any formal signal for the class to commence, he begins to talk. I notice that his hands seem enormously large, expressive, the thumb and little finger often moving in opposition to the middle fingers. Frequently, they hang limp from a forearm held parallel to the ground; at times, in this position, especially when he strains his chest forward, showing the motion of a dance movement, he looks like a baby chick emerging weakly from the egg, feebly pulling its head up into the light. And yet these movements are strong, timeless, and, through a slight twisting or raising of the arms, a twist of the torso, a thrust of the neck, the dropping of the jaw, a guttural sound in the throat (his flexibility makes it hard to believe he is eighty), his body appears capable of an infinite expressiveness. I have no idea really what he is talking about, but the gestures command my attention.

A dog barks in the yard, snapping through the sound of crickets, the wind. Onho's hands seem to move of their own accord, his voice breaking from time to time into repetition. He translates a few words from the last of the New Testament, and I try to connect the gestures, the cadences of the speech, the frail thinness and absolute strength of the body with the skinny Christ of the crucifix, his grace and agony. As the arms are swinging through the air, all I pick up through the Japanese is *"Kangaenai . . . kangaenai . . ."*—Don't think, don't think. I feel I might be wasting my time, it might have been a mistake to come. I keep hoping the sensei will not look at me, not see I don't understand. I edge back a bit; I bend my head closer, still attempting to listen. I don't understand. I think of Susie, visiting a friend and a Japanese family in a cabin near Mt. Fuji. I wish I were there.

A few minutes later, another student walks in. I am saved: Sekai, Ono says, will translate for me. Sekai is in his late twenties, with short cropped hair and thick, wire-rim glasses, with a puffiness about his features that makes him look slower than he is. I later learn that he's a photographer and is studying with Ono to learn more about the soul. Although Sekai's English is not really fluent, his translations help, and slowly I feel myself falling under Ono's spell.

As he talks, I watch the gentleness in Ono's hands, their strength, the repetition of certain words emphasized with repeated shakes—not the emphatic insistence of didacticism, but the repetition of dance, the retrieval of motion from randomness into expression, the cadence of music and body coming together. At times, he opens his hands as if presenting an offering. When he speaks about the cosmos, he spreads his arms up and then outward in a circle; when he speaks of hugging a dead man, he wraps his arms around himself and rolls gently back and forth. I feel less that I am listening to a harsh Japanese sensei, or even to the calm, pure wisdom and emptiness of a Buddhist master, and more that I'm in the presence of some shaman, some Native American wise man, a guide between this world and the next.

"Even if a person does not cry physical tears, that person may be sad inside. In dance, sadness does not just show itself on the outside, tears must be inside too. The body reacts because it's alive. I can't separate the two. And what is present is both the physical and non-physical. When you are sad, it is not just your single self who is sad, but all the dead people, the great number of souls who are living inside you . . .

"The dead people say they won't or can't cry. So I will cry

for them. And the cosmos is crying too. In Butoh, then, I have to enter the world of the dead, and even though I can't talk to the dead, because the dead do not talk, I know through my body, my body is there, and I feel very happy hugging a dead person.

"There are people who say the dead don't cry, and it's true, sometimes it's hard to tell if someone is crying or happy.

"When you dance, you must dance through the wall of the body. During my dance of Mozart, on the video, I am not doing a lot outside, but I am moving inside. If I move too much outside, I lose the within, the source or energy, the feeling that propels the dance. In order to break through the wall, I must hold on to and not forget what's inside. It's the relationship between what is living inside me and the living realm of the dead that is dance . . ."

And then the talking is done. It is time to dance. Ono motions for me to join the others. Not knowing whether I was coming here as an observer or a student, I hesitate. Will I make a fool of myself? Am I imposing? What right do I have to claim to be here as a student?

And then easily, quickly, my hesitations fall away. I join the others.

The Japanese are extremely polite and will go to immense lengths to avoid criticizing or confronting others. Foreign artists frequently remark that because of this lack of open criticism, Japanese artists don't develop and are unable to talk about their art with any vehemence or sense of the struggle to improve. These foreign artists often miss how much is imparted in Japanese society without words or direct expression. They also fail to see how, at least in the Japanese traditional arts, much of the learning that takes place is in the process of imitating the master. After years of study, most pupils don't need to be told how they fall short. Still, this charge that the Japanese lack the stomach for direct criticism has some truth.

Yet this attitude toward direct criticism provides a wonderful atmosphere for beginners; it allows one to develop an interest, to gain a foothold of understanding and technique, while overcoming self-doubts or self-consciousness. As Zeami, the great theorist of Noh, wrote: "At first [the apprentice actor] should be allowed to act as he pleases in what he happens to take up naturally and follow his own inclinations. He should not be instructed in minute detail, or told that this or that is good or bad. If he is taught too strictly he will lose heart and also become uninterested in the Noh and forthwith cease to make any progress in performance."

I'm sure I sensed such an attitude from Ono. Otherwise I would never have made such a fool of myself.

The dancers spread out across the wooden floor, doing knee bends and stretches, rolling their necks back and forth, in a ritual of loosening I try to imitate. Ono snaps a tape into the machine: a Japanese flute begins to play, the notes quavering, low, a series of drones and moans. The others around me start moving, very slowly, drifting, shifting into a trance.

I start with a squatting position, what seems the least affected to me. I put my hands on the floor in front of me and begin to lower myself into a crawling and then a prone position, all the while trying to keep thoughts about appearing ridiculous out of my mind, trying not to see the whole situation as an American, or someone unfamiliar with Butoh, might.

I look at the others around me, one woman lowering herself also into a crouch, and then slowly lowering herself to the ground; another man, staring forward, arms held as if in some karate pose called the praying mantis or the twisted crane; another moving with arms strapped across his chest, hugging his body as if trapped in a straitjacket. I am crawling on the floor, and as I close my eyes, Ono, who has been muttering, "Free, free" and *"Kangae-nai, kangaenai,"* stops everyone and says that in Butoh you keep your eyes open, slightly raised above eye-level vision. If you close your eyes, you lose the spirit, the process of giving and receiving, of creating a flow between what you see outside you and what is inside you; your eyes should take in the whole field of vision, but should not be focused on any particular object. Only the dead do not see, and when you are dancing you should be neither asleep nor dead, though you should be communicating, exchanging, with the world of the dead.

A bit later, he stops someone and tells him to slow down.

By slowing down you make your movements larger, says Ono; everything in the dance changes. After a few more minutes, he gives me an artificial oversized lily and tells me to look at it without focusing my eyes. It is an offering, he says. Somehow I sense he wants me to stop conceptualizing, to stop thinking how ridiculously or awkwardly or poorly I might be dancing, to forget what I am trying to represent with the dance, what I am trying to symbolize or imitate.

And, at certain moments, I do stop thinking. A brief, unnameable sadness seems to well up within me, and yet is offset by a rising joy. I start walking toward the screen door, where I see my grandfather and grandmother. I present them with the flower, a greeting bearing some part of me that has wandered through the world, unwhole, lost, bewildered, alien, fading in and out of the sense of playacting, of pleasing the sensei. I get a glimpse of what my self-consciousness misses.

3

Unlike most modern dance in Japan, Butoh has managed to escape being a pale pastiche of Western modern dance. Butoh finds its roots in the peasant culture of Japan, the movement of the rice fields, the grounding of the Japanese body close to the earth. It celebrates the short, stumpy legs and squat torso of the Japanese body, the body that sits on the floor, sleeps and dreams on the floor. In contrast to the leaps of a dance like ballet, the energy of Butoh is horizontal, close to the ground. The movements are stylized but not formalized, and are rarely choreographed with anywhere near the precision of Western modern dance. The faces and sometimes the entire bodies of Butoh dancers are generally white; often they wear only a loincloth; sometimes they are naked; sometimes they wear costumes, rags, or strange material, such as metal wires. The movements are the very opposite of graceful: jerky, halting, writhing, bumbling, almost spasmodic. As a Greek dancer who was a member of the Maijuku troupe told me, "Studying Butoh, I had to forget my classical training. I had to lose my sense of grace."

The effect of Butoh is enigmatic, muscular, ancient, dark. If one looks at present-day Japanese culture, one finds the delicate, aristocratic beauty of the feudal age preserved alongside the current culture of infinite silliness, cuteness, and fashionability. Butoh seems the almost necessary third dialectical element, the hidden side of the great postwar economic miracle. Originally, it was called "Ankoku Butoh" or "Dark Dance," and all its founders were from the north of Japan, the area of harsh winters and poor harvests. One Butoh dancer remarked, "When I came to Tokyo, I saw people who had hope. Where I came from, there is no hope."

To some, the twisted spasmodic movement of Butoh dancers seems to satirize the precision of contemporary Japan and its technology, or one of the by-products of that precision, the robot. To others, Butoh dancers seem reminiscent of hibakusha, survivors of some horrible apocalypse. This association is reinforced by the extreme slowness of a great deal of Butoh, a slowness perhaps derived from the slowness of Noh. There is also the technique, used particularly by the Hijikata troupe, of rolling the eyes up in the head, so only the whites show; at the same time, the dancer puckers his or her mouth so as to appear toothless. The lead dancer of the Hijikata troupe, Ashikawa, had her teeth pulled out to make this effect permanent.

Other associations come up with specific dancers—Min Tanaka often seems to be a parody or even an embodiment of the drunks who sleep in Shinjuku station: their glassy, wild-eyed gaze, their stumbling, herky-jerky movements. In "Admiring Argentina," Ono dresses in high heels, stockings, a long gown, a hat with a lace veil, a wig, whiteface, and makeup; the dance is a tribute to a flamenco dancer he saw from the balcony of the Tokyo theater in 1929, who inspired him to be a dancer. As Ono flounces about the stage, he resembles an aging Bette Davis, or Gloria Swanson in *Sunset Boulevard,* a grande dame trying to regain the grace and beauty of her youth and failing miserably, pathetically, heroically, falling on the stage, tangoing and twirling across it, clicking invisible castanets. In another piece, this time to Mozart, clad only in a loincloth, Ono leans against a piano and raises his arms slowly above his head. This gesture takes the length of the song and seems to mime the pathos of the Crucifixion, and yet at the same time to welcome a rainfall or some light from the heavens. Sometimes Ono will dance with his son, whose head is shaved and who dances in white silk culottes, a white blouse, and whiteface. The son's slow, impassive movements carry an otherworldly quality; he seems like some celestial space creature accidentally passing by, oblivious to Ono's pratfalls in a tuxedo.

But this attempt to read a definable content into Butoh is probably misguided. Presented most often with the starkness of the Noh stage or the plays of Beckett; freely using elements from Western music, but always managing to incorporate those elements into its essential Japaneseness; embracing the ugly or the grotesque, Butoh refuses to signify anything. Its dances are blank, impassive, without motivation or depth.

My choice to study Butoh with Ono was not arbitrary. Just as the fact that Ono was a good friend of Mishima was not arbitrary, despite Mishima's fierce militancy and fascist leanings and Ono's gentle, otherworldly manner. Both men represent a challenge to present-day Japan and to the increasing commercialization and trivialization of Japanese culture. Just as importantly for me, both represent a complicated non-Western investigation of sexuality. Mishima, the contemporary proponent of the samurai spirit, was a homosexual who lived his public life as a married man with two children. Ono, the portrayer and near-parodist of aging women, is a retired gym teacher who had been married for decades, yet seems to possess the sexual ambiguity one associates with a figure like Tiresias, an ambiguity brought on by wisdom, the body's withering, and the presence of death.

Before I came to Japan, the one Japanese author I felt a strong connection to was Mishima. I had written poems, even a play about him. What I identified with was the sense of transgression in his writing, a view of sexuality allied with rage, abasement, and self-loathing, and, therefore, with a sense of liberation, a vertigo that comes with letting go all ties to what seems socially sanctioned. Early on in Mishima's semiautobiographical novel, *Confessions of a Mask,* even before the protagonist reaches puberty and discovers his homosexual impulses, he speaks of a fascination with becoming someone other than himself and associates this impulse with tragedy and death. One day, after pulling out his mother's clothes, he dresses up as Tenkatsu, the geisha magician. Running about the house crying, "I'm Tenkatsu!" he suddenly encounters his mother, whose look of astonishment and horror causes him to lower his eyes and start to cry. In a fit of shame, he understands for the first time the motif of "remorse as prelude to sin" that is to characterize his life.

When I first read this scene, I felt the force of self-recognition. But how could this be? I had never had transsexual urges, nor was I homosexual. My parents were raised as Buddhist, then became Christian, but there was hardly a strong air of sexuality as sin in our Episcopalian household. Or was there? The isolation that Mishima speaks about followed me for years. And I often felt that it was tied to my sense of being Japanese, of looking different, less masterful, less masculine; my sexual self seemed charged with hints of inferiority and found it hard to believe in the reciprocation of desire.

Somehow this self had been drawn toward Ono. Why?

It has been argued that the white powder of Japanese makeup turns the face to a blank sheet, a space of writing. The white powder isn't meant to make a man resemble a woman; instead, it is an emptiness where, with black ink, the signs of womanhood are written. The makeup is a language, not a pictorial representation. This helps explain why an aging patriarch of a famous acting family, a married man with several children, can don each night the whiteface of a geisha in Kabuki or the woman's mask in Noh with an impunity and lack of parody impossible to conceive of in the West. And since Japanese social life so strongly emphasizes playing an assigned role, the Japanese are less apt to see or desire a strict congruence between what happens on stage and off. They realize the play is art, not life, is a system of signs and not the real thing.

Ono certainly drew on this sense of the self and sexual

identity when he took the stage to dance, though the hint of a Western aesthetic helped give his dance an element of parody and perhaps pushed it into both pathos and genius. It was as if he knew that the onnagata, the man who plays a woman on stage, could no longer retain the pure symbolic status of the feudal age; too much of the West had penetrated into the Japanese consciousness.

Ono's depictions of the grande dame, of the aging flamenco dancer, seemed a liberating pathway out of the rigid sexual images I'd grown up with in America, images which imprinted themselves on my consciousness while, at the same time, they excluded me. In the presence of Ono, the feminine traits I felt in my features, in my sensibility, seemed less odd, seemed something I shared with the other members of the class. This identity was more fluid, less neatly proscribed.

And yet my fascination with Ono held a hint of something morbid, as if it came out of the same impulses as my fascination with Mishima, his sense of longing and shame. Against Ono's airiness, his ethereal spirit, I also felt the presence of Mishima, a longing to embrace the most outrageous masquerade, to shock and therefore plummet, falling into and embracing my fears that I was weak, isolated, damned.

I also recognized this balancing between these two spirits as the tension out of which my writing appeared.

But there was more to my interest in Ono than a pull toward *frisson,* his ambiguous sexuality. He was also a man who talked more about the dead than anyone I had ever met before.

Although I know very little about my grandparents, I do know that my grandmother was reputed to be psychic. Her dreams sometimes predicted the future or sensed simultaneous events halfway around the world. My aunt has told me a few stories about these powers, but my father never mentions them. They're irrelevant, family lore, superstitions.

Perhaps Ono was as close as I could get to my grandparents. An eighty-year-old Japanese man, one who grew up with the ways of the Meiji era. Someone who spoke of the world of the dead, who walked as freely, perhaps even more freely, in their world as in the world of contemporary Tokyo, the fashion shops of Harajuku with their punks and bobby-soxers, the sarariman on the trains reading their comic books, the great auto factories of Honda and Toyota.

I went to Ono's class two, sometimes three, times a week. The trip took two hours each way on the train. Between the commute and the three-hour classes, Butoh took up a large part of my time. And in garages or warehouses on the outskirts of Tokyo, in the brand-new theater at the top of Seibu department store, Susie and I attended performances and rehearsals of other troupes. She was as intrigued as I was by the bizarreness of Butoh. But when I started going to see performances of Noh, in an attempt to get a better feel for the underlying similarities of the two art forms, she demurred. The chanting of Noh seemed dronelike to her, the movements slow to the point of boredom. It made her want to sleep.

"I like that feeling," I told her. "It's like a religious state. It reminds me of Episcopalian Communion, only there's not all that stuff about Jesus and a white man being God."

She laughed. "Well, I'm a Unitarian, and it's not for me."

"It's theater for introverts. Without all the strut and *Sturm und Drang* of Kabuki."

"Well, be glad that I at least like Butoh."

When I returned from my Butoh classes, Susie was usually asleep. In the other room of our apartment, I'd sit at my computer and write down my impressions.

Ono-san finishes and, smiling, asks if I understood, then asks one of the students to translate: There is thunder crashing—I see and hear again, Ono-san making the guttural, windy noises in his throat—and there is a horse galloping in the sky—I see Ono-san raise his head, lengthen his face, bring his legs, no, his arms up, as if clawing the air. When the horses, when the horse, bites the thunder, many colored horses burst out. It is the same as the creation of the cosmos, the creation of a child in the womb. The universe started as a tiny ball of dust and that ball exploded, creating the cosmos. This is the biting of the horse. A red horse, a white horse.

"It's hard," says the translator. "Do you understand?"

* * *

The record is the sound of rain falling, a train whistle, the train roaring in from the distance, closer, closer, right across my face, then slashing away from me, fading, lost in the rain. Over and over, a train coming, fading.

I am awkward, a thinker, a believer in French meals, new buildings, a man from the land of golf courses, highways, air-conditioned homes. I do not believe in spirits, I do not worship the night. I acknowledge no double, no movement of the drums. I have never danced in performance, have never studied any sort of steps. I have little relation to my body. I am a writer, an intellectual. An abstracter, a looker. One who does not let go.

Thinking is too noisy. I become three bright stones. Twisted. Fruitfall. My body knots itself. My eyes must be open, gazing at nothing, bringing everything in. Eyes open, says Ono-san, eyes open. My arm is shaking in front of me, sweeping across slowly, tensed, fighting itself. The fingers are bent, as if scorched, as if stiffened by a terrible pestilence. I feel myself twisting, a slow heat of pain. Rain leeching from the sky. The vast, open woof and filament, the sea escaped, a lightning dwarf.

The head bent, the mouth open, the teeth flared. The primordial refusal and screech of the horses of **Guernica,** *the eyes filled with the sibylline abyss, the spine twisted back, hoof and drum, futile, stranded, faltering, gallops of the mouth, bitter, open in the rain, rooted in terror to the sky, what is falling, the jaws that ache, jaws that shake and tremble with pain, that say no breath, the teeth flared, sweat sliding into froth, neck twisting, limbs leaping, and still the I, constant, remorseful, constantly critical, constantly saying, This is me, this is ridiculous, suddenly conscious: the eye of the teacher, the body beside me, the ruptured night, the crawling that comes, fixing suddenly; the eyes go upward, to the ceiling, expanding, exploding toward the rain; the hoof, the hand, claws the air. I am writhing in my sweat, quaking on the floor, each of my muscles tense, fighting against itself.* **Chotto,** chotto. *Ono-san stops us.*

Sweating, twisting. Hands, mouth. My shoulder hunches like a bentmaneback. **Itai,** itai *(pain, pain). My legs collapse, coming down inward, blown over and over, snapping limbs, collapsing, rising, pulling* *up, scraping at the sky, quivering, mane and head knocking the earth. I am faltering, I am tiring, my breath wants air.*

Ono-san chants, "Hai," releases me from the dance. I am happy, tired, sweating, pleased. I have moved for a time in the dance, have lost questions, entered my body.
Where did the dance come from?
It came from my mind's eye. It was much too constrained. From inside the muscles, the sunburst of bones. Another language. Not my own.

4

"What are they going to bring out next?" Susie whispered to me as she swallowed her cucumber finger sandwich. I looked up from my forkful of roast lamb to find the waiter carrying a steaming silver dish of beef Stroganoff.

We were sitting in a room with gold-paneled wallpaper, a chandelier overhead. It was a dinner for an Italian critic, Mario G., who was lecturing on modernism at Tokyo University. One of Reiko's college friends taught there, and she had arranged our invitations. Mario was a world-class critic, had written a definitive book on Pound, had taught at Harvard.

We'd been served, all at once, the following: sushi, quiche Lorraine, a seafood salad, fish and squid fried in a tonkatsu manner (breaded), fried potatoes, roasted lamb and gravy, and finger sandwiches. All of this was served cold, even the lamb and squid. After this, we were served the beef Stroganoff over rice on small plates, as if it were an appetizer. Then fruit for dessert. The clashes of the meal seemed quintessentially Japanese, like the fact that Ono, who dances in drag, was a Christian who had written in an essay that he also believed in Buddha. On another level, the serendipitous array and sequence reflected an aesthetic which eschews the center: there is no *pièce de résistance* to a Japanese meal. A series of dishes come in no particular order or in an order determined by the whims of the eater or the whims of the kitchen. This principle was particularly evident at the *yakitori-ya,* the Japanese equivalent of a bar-and-grill.

The conversation at the table, which had been mainly small talk about Mario's trip, turned to literature. Mario began characterizing post-structuralism and deconstruction as recycled Hegel: "You have these magazines like that one in New York, what's its name? Oh yes, *The New York Review of Books.* It pretends to be intellectual, but, you know . . . Americans always seem to be picking up on things like deconstruction, the latest fad in Europe."

On a certain level, what Mario was saying was true, and I knew my own interest in writers like Walter Benjamin or Roland Barthes or Michel Foucault carried a certain eagerness for European glamour. And yet, underneath Mario's bravado, I felt more complicated currents. Europeans are no longer the center of the world, and they feel this loss greatly. In many ways, America, whatever its crassness, whatever its ugly foreign policy, has rendered them secondary, and one reaction against this is to put down Americans as cultural yahoos.

After the meal, one of the Japanese professors brought out a poem, the first he had written in English, and an Italian translation that he had done in Mario's honor. It was a poem on Penelope, which, considering the language problems he faced, was a game effort. Then he read the poem in Italian. Someone asked Mario to read it, and after a show of reluctance, he replied, "Sure, and I'll correct the Italian as I read it."

Everyone laughed, including the professor, and yet Mario's wit seemed incredibly rude in contrast to the humility of the Japanese, their reluctance to assert themselves or criticize others. Mario read the poem quickly, in a rather jaunty manner, not stopping at the line breaks. I couldn't tell whether the Japanese picked up his tone; it was obviously different from the way Mario recited Dante a bit later.

What Mario had done was something a Japanese simply would not do, especially as a guest. Instead, another Japanese would treat the professor's poem with the same care as Dante's. But the Japanese professor, who was a Pound scholar, did not take Mario's actions as an affront. After Mario left, the professor remarked to me, "When I think of how deeply Mario understands Pound, how easily it comes to him, and I think of the way I struggle to understand, I feel a bit hopeless and wonder why I'm doing what I'm doing."

Writing about this encounter in my diary afterward, I wondered why, faced with Mario's wit, cynicism, and arrogance, the Japanese professor reacted as he did. Was it the Japanese social code of self-effacement and the avoidance of confrontation? Or was it the Japanese admiration for and sense of inferiority before certain cultural aspects of the West?

I felt I understood Mario's behavior a bit more clearly. He mistook the Japanese etiquette of humility as an open acknowledgment of his superiority, an implicit and overwhelming acceptance of European superiority. This misperception was then exaggerated by the generosity of the Japanese, their unwillingness to refuse the guest any request. Europeans in Japan, as well as Americans, often come to view this hospitality as something expected, and, since their requests are not refused, believe they are not causing any trouble and there is no limit to what they can ask.

My analysis was hardly objective. I felt a strong identification with the Japanese professor and his envy of Mario's learning. Mario's assumption of superiority had also unnerved me. He was from an aristocratic family, was friends with Italo Calvino, Eugenio Montale, Umberto Eco. He had a seemingly natural access to a cultural heritage which I desired and yet made me feel like an upstart, an outsider.

My encounter with Mario reminded me of the ways in which graduate school in English slowly undermined my sense of self. At first, it was just small things. In my second year, for instance, I was teaching a special section of Freshman English for Southeast Asian refugees. When my teaching assistant first entered the class, she looked at all the Asian students, saw my face, and thought, Oh, God, not only am I going to have to teach English to non-native speakers, but the teacher's also a foreigner. As a way of getting back at her, I made jokes about her mistakes in grammar, as if to prove my superior command of English. Somehow I needed to prove that I had the same rights to the language that she had.

A more difficult incident occurred in my third year in grad school. I was in a professor's office, arguing with him about my grade on a paper on T. S. Eliot's "Gerontion." He'd given me a B-plus, and as a graduate student, I knew nothing less than an A would do.

My professor said that I'd taken too many liberties with my interpretation. The author of a book on T. S. Eliot, he was a New Critic; he believed literature should be read as literature, should not be used in the service of sociology or political analysis. One should not, God forbid, surmise about the author's intentions or include one's own subjective, personal reactions in interpretation.

"You can't know what Eliot was thinking," he said. "You can't simply go against the obvious meaning of the lines, just to show your ingenuity. And then you bring in all this philosophical material about Freud and consciousness. There are also some problems with your prose style."

I looked down at the paper as if it were to blame.

"Besides, it's still a B plus," he said. Seeing my face, he added, "You know, I liked your poem that appeared in the *Daily* the other day. It seemed much better written than your prose here."

I felt humiliated. I couldn't write prose, couldn't analyze T. S. Eliot properly, my intellect was a wasteland. I hardly noticed my professor's compliment about my poem. Just as I hardly noticed that the subject matter of my poem "Grandfather" was different from Lowell's or Berryman's, much less Eliot's. My Japanese-American identity was something I shunned, both consciously and subconsciously. I felt it relegated me to secondary status, kept me from being with Lowell, Berryman, and the boys.

After this incident, things seemed only to get worse. I piled up seven incompletes, and eventually the director of the graduate school suspended my teaching assistantship and asked me to take a leave of absence.

Although my leaving grad school seemed like a failure at

the time, over the years I've come to view it as a blessing. A few months after I left I won a small State Arts Board grant for my poetry. I also joined the Writers-in-the-Schools program, and found myself teaching not as a scholar but as a real live poet.

On my first day in the program, as I stood before a group of fourth-graders in a suburban elementary school, I was very nervous. I decided to open with questions.

"Where do you come from?" one of the students asked.

I knew what the student meant, but answered, "Minneapolis."

"No, where were you born?"

"I was born at Great Lakes Naval Training Center."

"But where did you learn English?" Later, I got this same question from some of the teachers.

I told them I learned English in the same way they had, at home, in school, on the streets of my hometown, Chicago.

"Do you know karate or judo?" a boy in the back asked.

"No, but I do play jazz piano, and when I was in high school, I played football and basketball."

Well, I thought, what did you expect, and I quickly decided to turn to my opening lesson, a small surrealist poem that began, "In my next life . . ."

As I wrote about some of these incidents, some of which, like the scene in the elementary school, had seemed trivial at the time, I suddenly began to see, in a way I never had before, that they were not just obstacles to overcome, they were my subjects. This was what I should be writing about. I couldn't possess, or even pretend to possess, Mario's European mixture of confidence and arrogance. I had a much different, more wayward and contradictory, story to tell.

About a week after the dinner with Mario, I came across a poem by Derek Walcott, the brilliant black West Indian poet whose technical resources rival those of any poet writing now in English. In the poem, Walcott pictures himself in Westminster Abbey, amid the graves and gravestones of the great English poets, wondering, What am I doing here? A black man from the islands?

In its anguish and irony, Walcott's expression of his plight helped me clarify my own. I might love T. S. Eliot or John Donne, but I realized that were I to have met them, they would have considered me either a curiosity or a savage; in any case, an unlikely candidate for a poet of the English language. And I could not help but recognize Eliot, the Anglican, royalist defender of the poetic tradition, and the cleric John Donne as two members of the elite, the voices of power. My admiration for their work would always be tinged with detachment, even anger, and a political awareness of my place in the world. Those who think this detachment and anger mean I want to dispose of Eliot or Donne distort my position out of fear and an unconscious desire to keep the tradition white and intact.

The trick, then, was to learn to write out of my sense of duality, or rather plurality, to write not in slavish imitation of the European tradition but to use it and combine it with other elements of my background, trying to achieve a difficult balance. In order to understand who I was and who I would become, I would have to listen to voices that my father, or T. S. Eliot or Robert Lowell, did not dream of. Voices of my family, of Japan, of my own wayward and unassimilated past. In the world of the tradition, I was unimagined. I would have to imagine myself.

V

"The language of the dialogue constantly destroyed the possibility of saying what the dialogue was about."
—Professor Tezuka to Heidegger

" 'There is no sky in Tokyo,' Chieko said . . ."
—Takamura Kotaro, "Artless Talk"

1

The days were growing cooler, clearer. The time of leaf viewing had almost passed, the crisp red stars of the *momiji* maple, each perfect as an illustration in a children's book, rustled down the slopes of the mountains, floated in the shallows at Lake Nikko. It was the season of the moon, winds from the north. The light in the city seemed sliced in thin strips; the shadows of buildings came down early.

In the windows of coffee shops, coats hung over the backs of chairs. Young women brushed thick black sheaths of hair from their face and sipped the coffee. The waitresses bustled about like bees around a queen, quick, obedient, their only object to serve. The tables were white, the booths railed by chrome, the music American rock. When the women left, there were ashes in the trays, lipstick stains on the cups. Walking down the avenues, they passed racks of magazines with movie stars on the covers, shop windows with Italian shoes or dark loose dresses, ambiguous as kimonos. In the love hotels, in rooms sealed by mirrors, dresses slipped from shoulders, revealing a white strip.

No, that never happened; the women went home to the small rabbit hutches of their parents, saved half their salary for these dresses, slept at night, chaste, protected, anxious about the days before them when they would have to find the right partner for their lives to begin. In the morning they went to school, to jobs as secretaries, office girls. Their jobs meant nothing to them. There was only the future.

All of this was only speculation. Walking down Roppongi-dorii to a reception for the U.S./Japan fellows, we sensed that the lives of the people rushing back and forth around us were sealed off, that whatever was private and secret and passionate was obscured, hidden, or perhaps, did not even exist at all. There was only this constant motion, this world of commuting and commerce. I was reading Enchi's *The Waiting Years,* stories of the life beneath the surface, the hidden angers of women, dances of manipulation, the affairs of arrogant, important men.

None of that connected with the polite, banal chatter at the reception, the questions about our impressions of the country, the poets I had read. The hosts were administrators, a few professors, secretaries; they were performing their roles, that was all. Mikio Kata, the head of International House, came up to me and mentioned that he had a book by a Japanese poet he wanted to give me. I hadn't seen him since the first week I'd arrived. His face was pointed and gaunt, there was a mole on his cheek. His manner was stiffer than Reiko's or that of the Butoh students. He quickly moved on to talk to Hasegawa, his assistant. I recalled that I needed to ask if I could get my stipend before the end of the month. We still hadn't quite recovered from the blow of the key money for our apartment.

On the table, the ever-present trays of sushi were laid out in precise rows. Japanese food is a delight of textures and vision rather than taste. Another demonstration of the art of the surface. Through the picture windows, I could see the stones of the garden, the carefully clipped pines and cedars, a small pool.

Each of the fellows had come to the country at a different time, and some were staying in different places (a couple of them in Kyoto). Shauna, whom we'd met just after we arrived, was about to end her visit. Daniel, a mime, arrived shortly after me, and we'd quickly become friends. With his bony, six-three frame and his flurry of hands, and the way he bent down intensely to listen, then pulled back and pointed his finger and laughed, Daniel seemed overly animated, like someone who had been assigned to teach the Japanese how to party. His hair was thinning and turning gray. If you didn't watch him move, he sometimes seemed much older than he was. It was as if the ghost of his old age had popped out too early and was reluctant to go back into hiding. Only his manic energy kept it at bay.

He had the ease of someone used to a foreign climate.

Though he grew up in Milwaukee, he'd lived the last fourteen years in France, had studied mime under the great Etienne Decroux, former partner of Jean-Louis Barrault. Daniel talked often about Decroux, his autocratic ways—he'd kicked Daniel out when he discovered Daniel had arranged secretly to give a performance. "You obviously can't be serious about your art," said Decroux, "or perhaps you think I have nothing more to teach you . . ." It broke Daniel's heart to be let go. He had delicious gossip about Marcel Marceau, about Jessica Lange, who'd studied with Decroux. A short while after being kicked out by Decroux, Daniel married a French sculptor, a woman who did masks and costumes for the movies, the Paris opera. She was back in France, working on a shoot. Daniel was in Japan to study *sumo.*

In the middle of the party, we began to argue about Butoh. Daniel thought it was trash. The performers never knew what they were going to do, they just improvised. Their sloppiness astounded him. He preferred sumo, went every day to watch the training sessions. The beefy wrestlers would squat and go into three- or four-point stances, like NFL linemen staring each other down; then they'd smack into each other with a noise like the crack of a wrecking ball, grunting and tugging, scurrying across a ring of dirt and clay. I didn't understand how Daniel could prefer that to Butoh. But there was so much ceremony in it all, said Daniel, and he began to show me how the wrestlers before the match would raise one leg up to the side, tilting their bodies, until the leg was pointing to the sky. "They have such incredible balance," he said. "They train, they work." I said Butoh seemed to partake of both the spirit of Noh and the peasant culture, an incredible combination. "You can't believe that," Daniel shouted. "They get away with so much crap. It's disgusting. Ugly. They actually try to look like zombies, like people with a disease. That's not art."

At this point, I could feel people's eyes on us. What did they make of this towering *gaijin* (foreigner), tipping himself up and down in the movements of a sumo wrestler? Or the way I tapped Daniel on his shoulder in a joking, patronizing manner, as if talking to a child? Back and forth we went, like two wrestlers, enjoying our argument for argument's sake. We were like two Talmudic scholars. Very un-Japanese.

As Daniel, Susie, and I left the party for a bar down the street, I wondered if I would ever get closer to the Japanese than discussing their art. What about their passions, I thought, not realizing this was perhaps the wrong question to ask.

The sidewalks of Roppongi were jammed as usual with young people dressed for the dance clubs and other night life of the area. We passed the McDonald's, the white sparse makeup boutique of Shu Uemura, my namesake, the tacky pink neon of the Almond Coffee Shop. At the corner of Roppongi crossing, Susie and Daniel rushed on, crossing against the light. When they arrived at the other side, they started yelling at me to come on, gesturing above the crowd. Daniel, with his lanky six-three body and mime's motions, like a scarecrow flapping in the wind, was attracting not only my attention but the attention of those around him.

As I stood across from them, with the rest of the Japanese, I felt uncomfortable and was embarrassed by Susie and Daniel's minor breach of the law. Somehow I had less gaijin license—the freedom of foreigners in Japan to break the rules, a freedom that comes from the Japanese assumption that foreigners do not know the rules. It didn't matter that I too was a foreigner. I didn't look like one, and I sensed the Japanese would silently chastise me if I crossed in brazen American freedom. It shouldn't have mattered to me what they, the Japanese, thought, but it did. Beneath that concern, I felt somehow the smugness that the well-mannered feel among the ill-mannered. And beneath that, I felt privileged: somehow I was more in tune, more at home, with the Japanese than Susie and Daniel. Such a feeling relieved my embarrassment at being a beginner gaijin and allowed me to emphasize my "familial" closeness.

I looked across the street and sensed a rift opening up between me and Susie—not a large one, but one which had never been there before. It would take us a long time to understand what this rift meant.

But as the schoolgirls gossiped around me, and the sarariman jabbered, I was also aware of another rift. Despite looking like everyone else, I would never be Japanese. This fact was not entirely negative. It meant I possessed a secret source of power—I was an American; I mingled with the white foreigners in a way no Japanese could. When I walked down the street with Susie and Daniel, we formed an island of English, bearing the glamour of the West.

Daniel and Susie were waving. The light changed. Caught at the tip of a wave of pedestrians, I crossed the street.

"Gaijin no laisensu ja nai," I said. "You Americans. You think you own the world."

2

Most of the women on the Tokyo streets were thin as wisps. In contrast, my friend Reiko was built like a sumo wrestler. Sometimes she gave performances of her own choreography. She lumbered about the stage like one of the oversized Greek women in Picasso's painting of the pair running down the beach. The dances, I felt, weren't very effective. Still, I admired her boldness, her lack of Japanese reticence.

After the performance, she'd appear in a leather jacket, carrying a white helmet, and then she'd lift her leg skyward like Chiyonofuji, the sumo champion, and plop herself down, straddling the largest motorcycle you could buy in Japan. She worked as an architect, made money for her magazine. She drank me under the table time after time. Her face was broad, wore a sly smile; when drunk, she turned red with laughter. She illustrated a certain principle about Japanese conformity—when a Japanese decides to break the rules, there's little opportunity to go back; therefore, once someone breaks with society, she might as well go as far as she can. There's not much gradation: either one conforms or one is extremely eccentric. This seemed especially true for Japanese women, who were even more constricted than the men.

Our first Japanese friends were friends of Reiko, who admitted us to her social family. One evening she called and told us we were invited to a party at the house of her friend Haruki. She gave us train directions and told us that her friend Mieko would meet us at the station.

The train clattered off behind us; the bells of the crossing clanged. Waiting at the bottom of the stairs, Mieko was short, slight, her hair cut in bangs. She wore a pleated skirt and a blouse with the Japanese equivalent of a Peter Pan collar. Her nose was small, her mouth even smaller, a face like a drawing without depth. She looked like a schoolmarm and displayed little of the flair of the typical fashionable Tokyo young. She was studying to be a classical composer. Her idols were Takemitsu, Kondo Jo, Schoenberg, and Webern. She had written little, had much to learn.

She greeted us politely, guided us down the street. Next to Mieko, Susie looked like a giant, an adopted mother. Her brown hair seemed lighter, her face foreign, intelligent with age. Her long, loose coat, like a doctor's whites, ballooned in the breeze. Bright plastic flags and flowers of a local festival were strung up over the two-lane street, and women rushed past with baskets of *dashi, shoyu* (soy sauce), spinach, rice, slabs of sushi, going home for dinner. Their toddlers trailed behind them like goslings. Mieko seemed encaged by a reticence, an unsureness that was due to her age—twenty—and to her own natural shyness. I tried to think of her sitting on the floor of one of the garages where Butoh is performed, of what she'd look like if she were wearing loose black pants, a turtleneck sweater instead of her prim outfit. It was as if she was at a crossing: she could either go the way of Reiko or she could go the way of most Japanese young women—get a good education, work for a few years, find a husband, and spend all her time raising a family.

What did she think of Reiko, I wondered, and did not ask. Though Reiko had a daughter of fourteen, she enjoyed an independence unheard of for married women in Japan. She never talked about her husband. I assumed she was divorced. Later, when I asked Haruki, he replied that he had never met Reiko's husband and didn't even know if Reiko's husband was dead or alive. "We are friends," Haruki said. "We don't need to know about each other's private life."

Following Mieko, we entered alleys no wider than a car, passageways where we walked in single file. The two-story buildings were dark, wooden, or white slab concrete, with slate-shingled roofs. Caught in a cul-de-sac, fronted by a few shrubs of jade and pine, the door of Haruki's house opened to a small kitchen lit by a fluorescent light. Haruki was cutting vegetables at the sink, a cigarette dangling from the corner of his mouth. Dressed in a blue kimono, he looked unshaven, drowsy. His hair was prematurely salt-and-pepper; at thirty-five he was considerably older than Mieko.

We entered, took off our shoes. It struck me that taking off my shoes at the entrance to any house was automatic with me in a way it wasn't with Susie. Haruki greeted us with a bow. We bowed back.

Haruki was shorter, slighter than I, yet his body still didn't quite fit with Mieko's. Reiko had told us that Haruki and Mieko were interested in each other, but weren't boyfriend and girlfriend yet. They seemed comfortable with each other, Haruki wry, smiling, Mieko laughing.

An artist and a high-school teacher, Haruki seemed already on the downside of promise. His apartment was small and cramped and gave me the impression he was managing a living but not much more. The main room was divided in two—one half a desk, with brushes, pens, tubes of paint; the other with a bed, a small low table. His paintings were on the walls; some were album covers. The figures were like Giacometti sculptures, thin wisps of swirling colors dominated by Japanese greens—the green of ferns, moss, tea, the fading iridescence of a court lady's kimono. It was commercial work, a minor talent.

Mieko played us albums of Japanese composers, shamisen and the Noh flute interwoven with Western instruments; then Haruki put on Carmen McRae, Ann Burton, Billie Holiday. "God Bless the Child." Singles came on, the Beach Boys, the Animals, Billy J. Kramer and the Dakotas. A wash of memories. Boy-girl parties, *Sixteen* magazine, Lloyd Thaxton. How do these songs sound to Japanese ears?

Reiko arrived like a Bourbon prince, a stockbroker with bottles of wine, or boxes of cigars in his arms. She was an earth mother, a patriarch; sake sank inside her as in an ocean, never making a dent. Mieko faded into the background. She seemed like one of the children allowed to sit at the grownups' table. Haruki put on Janis Joplin, Ball and Chain, "a piece of my heart." "She was from the springtime of my life," said Reiko. Haruki began laying out the sashimi, raw oysters, squid, fish cakes, pickled vegetables, in patterns of stars and circles, the garnishes framing them placed like the strokes of his brush. A friend of his arrived, Naoko; she taught at a high school, had the high cheekbones of a Chinese; her cheeks were spotted with freckles. She was intelligent, quiet. Haruki began to juggle oranges, Reiko followed. The orange globes popped in the air like fireworks. The conversation switched to Japanese, too quick for me to follow. Cards for *hana* came out, Haruki tried to teach me to play. Sake, poured into thimble-sized cups, disappeared in a gulp. The cards whirled before me, figures of feudal lords and ladies, momiji, chrysanthemum, Prince Genji himself, lover of hundreds of women, unattainable beauty.

Suddenly I thought I heard the word "virgin," or more accurately, "burgin." Haruki pointed at Mieko. He was like a little boy telling the crowd she has a crush on someone, that her mother still walks her to school. He turned to me and said, this time in English, "She's a burgin."

I turned to Reiko quizzically. Reiko laughed. "He says he knows what she's interested in, and I know what she's interested in, but she doesn't know what she's interested in."

Mieko blushed. Susie was going, "What? What?" Remembering Mieko's remark that she couldn't decide what musical style she wanted to work in, Susie asked, "You mean she doesn't know what kind of music she's interested in?"

Everyone laughed. Susie looked at me. "Did you understand?"

Later we told everyone we'd like to have them over to our house, a reciprocal gesture. Haruki slurred something in Japanese. I caught only the question "Do you like?"

"Do I like Susie's cooking?" I ask. He waves his hand. No, no.

More Japanese. "Do I like Susie?" I ask. Susie leaps in: "No, he's asking about my cooking."

Haruki brushes her away. More Japanese.

Reiko: "Haruki says he's jealous . . ."

Of what?

"Of you."

Suddenly Mieko interrupts: "It's just drunken talk. *Yopa-ratta.*" Susie still thought Haruki was talking about her cooking.

It was getting near time for the last train. Reiko said Japanese parties go on into the morning, tomorrow is a holiday. Haruki had a room next door, everyone could sleep there. But we were tired, we'd been at Haruki's for seven hours. We'd drunk too much sake, we wanted to go home.

The air outside was cool. Our breath seeped out in white puffs. Overhead the moon was pale, pouring light. Haruki put his hand on my shoulder. I felt uneasy. Japanese touch each other so seldom. What did this mean? I smiled, put my arm on his shoulder, and thanked him. Something in Japanese. I turned to Mieko, who said again, "It's just drunken talk."

"Bakka-rashii?"—nonsense—I ask. Everyone laughs.

What had happened? We didn't know. Talking about the night, we sensed a darkness there we hadn't seen before, some hidden depth. Or perhaps it was nothing, as Mieko said. The relationships seemed murky. The party was like a Noh mask, the white-painted face of a woman which changes with the light, from joy to sorrow to suspicion to fear, as it turns back and forth. Naoko accompanied us on the way back. She told us she sometimes stayed at Haruki's all night, slept there till morning. But she didn't do that too often, her husband didn't like it. That night, her husband had been painting. He really didn't like Haruki's parties. She spoke as if the nature of her relationship with Haruki was clear. We felt stupid, childish.

The next week we went with Reiko, Naoko, Haruki, and Mieko to a performance of the Yuki-za. A puppet troupe, they used puppets with strings rather than the large puppets of *Bunraku,* which take three puppeteers to manage properly. At this post-modernist rendition of Cocteau's *Beauty and the Beast,* there were pictures on a screen, video, rock music, jazz, shamisen, and en-trances from all sides of the theater, including the ceiling. Dressed in kimonos and Western clothes, the troupe both acted and manipulated the puppets. First, the woman who played Beauty talked to the puppet of the Beast; in the next scene, she had a puppet Beauty, who talked to an actor who wore a mask of the Beast; then the two puppets of Beauty and the Beast spoke to each other, while the actors playing Beauty and the Beast did the same. The characters moved like figures in a fairy tale, a cheap romance, a farce, a soap opera, as if hovering on the edge of a violent sexual passion. It's said the Japanese self shifts with the role it has to play, is like the Japanese house, whose rooms change shape in an instant with the sliding of screens, where there is no center. We were watching a vision of the self as multiples; there was no true Beauty or Beast, no unitary self.

We walked back to the train through a mall lighted like a ballpark, bright enough to spot a speck of whiteness at a hundred yards. Pachinko parlors, restaurants, bars, grocery stores. Awnings were coming down, steel doors sliding. One by one, the lights went off. Reiko explained to us that the troupe was three hundred years old, that the old man who worked the Kabuki puppet and the old woman who played shamisen were the grandfather and grandmother of the head of the troupe. When they would come on stage, it was as if time had shifted, Tokyo was still Edo, the samurai still reigned.

Mieko and Haruki walked ahead of us. They did not touch. We felt like a chorus watching the action of the players. We sensed something was coming, we didn't know what. Reiko said Mieko's parents hadn't met Haruki. Would they disapprove? She didn't know. Mieko's father was an engineer; they had a house in the suburbs, small by American standards, large by Japanese. She was an only child. Haruki's mother was a widow, who lived in the provinces.

We passed an alley where the pink neon of a love hotel throbbed quietly. These hotels were hidden in nooks and crannies of the city, existed because there was no space here, because the walls were thin, the neighbors close, because sex was casual, without sin. Reporters from the tabloids would stake themselves in the passageways next to these places, leap out and shoot movie stars, politicians, baseball heroes. The flash pops, the lovers turn, the reporter is gone. Their faces, bewildered, awkward, unfold from glossy pages a few days later.

Haruki and Mieko, Mieko and Haruki. The one old enough so that the women his age were already home in bed, had fed their children, were waiting in the dark for the sound of a husband at the front door, his clumsy steps, his erratic breath. The other moving into a world where women are nothing, where anything can happen. She had no knowledge of her body. You could tell by her walk, by the way her limbs in motion were dainty, tentative. Haruki seemed more boyish with her. They stood before the crossing. Rushing like film that has jumped its sockets, the train roared past, window after window of shuttling light.

3

A pattern takes hold, the days gather substance. We could feel it in the air, the season turning. It was December, the air crisp, cold. We bought a heater for our room. Just one. That was all we could afford. Gradually our house had begun to fill up. "We're like pack rats," I said to Susie, "even in a place where the aesthetic is simple and sparse, we keep buying things. Especially you." I was worried about money. Near the end of each month, when our stipend was just about depleted, we'd find ourselves charging things on our credit cards. "Don't be a Scrooge," she said. "We're only going to be here once." She bought bowls at the grocery, tea cups and tiny plates from the pottery shop. Their colors were rough, brilliant. Each meal, each implement, each gesture was an art.

She and Daniel began tea ceremony classes. She sat for long minutes on her knees, till her legs went numb and the pain became unbearable. The art was not simply the gestures of preparing and sipping the tea, breathing in the aroma of the leaves, heavy as incense. After you finish drinking, you take the cup, the saucer, lift each up, examine it in the light. Turn it over, note who made it. Hold it loosely, lightly, sense the texture. Even cleaning up was an art: wiping the tray in six strokes, starting with a half moon; folding the towel as intricately as origami. More precise than a surgeon, nothing left to chance.

She learned the names of sashimi in the store: *maguro, taiko, anago, hotate;* the names of vegetables, of sauces, how to prepare *nabe* (soups), the difference between *shabu-shabu* and *sukiyaki* (one is boiled, the other uses a mixture of shoyu, rice wine, sake, and sugar). "I learn about the world through my taste buds," she said. She bought flowers at a local stand, made friends with the owner. She placed them in vases, in sake containers. My books were lined against the wall, prints by Utamaro hung in our rooms. We made a home.

She lost weight from the diet of fish and rice, grew as slim as she had been at seventeen, when I met her. Her hair grew long, the permanent loosened. She wore jeans, large cable-knit sweaters, dresses of corduroy, of rough-cut dark wool. She soon gave up shopping in Tokyo. Nothing fit her; the clothes were for girls, for the incredibly slight creatures who walked the avenues, poured through the turnstile at the station. No matter how she slimmed down, they would always be thinner. She felt hearty, like a peasant. She felt free, incredibly young. People stared at her on the streets. I said she was imagining things. Time passed. She no longer noticed whether anyone was staring.

In America, all our friends had gone through therapy, some through divorce, some had broken up with lovers they had lived with for years, some went into AA or Adult Children's; serenity had finally taken hold. Next came the summer when everyone got married. A few years passed and the women were pregnant, a new stage had begun. But Susie was still a resident, she was thirty, there was time. We'd been given this year. The children would come. A door had opened unexpectedly, like the friend one makes in late middle age. We were younger than that, had suddenly grown incredibly young.

We talked about everything late into the night, no work the next day. It was like the first days of college. Noh, Kabuki, shiatsu. Her shiatsu teacher showed her how to press spots on the body to wipe away headaches, back pains, arthritis. His hands probed like X-rays, held an intimate knowledge, more intimate than love. We traveled to the shrines at Kamakura, at Nikko, the baths of Hakone, the open-air sculpture museum where Calders and Niki de Saint-Phalles and Henry Moores strode out of the mist. On the far mountains, from volcanic holes, the steam hissed upward with a smell of sulphur, like a vision of hell. In the inn we soaked for hours, luxuriating in the baths, our skin turning pink and wrinkled, our muscles nonexistent. Folded into the futon, we slipped into a sleep like the dead, woke to breakfasts of cold fish, rice, a raw egg for dipping, *nori* (seaweed). They turned my bowels inward. Susie devoured everything with a gleeful delight.

Through a friend of her father's, she met a woman general practitioner. Takako Inada's hair was cut like a helmet, and her body was broader than that of most Japanese women. She waved her hands about constantly, as if a cloud of bees were buzzing at her head; and she always seemed to be smiling, at least at first. Her practice was in the most fashionable district of Tokyo. She helped Susie find a shiatsu teacher and meet pediatricians; Susie helped her with her marriage.

Well, not quite. One day Takako told her a secret. She must never tell a soul, she must promise. Susie has this way of eliciting secrets. People meet her, they pour forth things they have never told a soul. She is one of the healers, knows the sources of pain.

Takako took a deep breath. She and her husband were living separately. No one knew. Not his parents (hers were dead), not the children. They'd been told their father was away on business. "I can't help it. I can't even stand the way he holds his chopsticks . . . I don't think I ever loved him."

That, Susie said, is the time for divorce. Takako objected. The children wouldn't be able to marry, to get into the university, other children would shun them, they'd grow up crazy. Her in-laws adored her, it would tear them apart. She was almost implacable, rigid with fear of the shame, the gossip.

"It's as if the Japanese are at the same stage America was at in the fifties," Susie said. I could tell Takako's marriage was not long for this world. "It's almost as if I've come across a dinosaur egg. They're just beginning to discover divorce."

Another party, this time at Naoko's house. Reiko, her cousin, a few friends of Naoko, Naoko's husband, Mieko, and Haruki. There was an enormous amount of food; course after course poured from the kitchen: grilled fish, chicken balls, sushi, eggplant, slices of beef and potatoes, *miso* soup, a custard with mushrooms and vegetables inside, sake, bowls of rice. An army of Kirin beer bottles guarded the table.

At about ten o'clock, Mieko announced that she had to call home. Her mother, Mieko said, had been angry that Mieko stayed out all night a few times at Haruki's. Mieko's mother thought Haruki had "spoiled" Mieko, though that was not the case. As Mieko told this to the table, she seemed a bit embarrassed. When she called her mother, all she said was, "I'm going to have dinner and then I'll be home."

Everyone burst out laughing. Since Mieko was no longer allowed to go to late-night parties, she had told her mother that she had gone to the theater with some girlfriends.

Chiba, a woman of about forty, remarked that before she was married she was shy around men. Now she didn't feel shy and was able to have several boyfriends. Susie and I expressed some confusion at this. Was she some kind of female Genji?

No, no, laughed Reiko. It turned out that "boyfriend" or *"boiyo furendo,"* as it's pronounced in Japanese, refers only to friends who are male; *koibito* is the word for lover. As we laughed about this misunderstanding, Haruki began flirting with Chiba and asked her if she wanted a lover. Chiba replied that Haruki was not her type. Haruki answered that she could just close her eyes and it wouldn't matter. Mieko sat in the corner, sipping her tea.

A short time later, Mieko left quietly. Her youth, the presence of her mother, hovered about her like a ghost, separating her from the others.

Later, as we walked to the station, I asked Haruki how he felt about her.

"I like her," he said. "I admire her seriousness. Japanese culture now, like American culture, is light, there's no room for seriousness. Mieko is exceptional. But since I haven't slept with her, I cannot feel romantic toward her."

There was no passion in his voice. It was simply the way things were. His face was lit on one side by the streetlight. His eyes were slitted, bleary with drink. And then he smiled briefly at some irony only he could see.

As we rounded the corner near the station, something leapt from the shadows and swiped at Susie, who bumped against me. A bearded, snarling face, reddened and greased with dirt, rushed past, and I turned to see one of the homeless drunks who lived inside the subway stations flailing the arms of his torn raincoat at us. I smelled sake, debated whether or not to swing, but Haruki pulled us away and pushed us into the station.

"Jesus Christ, what was that?" Susie cried.

The three of us were spilling out laughter. "The Phantom of Takadanobaba," I told her. "You broke his heart."

For three stations I tried to explain to Haruki about the Phantom of the Opera. I gave up. We were all too drunk. The city passed beneath us—the signs of banks, bars, the lights of love hotels; a huge surreal gorilla protruding from the side of a building, followed by a mannequin couple twelve feet high, dancing on a wedding cake. I looked up at the advertisements inside the car—a porno magazine, trips to Nikko, razors, the department store Marui 101, weddings that cost, as I totaled it up, thirty thousand dollars. I looked over at Haruki. He was fast asleep.

That night in bed, Susie and I discussed the possibilities of parental disapproval, Haruki's impatience. We agreed that things between Mieko and Haruki could not go on like this very much longer.

We were spending a lot of time with Reiko and her friends. We'd meet them at dance performances, at concerts, at an Indian restaurant in Roppongi, a Vietnamese restaurant in Shinjuku. One week we went traveling with Haruki, Reiko, and a couple of her friends. Mieko did not come; probably her mother had refused permission.

We spent a night at the Hotel Ureshima, which was on an island in a small bay about three hundred miles from Tokyo. We arrived late and ferried out from the small fishing village, looking back at the lights on the dock, at the shadows of the mountains that reared up just above the shore. The fishing boats at their moorings were empty, ghostly. A stretch of black water, and then, all aglitter with lights, the hotel loomed ahead like a giant ocean liner, dwarfing its small island setting.

Susie was the one hakujin among ten thousand nihonjin who would spend the night in that hotel. We all were to sleep in a single room with a tatami floor and six futons rolled up like thick padded carpets. Japanese hotels charge by the person, not the room, so they crowd as many people into one room as possible. Shortly after we arrived, there was a knock at the door and a woman in a kimono came in bearing tray after tray of food. Four kinds of fish, a boiled course, a fried course, a grilled course, several types of tofu, pickles, soup. And of course, beer, sake, beer, sake. Susie and I were both recovering from the Hong Kong flu, but even at the peak of health we would never have been able to, or would have wanted to, keep up. After dinner Reiko told us the hotel was famous for having four hot springs. We all put on our *yukata* (cotton bathrobes) and set off to take a bath.

At the bottom of a stairwell, we entered a long tunnel, which kept turning and twisting, like a giant snake meandering beneath the hotel. The tunnel grew craggier and dimmer, and then came a wash of lights, marking the entrance to the hot springs. Susie and the women went to one side, Haruki and I to the other. I felt a bit nervous being alone with him, since we would have to speak entirely in Japanese. What would we talk about?

We took off our robes and sat on benches, and joined a dozen other men lathering themselves before spigots on the wall. The room was blue tile and opened at one end to the hot spring. As I doused myself with a bucket of water, I looked at the large steaming pool. Overhead, a rocky ceiling arched like a cathedral. The arch opened onto rocks below where waves crashed, and beyond, the moon spilled out on the ocean rippling toward us in tiny rivulets. I slipped myself over the edge of the spring, sliding on my backside. Haruki followed me.

"*Ii na,*" he said.

And we began a conversation of several sentences about the goodness of the bath. He pointed out to me that the women's side was smaller, and the men had the better view.

After that we didn't say much. The heat of the springs was soaking through my muscles and bones, melting my body into a pool of mush. I didn't care about anything. This was paradise. I realized it probably didn't matter that we didn't have much to say to each other. What mattered was that I had become a part of the circle of his friends. What gave me entrance, I suppose, was that I was Reiko's friend, but I didn't know her much better than I knew Haruki. That was the freedom of Japan. Once in a group, if you performed your social obligations, you could belong. You didn't have to be a scintillating conversationalist, people didn't have to love your wit or your charisma. What the group did together was what mattered, and what we were doing together was taking a bath. That was our intimacy.

Or so I thought, looking out at the waves and the long, thin point of the moon on the water and the real moon propped up above, like some traditional painting. A cold wind blew across my face, and the contrast with the water around my body warmed me even more. I could feel the sake humming slowly through my veins. I was ready to sleep.

But when we got back to our rooms, Reiko, Haruki, and the others, still in their robes, went off to the hotel disco and danced until three. Alone in the room, lying on the futons, Susie and I talked.

"Reiko had a mastectomy."

"What?"

"She had a mastectomy. They removed both breasts. It happened a few years ago."

"She told you?" Cancer in Japan is more taboo than sex. It's standard practice not to tell patients they have cancer, since such knowledge may destroy the patient's will to live. In fact, 50 percent of the patients at the Japanese National Cancer Institute don't think they have cancer. The Japanese have carried the view of cancer as the symbol of death and disease further than we ever have.

"Yes. Well, I asked her about it."

"I can't believe you."

"She told me that she had wept afterward. She felt she had lost her womanhood, that she'd never even had her womanhood despite the birth of her daughter. She said she'd never felt sexual with her husband. And then, after the operation, when she healed, she felt changed. She suddenly felt sexual. It was as if she'd been given a second chance."

"But what about her husband?"

"She didn't say."

"I'll never understand this country."

"Neither will I."

The next night, we stayed in a temple. The building itself was quite old and lovely; all temples have a garden heavy with symbolic meaning, as well as a large room for religious ceremonies and rooms for guests. The fare at such places is supposed to be strictly vegetarian, but the priest at this temple was an old friend of Reiko, and he had smuggled in chicken and sashimi enough for an army. Thirty-three, Ouchi had been a priest for four years. Before that, he'd been an editor for a "very sexual magazine," and before that, he'd gotten a Ph.D. with a thesis about prostitution in old Tokyo. In his broken English he told us very straightforwardly that his parents had been divorced when he was quite small, and thus he's been obsessed with finding the role of sexual love in marriage. As a monk, he was allowed to get married, and though he said he was uncertain about marriage, he did have a girlfriend whom he loved very much; he'd met her when she was a guest at the temple. Buddhist monks can also smoke and drink alcohol, which he did with abandon, along with the Japanese members of our party. The next morning, we all got up at 5:45 for the prayer ceremony, complete with sutras, chanting, incense, gongs, bells, and a very sober and somber monk. As I watched Reiko sitting behind Ouchi, I suddenly wondered if they had ever been lovers. I didn't think it likely, but then again, what did I know?

When Susie and I got back to Tokyo we were exhausted. After three days of constantly trying to keep up a continuous Japanese conversation, our jaws and brains were aching. We felt as if we'd just run a marathon.

And then it was Christmas time. Holiday lights were up in the street. The Seibu building in Shibuya sported a huge Christmas tree. In front of the Kentucky Fried Chicken near our station, Colonel Sanders was dressed up in a Santa suit. I was reminded of a story my aunt had told me about when Christmas was first becoming popular in Japan after the war. One of the department stores put up a Santa in front of the entrance. This Santa, however, was nailed to a cross.

I began to feel homesick, so I went to the English bookstore in Shinjuku and bought a book of short stories by Saul Bellow and a novel by Philip Roth instead of Japanese novels or books about Japan. I felt as if I was returning to my roots in Skokie, to the world of American Jews.

We called up Daniel, arranged to have Christmas dinner together. He said he'd cook. He'd learned to cook during his years in France, and he told us he'd serve us *coq au vin* like we'd never tasted. We'd bring dessert, rent a video machine and some tapes.

The meal was superb. As we ate and before we plopped *Once Upon a Time in America* into the video machine—"Well, that's hardly a Christmas video," Susie had said—we talked, as always, about Japan.

"This is a strange life we're leading here," said Susie. "Yesterday I got a phone call from a woman who speaks no English, whom I met on the Shinkansen [the bullet train] for an hour as I was going to meet David and our friends a week ago. Some people are so happy to meet Americans and discover that they don't have horns that they want to be friends forever."

"It does seem that casual friendships don't exist here the way they do in the States," I said. "Men have casual drinking buddies, and women have neighbors, but once you've been admitted into the realm of friends, then it's supposed to be a lifelong relationship. Americans are notorious here for being friendly but then not continuing the relationship once they return to the States."

"I feel as if we have to be careful about which acquaintances we pursue," said Susie. "Still, I've been overwhelmed with how nice people have been—none of the coldness and reserve that we were told to expect."

She began telling Daniel about Takako, while taking care not to give away her secret. "My friend Takako is interesting because she's a working woman and a doctor. Most women devote themselves solely to home and children. Most husbands leave the house at 7:30, work until 6:30, and then go out drinking with their co-workers until midnight—every night. They rarely see their children. I think Takako would call herself a feminist if she knew the word. She's committed to being a working woman. But it's really difficult being an unusual Japanese woman. I think I give her support she could never get from another Japanese woman."

"That's part of our attraction," said Daniel. "We're strangers, outsiders."

"But that's not quite the case with me," I said. I was feeling jealous about Susie's friendship with Takako.

"But what about you?" Susie asked Daniel.

"Well, I love going to the sumo stable," he said. "The attention to detail here amazes me. Just the way the underlings sweep the ring after their morning practice. They pile up the dirt in a little mound in the middle. Very precise. But I can't say I understand or even know the wrestlers very well. My Japanese is pretty nonexistent and most of them don't speak English. Still, I did get invited to one of their meals. I was astonished at what they put away. And always there's this pecking order. The better and bigger wrestlers—though the two aren't always synonymous—get served first. Sometimes before practice I've watched their underlings do up their hair into a top knot. Their hair is past their shoulders, and it makes them seem both womanly and not. After all, once you see them in the ring . . ."

He took a swig of sake. I poured some more in his cup, just as the Japanese do for each other.

"This morning I was watching the underlings sweep up. And I don't know why, but the bigger one suddenly got angry. He started shouting at the other one and began slapping him. Over and over. And the smaller one just stood there and took it. It was the most amazing thing."

"Yes," I said, "there's this tension under all that discipline. And the way the hierarchy is so rigid can seem cruel."

"But that's what I admire," said Daniel. "The discipline. We Americans just don't have that."

I felt chagrined. How had I gotten myself in the position of siding with America? Some part of me knew I could never live with the Japanese sense of hierarchy. I couldn't stand authority, I was too filled with resentment. I believed too much in independence, in thinking freely.

"You can't be an artist without discipline," Daniel added.

What I liked about Daniel was his seriousness, his ambition. We both shared that. But discipline? I knew I certainly wasn't taking my Butoh training as seriously as I might. But I wasn't a dancer. I wasn't a performing artist. The discipline I needed was something else, but what that was I hadn't yet learned.

Susie began to put our presents on the table. She raised her sake cup. "Merry *Kurismasu,* Daniel-san," she said.

"Omedeto gozaimasu," I chimed in.

"Happy Hanukkah!" he replied.

"Kampai!" we all shouted.

5

The day after New Year's Eve. I wake with the taste of something sour in my mouth. A gray light squeezes through the small window. The walls are bare board, the room cold, my breath hangs in the air. Susie turns over beside me, groans. All the city is hung over. The schools, the skyscrapers are empty. The alleys smell of urine. I squint at the light. In a few hours we will be at another party, Dr. Kobayashi's, a friend of Takako, and then at the house of Naoko's brother, who is also a doctor. Our bellies will grow solid like sumo wrestlers'. All the food will be cold, cooked beforehand: rice cakes, rice balls, teriyaki, sushi. Underlings will come to the houses of their bosses and stand about paying homage. Their suits dark, like at funerals. A drink in their hand.

We are in the room out behind Haruki's house. Susie stands, lets her yukata drop to the futon: the cloth leaves a web of wrinkles on her back. Last night, Reiko dressed Susie and Mieko in kimonos, put their hair up in chignons, painted their faces white. They looked like toy dolls. Haruki also donned a kimono. Reiko of course wore jeans, a sweater, a leather jacket. We drove to the local temple: there we found drummers and flute players and celebrants drinking cups of rice wine. Many of the women were in kimonos. A huge bonfire in an oil drum was shooting up sparks to the stars, and we huddled around it, then lined up to ring the prayer bell. The big brass Buddha was impassive, remote. Old men posed for photos with Susie and Mieko. They could tell Susie was white and seemed amused by her makeup. Haruki snuck into one photo, wearing a porkpie hat cocked at an angle. The three of them looked like a pimp and his contingent. Everyone was plastered, stumbling about. Somewhere after midnight Reiko disappeared.

Six hours later, Susie turns to me. We both ask at once: "Well, what do you think happened?"

Haruki and Mieko are sleeping in the next room.

"Yes, yes," we are applauding. Mieko is blushing, trying to stand up, push the piano bench away. We ask for more. She shakes her head, waves her hand, backs away. She cannot keep from laughing. She sits down. Again, the music begins.

Reiko directs it all. The applause, Mieko's performance. She has Mieko bring out her parents, who have been hiding in the kitchen. We, the foreigners, are introduced first. There's a flurry of urgings. Mieko's mother seems to back away. Mieko scurries from the room and returns lugging an accordion. It looks like a small refrigerator against her body. Her mother shrieks in embarrassment. It's no use. She plays show tunes: "Memories," "Send in the Clowns." Reiko has her way, sings in accompaniment in a flat, off-key voice. Everyone joins in, humming. Even Susie and I don't know the words.

Afterward Mieko's mother stays in the room. She seems

relieved. We feel she expected a band of demons, with Haruki, the potential suitor, at the head, gruff and smelling of fleas, scratching his underarm like Toshiro Mifune in *Yojimbo*. Instead, he's polite, quiet, dressed in a sober dark kimono; he fades into the backdrop behind the energy of Reiko.

At the end of the evening, we all bow goodbye. Everyone is smiling. The evening, we all think, has been a success.

Mieko follows us to the gate, waving goodbye. Her mother stands in the doorway. The air is clear, the snow has stopped. Reiko and Haruki strap on their helmets, mount their motorcycles. The night explodes with their engines. Smoke pours out of their exhaust. The Wild Ones are off.

Haruki lived on the outskirts of Tokyo. No, this is wrong. There are no outskirts of Tokyo, it stretches on as far as the trains can run, across the great Kando plain, millions upon millions, neighborhood after neighborhood, small, circumscribed villages around a train stop. The cramped two-story homes, the apartment buildings with rooms like closets. There is no space there, no room to breathe, to see the sky. Everything is dark, enclosed, the rooms without windows. The art of the Japanese is flat, two-dimensional, no play of light like the landscapes of Monet. There are only gardens, shaped, pruned, molded as if by brushstrokes or by a potter's hands. There are only dark interiors, neither day nor night.

Next to the train stations in the tiny alleys are the places where men go to drink. *Snakku-barru*—the name is generic, with connotations of American junk food. Inside, after work, after the last train, before going home to the wives, the family they never see, the men sat intently with glasses of *shochu* and lemon, bourbon and water, sake, beer. Each of them had a bottle with his name on it behind the bar; this was how they made it their home. The air was thick with smoke; the light like the rooms of Caravaggio, an underworld of shadows, dark bronzes, a cone of light. There was only one counter, the room was no wider than the span of a large man's arms. One, maybe two of the patrons slumped their heads on the bar. One stared off into the corners of the room, one jabbered incessantly with the owner about sumo, baseball, about troubles at the office. He was drunk, the words poured from him as out of a magical jar, never exhausted, an explosion of invective and complaint. A joke. His body rocked with laughter, his eyes squinted, his face was red. In the hours before dawn, he would climb the stairs to a small apartment, where his wife and children had long been sleeping. His body would stand at the open doorway, a shadowy presence. A few hours later he would be leaving. He might or might not see his children. Why wasn't he home earlier, why did he linger at the bar? Everyone was already asleep. He'd gotten off the last train an hour after waving his co-workers goodbye in Shinjuku. It was his life.

Haruki was not one of these men; he had opted out. He was an artist. He would find his dissolution in other ways. He was thirty-five. It was time for a change. Near the station by his house he bought a snakku bar. He would sleep late, he would work at night. His skill at cooking would come in handy: tiny snacks of tofu or *udon* noodles, of fish smaller than your little finger, slabs of whale meat, thick, marbled like bacon. He held an opening party for his friends. After that Susie and I went there occasionally. Each time, he kept sliding before us dish after dish, no matter how we protested we had had enough. When the bill came, it was always halved. We protested. There was nothing we could do. We worried about him as a businessman, he had no head for money, the bar would go under. Reiko didn't share our worries. If the bar failed, he would find something else. He wasn't a sarariman. He had no career. Reiko was always there when we visited. Mieko too was often there.

And then she was not.

It seems strange to blame the end on the snakku bar. That wasn't it completely. But there was something resigned and sad about that decision in Haruki's life. He had settled at the margins. Mieko must have seen that more clearly. Surely she would have found it impossible to live her life there, cooking these dishes with Haruki, washing the small mismatched plates and sake cups, the shot glasses. Oh, she did this gladly when she was there, but a lifetime of it? He had opened up something inside her, but to stay longer—that would have been a closing down.

But perhaps I am wrong. Perhaps it was not Mieko who saw all this but Haruki. Perhaps he was clearer, kinder, than I thought. Perhaps he had known what she would be feeling even before she felt it. Or else he was bored with the struggle, the insistence of her innocence. She was serious, but she lacked the coarseness, the earthiness, of the older women he knew. With them he needed no pretensions, no dealing with the future.

We saw Mieko less then. Reiko saw her separately occasionally. It would have been awkward for all of us to get together again. The winter deepened. We lost touch.

VI

"The Japanese race is an enemy race and while many second and third generation Japanese born on United States soil, possessed of United States citizenship, have become 'Americanized,' the racial strains are undiluted. That Japan is allied with Germany and Italy in this struggle is no ground for assuming that any Japanese, barred from assimilation by convention as he is, though born and raised in the United States, will not turn against this nation, when the final test of loyalty comes. It, therefore, follows that along the vital Pacific Coast over 112,000 potential enemies, of Japanese extraction, are at large today. There are indications that these are organized and ready for concerted action at a favorable opportunity. The very fact that no sabotage has taken place to date is a disturbing and confirming indication that such action will be taken."

> —Lieutenant General
> John DeWitt, Western
> Defense Command
> (in charge of the
> relocation plan)

"I had a presentiment then that there is in this world a kind of desire like stinging pain . . ."

> —Yukio Mishima,
> *Confessions of a Mask*

1

The slush of the Tokyo streets had chilled our soaked feet. We ducked beneath the banner at the entrance and took off our shoes with the others, glad to have reached the restaurant. The genkan was cramped, dimly lit. The air smelled of shoyu and cigarettes. Ono was in the middle of us. Tiny, rail-like, and resilient, he had the strength of an insect, of creatures who can carry many times their weight. His hair was long, thinning; his face flecked with age spots, his cheeks deep and hollow. Around him were students, admirers, friends. He had just given a performance at the huge hall in the Asahi Shinbun building, headquarters of Japan's largest newspaper, with the poet Kazuko Shiraishi. This was the obligatory celebration afterward. He disappeared up the stairs behind the waitress. We followed.

In the performance, Ono had ended with a dance in a tuxedo and whiteface. He looked like a clown, and his stumbling, halting movements combined pathos and humor. At times, he was Emmet Kelly, then Chaplin, then a Japanese parody of everything Western, a duplicate that advertised itself as a fake, a copy that called the original into question. The accompaniment was a single violin, gypsy music. He fell to the floor, got up, fell again. He rose, and seemed to fall into an accident of grace, a series of skipping spins that got more and more jagged, like a rope unraveling. And then the music changed to synthesizers, a wall of sound. Ono's son came out, dressed in white culottes, his head shaved, his flesh whitened. He was the ghost of a monk, an extraterrestrial, an otherworldly creature whose tediously slow and lyrical movements counterparted Ono's falls.

In the large tatami room, the group crowded around the tables, kneeling on the mats. Some of the students had danced with Ono earlier in the performance. They were seated nearest him. I had decided not to perform. I wasn't ready. I wondered if I ever would be, or if I wanted to. I felt envious, relieved.

Beer, sake, a series of toasts. As often happened in such parties, we were seated at one end with an American. We'd met John before at other gatherings. Blond hair parted in the middle, wire-rim glasses on a pointed nose, he looked like Ichabod Crane in a plaid shirt and jeans, like an aging grad student. He had grown up in San Francisco, idolizing Rexroth, Snyder, and the Beats. A Fulbright fellow in Japanese studies, he was married to a Japanese woman.

He started to talk about the Japanese sex clubs. "It's all quite mechanical, almost like wind-up toys. A woman comes out in a G-string and picks a member of the audience and then engages him there on stage. At the end she holds up the condom and everyone cheers."

John explained that he went to the clubs strictly as an observer. "It's tough. Some of the women aren't really good-looking and the men can be kind of cruel. They'll yell out for people not to waste themselves on such an ugly woman." He gripped the bottle of Kirin. "It's known as the cheapest fuck in town."

Susie said she wasn't surprised at the mechanical aspect of the shows. She'd already begun to tire of Japanese sexism. She told him about her friend Takako's fears of divorce, the pressures for a Japanese woman to become a housewife.

"I think the feminists need to be less uptight," John replied. "Yes, there are Japanese feminists that want to be exactly like American feminists, but a lot of them are angered by American feminists who come to Japan and spend all their time condemning Japanese society. Japanese feminism needs to come out of Japanese culture. It has to be different from American feminism."

"That's all nice in theory," said Susie. "But what does it mean?"

"It's hard to say. But you know that the *ko* at the end of

women's names means child. Well, many Japanese feminists, like my wife, have dropped the *ko*. My wife is Yoshi, not Yoshiko.''

I could tell Susie wasn't impressed by this. Neither was I. The waitress began setting little appetizer dishes on the table.

John pointed to the *konyaku,* an agar-agar gelatin, and told us that all Japanese boys know it's perfect material to masturbate with. ''I wrote a whole article about sexual terms in different languages. For instance, there are two words for masturbation in Japanese. One is *senzuri,* which is for the male and means a thousand rubs. The other is *manzuri,* which is for the female and means ten thousand rubs. Isn't that far out? They acknowledge it takes longer for a woman to get it off . . .''

I expressed skepticism about the konyaku.

''Ask him.'' John pointed to Oiga, who was sitting across from us. ''He knows.''

Oiga was a barber, but with his crew cut and bulky build, he looked a bit like a *yakuza,* a member of the Japanese mafia.

John translated Oiga's reply. ''He says sure, he knows it. Only you have to warm up the konyaku . . . But the Japanese are cooler about these things,'' John went on. ''They don't get so uptight and think sex is dirty.'' I told him about the discussion of Mieko's virginity, the way Haruki and Chiba flirted with each other.

''That's just another example. They don't have all these restrictions about talking about sex.''

I asked some questions about Japanese marriages; Susie alternated between feigning blushes and holding back her outrage.

What did the Japanese think about having a lover when they're married?

''It depends on the person,'' Oiga answered with a smile just this side of a leer. ''I have several.''

''And your wife?''

''My wife doesn't know. Americans are too logical. For you marriage is fifty-fifty. The Japanese aren't so logical. But in America the divorce rate is very high, while in Japan there are few divorces. That's because the Japanese mother takes a different attitude toward her children. They are more a part of her than separate beings. So she would never break up the family.''

I explained that though many of my friends grew up in the sixties with the idea of free love, we've decided that if you're going to get married, you ought to stay faithful. Besides, I didn't think I could keep any infidelities a secret from my wife.

Oiga laughed. "Americans are too logical," he repeated.

But are Japanese women happy in their marriages?

John said that Americans don't understand Japanese marriages. They see something that's unlike American marriages and automatically judge it as backward.

"The Japanese wife has a lot of power in the family," he argued. "She controls the books, where the children go to school, how the household is run. The husband has to go to her to ask for an allowance. She's not just subservient. Most Japanese women don't want things to change, because they'll lose that power . . .''

A few days later, Susie talked to a woman doctor who had the same complaint: "American women think it's so bad that the husband stays out late after work drinking with people from his company. But the Japanese man is like a king in his house. He has to be obeyed and served. So often, the wives like it better if the man is out all the time. It makes things easier for them.'' Susie thought the irony of the situation was not quite apparent to this woman.

I tried to ask Oiga about the anger of Japanese women that seems to seethe beneath the surface of many Japanese novels; I wanted to explain that Americans are not necessarily cold and logical.

"If my marriage with Susie is fifty-fifty, it's because I love her. That's what's behind the drive toward equality, not logic.''

I'm not sure if John, much less Oiga, understood.

"Did you know there's no equivalent for 'fuck you' in Japanese?'' said John. "The sex act isn't associated with that sort of anger and violence.''

Then what about the tremendous amount of S&M porn in Japan, in both comic books and magazines? Riding on the subway, I had seen numerous sarariman casually perusing such fare.

"The Japanese are better at maintaining the distance between fantasy and reality," John said. "Look at the crime statistics. A woman can walk the streets at any time of night and feel safe."

"That's true," said Susie. "That's one of the things I love about being here."

But as the sexual topics kept spinning up, something about Oiga disturbed me. A look in his eye advertised his disdain toward American marriages. His casual chatter about mistresses and his openness came less from friendliness than from something rigid in his nature, an assurance that refused the least shudder of questioning. I looked down the table at Ono, gesturing with hands expressive as butterflies. A man of ambiguous sexuality, a performer of gentleness and strength. Who was the typical Japanese, Oiga or Ono? Or was that the wrong question to ask?

At the end of the evening, when Oiga shook Susie's hand to say goodbye, he took his middle finger and wiggled it in her palm.

"Japanese subtlety and openness," I said. I concluded that Oiga was probably one of those men who pore over S&M comic books on the subway.

That night, after we had turned on the heater and rolled out our futons onto the tatami, Susie announced that she needed to decide how she would spend the next six months.

"Today I'm leaning toward reading and studying as much pediatrics as I can. Shiatsu didn't excite me enough to continue," she said. "It takes an hour on trains to go anywhere in this city; classes mean that most of a day is shot. I want to slow down a bit. After all, I'm going back to the land of craziness in July." Because of work she had to be back in the States two months ahead of me. "But I don't seem to be able to sit still for long."

"I can't believe you thought you'd take up knitting here," I said. "If there was ever an activity you were less suited for—"

"I feel like Ms. Worrywart of 1985 . . ." she said.

". . . and '86, '87, '88," I interjected.

"Maybe I should be storing up energy and good vibes for the next fifty years," she continued, "or maybe I should be writing the Great American Medical Book. So much of my energy goes into learning Japanese. I have no idea if that will end up being a good investment. Of course, I hope that we come back, but I'm not sure I can see living here again. It's almost impossible for a foreign doctor to be able to practice in Japan." She paused. "At least I've realized here how much I miss my work."

All this made me a bit uneasy. I was hardly ready to think about leaving.

"And then there's the whole question of children," she said.

We'd stopped using birth control. It wasn't something we'd thought out in any thorough way. It just seemed to be the thing to do. Japan was like a huge experiment, a play life, not a real one.

"On the one hand, I'd like to be childless forever, to live this carefree life. And on the other hand, when I think of all our friends back home who've just had babies, I'm afraid we won't be able to conceive."

This, of course, wasn't my fear. But I said nothing. I was too scared of her reaction to say what I felt. "It'll be fine, hon. It'll be fine."

I turned off the heater. In the dark, the coils still glowed.

2

"Kono denki wa benri desu ne," said Mrs. Hayashi, pointing to our new heater.

I poured her tea. The steam rose from the cup with a smoky scent.

The heater was *benri*—convenient—because our apartment, like most Japanese houses, lacked central heating. Mrs. Hayashi said that Japanese bodies get colder more quickly than Caucasian bodies. Was that why I always seemed to be colder than

Susie during the winter, why we were always fighting about where to set the thermostat?

I shifted my cramped legs beneath the table, and told her about my Butoh teacher, Ono. It seemed this dance form was better known in the States than to the average Japanese. I described the drag costumes Ono wore, the hat, the veil and boa, the velvet dress and high heels. I got up and tried to show how he flounced about the stage. Mrs. Hayashi broke into laughter.

Gradually, we had reached a stage where our conversations felt freer. Later, when I told her about a political demonstration at Narita, complete with tear gas and riot police, or one night when a drunken Japanese bartender had seemed to be making passes at me, I couldn't tell whether she approved or not, but she found my experiences quite fascinating. "You people do the strangest things," she'd say. I sensed that we talked to her in ways her other students did not—she and Daniel, for instance, had a more formal relationship—but perhaps she was simply being discreet about what her other students told her.

After teaching foreigners for twenty years, Mrs. Hayashi was not a typical Japanese woman. She was more independent—she had helped found the Association of Japanese Language Teachers—and less willing to put up with certain constraints of Japanese society. She was always careful, though, to tell us where she differed from Japanese custom. I felt I could trust her as a cultural guide.

For instance, she thought her son should be able to cook and give compliments to people, in contrast to the traditionally house-helpless, taciturn Japanese male. Again, I felt relieved. I'd always found it hard to compliment others heartily. Susie had complained about this for years. Perhaps my fault was cultural in part, not entirely mine.

Since she had raised her children carefully, Mrs. Hayashi trusted their judgment and planned to let them pick their own marriage partners. But this was not typical, she said. Although Japanese parents no longer force a child to marry against the child's wishes, the parents will often pick suitable mates; while the child has the right of refusal, he or she cannot go out and find someone independently.

Susie told Mrs. Hayashi that a young woman she tutored in English had gone through arranged meetings with over two dozen men before she finally got engaged. It seemed all of Tomoko's life was a preparation to get married; she took flower arranging and *koto* (a thirteen-string harp) classes, and added English classes because her future father-in-law had demanded it. At first, Tomoko found her future husband unattractive and awkward, but he was obviously quite a catch. "Truly, he is truly a rich man," she had told Susie. Gradually, Tomoko began to change her mind, as though she was consciously teaching herself to fall in love with him. "Well, he really isn't that bad-looking when he takes his glasses off," she said after their third date.

Mrs. Hayashi told us that this young woman was an *ojo-sama,* the Japanese equivalent of a debutante. Mrs. Hayashi's daughter, who was studying international law, didn't have time for *ikebana* or koto.

In a certain way, Mrs. Hayashi reminded us of some generic middle-aged, middle-class, working housewife, and we found something comforting about this. Although she worked, she generally made breakfast for her family and returned home in time for dinner. She expected her daughter to call if she was late, and her expectation that her daughter would never come home at 6 A.M. seemed neither rigid nor self-deluding, but simply her use of common sense and care in raising her children.

I asked Mrs. Hayashi how Oiga could have a mistress, frequent sex shows in Shinjuku, and claim none of this had an effect on his marriage.

Mrs. Hayashi said Oiga talked too much. She implied that she would never put up with a husband like that. But she added, "Most Japanese wives, if they found out their husband had a lover, would simply have *gaman* [patience] and not get divorced." The wife wants to keep the family together for the sake of the children; also, it's extremely difficult for a woman to support a family. Japanese women simply don't have enough economic opportunities.

Unlike American divorces, said Mrs. Hayashi, most Japanese divorces take place later in life, at the time the man is going to retire, when he is around fifty-five. The woman waits until her children are through college; then she thinks of divorce. When her husband retires, she can take half his pension and live with her children. In many such cases, the children will willingly take in the mother, but will have nothing to do with the father, since he has been absent from their lives for so many years. As a result, a number of old men live virtually all alone and sink into early senility.

Susie asked Mrs. Hayashi what would happen to all the young couples we'd seen on the trains, in Yoyogi Park, in the Shinjuku department stores, the Roppongi discos. Unlike married couples, whom you rarely saw together, these young people were always holding hands or draping their arms around each other or falling asleep together on the trains, as if there were no one else in the world, their physical closeness and display of affection seeming more intimate for its rarity in the rest of Japanese life.

Mrs. Hayashi told us that those couples do not get married. They have college romances that end when the young man graduates and finds his first job; at that point, he has no time for romance, all his efforts go toward his work. Everyone knows this will happen. They also know that later the young man will probably meet someone through a go-between, someone chosen by his parents; the same will happen to his college girlfriend. A photo will be presented to the young man and his parents, along with a résumé. If the young woman seems a good prospect, the young man will meet her. Then they will date for a half year to a year, and if both agree, they will marry.

The criteria in choosing a person to marry, then, is not love but whether he or she will make a suitable match, whether he or she will provide economic security or the type of family and home and background one should have.

I began to see why fidelity might seem less important in Japanese marriages than in American ones. Marriage in Japan means obligation, particularly for the man: if he is able to meet his social obligations and perform the expected duties of the husband, the wife has less reason to complain than an American wife, or so the thinking goes, since love was never part of the bargain.

I recalled my aunt's story of how my grandfather was so

handsome that he could return to Japan and arrange his marriage in person rather than sending someone else's photo. Was there love in my grandparents' arranged marriage? I know he gambled, was often lazy; he loved to sit on the porch in the afternoon strumming his *biwa* rather than working in his nursery. He was a dandy, there were rumors of another woman. And yet my aunt Ruby recalls a time, shortly before my grandmother died, when she and her husband went to a movie with my grandparents. In the middle of the movie, my aunt Ruby turned to see my grandparents holding hands and cuddling. "Here my honey and I were sitting together, watching this movie as if we were strangers. And there they were like teenagers, after what, forty years?"

Sitting on the tatami in the small bedroom enclosed by shoji, Susie and I listened like children to Mrs. Hayashi. These differing attitudes toward marriage seemed like a problem to be solved, a puzzling mathematical equation. On our newly bought Japanese pottery, Susie served mochi. I showed Mrs. Hayashi pictures of the dancers, Ono, Hijikata Tatsume, Min Tanaka. Susie mentioned our upcoming trip to Hiroshima and the doctor she was going to meet there.

I thought Susie and I were certain about each other, our American marriage, and in the end I was right. And yet, in the splintering confusion of my new sense of identity, in the heady encounter with the Japanese and their culture—Butoh, Noh, the fashions of Tokyo, the tiny bars and restaurants, the baths, the temples—I did not realize how deeply Japan was pulling me back into my past, how far I was drifting from the certainties of my American life.

3

The bus passed through crowd-thronged boulevards, past billboards, neon signs, huge depato and office buildings, the baseball stadium of the Hiroshima Tigers, pennants snapping above the empty stands. The city looked like any other middle-sized Japanese city, another Nagoya. We got off at the river, strolled down the walk lined with leafless trees. A grassy mall with empty flower beds lay a few blocks in the distance. In the morning light, the river was the color of steel. An old man was fishing on the bank. He tossed a cigarette in the slow-moving current. The air was cool, the edges of winter starting to wear off. Rowboats were moored at a dock. On the opposite bank, a crowd of schoolchildren trudged toward us. They saw Susie and started to shout, "Haro, haro."

We passed the one preserved remnant of destruction, the domed structure seen in thousands of photographs and newsreels. Only this emblem jarred the mild late January day, the ordinariness of the city. I kept thinking of the scenes in Alan Resnais's *Hiroshima, Mon Amour* where the Japanese man pursues a French woman through the streets of the city. In the film, the black skeleton of the dome cuts across the sky, seems to frame the lovers both visually and emotionally, makes them seem housed by destruction, haunted by ghosts.

And then Susie and I were in the Peace Museum, the long, dimly lit corridor of displays before us. More masses of schoolchildren, in blue-and-white uniforms, scurried from display window to display window, crowding for a look, their voices and footsteps echoing off the marble floors. We passed the wax figures of the victims, their skin seeming to melt from their fingers, their hair white with ash, the faces burned and gaunt. Though I could understand the desire to show something beyond photos or pieces from the rubble, the lifeless wax art seemed to mock the memory of the victims, to relegate them to the confines of the museum by a staleness—you could see the dust on the figures—with no relationship to the present.

In the opening scenes of *Hiroshima, Mon Amour* the viewer sees limbs entwined together, black-and-white shadows, a dark cylinder of an arm, the sweat of the woman's back, which suddenly turns to the bubbles of burns on the skin in the photos of victims: smooth flesh to beads of water to scars and scabs to rubble and ash—the frames keep flipping over on each other. In the memorial museum, each exhibit we passed seemed to move inside my head with the memory of those lovers. There were photos of the rubble, the girders of the city spilled and split apart, scattered like matchsticks. There were photos of a ward of bodies, heads, arms, legs, torsos, wrapped in bandages, or unwrapped, the milky gnarled flesh abstracted by the lack of color, the black-and-white distance of history. There was the block of concrete imprinted with a man's shadow, another with a leaf's. There were the technical explanations, in English and Japanese, of the damage done. I tried to block out the rush of schoolchildren and tourists, the mistake-ridden, overwritten translations on the displays.

And then Susie stopped me: there behind the glass was the black charred *bento* (a lunch box) of a schoolgirl. Inside it, instantly transformed to carbonized blackness, was a rice ball, the tiny grains perfectly preserved. We stood and stared at it, at the watch beside it, the hands stopped to the exact time, at the flower swirls of the bento, black and rough and delicate as a moth's wing, at the black powdery grains of rice.

And then we moved on.

The sunlight flooded through the window. Korematsu stubbed his cigarette in a ceramic bowl. His fingers were stained yellow, his white coat spotted with tiny flecks of ash. The smoke rose into the shaft of light. Behind him, through the leaves of a jade tree, down the winding hills, we could see the city laid out in a grid, the river running through it. Along the river, the wide boulevard of the peace garden.

Korematsu was a friend of a doctor Susie knew in Tokyo, another connection from Todai or Keio University, the graduates from prestigious schools who run the country, a Japanese version of the old boys' club. A tall thin man, Korematsu had short cropped hair and black glasses that made him seem serious, intense. He worked at the medical research center for the bomb victims. He remarked on the changes in Japanese youth—"We call them the people from outer space"; he described his research on the children of Hiroshima, and spoke of probing their fears, the extent of their knowledge of atomic weapons, their memory of history.

"Do they think about the atomic bomb more than other Japanese children?" he said. "More than American children? Are their dreams different?"

Susie started to ask about the parameters of his study, the type of questions he asked. I wondered what it would be like to have grown up here, where the museum and the blackened dome would be as much a part of the city as the baseball stadium. But I said nothing. I felt awkward. Irrelevant.

It seemed to make no difference to Korematsu that Susie was a woman. He was consumed by his work. He asked if she could help him set up a study in Minnesota as a cross-cultural comparison. By the end of the meeting, she'd become a partner in his research.

He took us down the hall to meet Matsumoto, the head of the center. The corridors of the building were windowless, dark, like a school at night. Here researchers studied cancer rates, examined tissues, blood; in the rooms were huge machines, their arms like giant insects, looming over examination tables. To our right, a window opened onto a small rock garden with pines, raked stones, a pool.

Matsumoto's office was large, well furnished by Japanese standards. He greeted us with a handshake. Gray-haired, fleshy, his torso round as a seal's, he was dressed in a dark suit. His eyes sparkled as he told jokes. He asked about Susie's background. It turned out he had been a classmate and friend of Susie's father at the Harvard Public Health School.

"My father told me about you," said Susie. "I kept trying to find you in Tokyo."

Matsumoto seemed to be enjoying this respite from work. A beautiful young foreign doctor, the daughter of an old colleague. Yes, yes, he remembered when they were in school together, their meals in Boston.

As we left, he pointed out an old woman who had just arrived. "Once a month they come here to be examined," he said.

A hibakusha. In her gray print dress, with a small hat propped like a bow on her head, she seemed no different from thousands of older women I had seen on trains, in the streets, in the depato.

We rode back to the city in a taxi, shifting back and forth with the curves of the road, edging down through the hills. Susie marveled at the coincidence of meeting her father's friend. She felt she was making more and more connections with the medical world in Japan. In comparison, I had met few writers. She was pleased to step out of the role of a wife following her husband.

As for me, I had bought some books in the museum and later, in a bookstore nearby, picked up a copy of Marguerite Duras's filmscript for *Hiroshima, Mon Amour.* I was caught by the conjunction of the images of destruction with the image of a Japanese man and a Caucasian woman. The city had somehow made me aware of our racial differences in a rather disturbing way; after all, I felt, it's partially because she's a white gaijin that the Japanese doctors like her so much. She's like a prize to them. Immediately a voice inside echoed: "And to you."

What am I doing here? I wondered. Whom have I met?

That night we slept in a small ramshackle inn we picked out at random from a guidebook. The food was not fresh, and we were served udon, a noodle soup which I've hated since childhood and which Susie loved. There was a rank odor in the hall. Cold and the sounds of traffic drifted in through the paper-thin walls. The blankets were thin, frayed at the edges. In the next room, a group of drunken revelers kept singing on into the night. A telephone rang, shrill as an infant's wail. It rang again. I wanted to complain, but the inn was cheap. We were nearing the end of the month and our stipend was almost gone. Besides, I thought, what would I say? I didn't have the language to tell the owners what was wrong, and I feared I might offend them. As I lay in the dark, my feet were cold, my legs tired. My chest tightened, I could feel a cold coming on. An eczema patch was starting to appear on my neck. It was the hot baths, the dry winter weather. I scratched. I scratched again. I looked over. Susie was asleep.

The next morning we overslept. We paid in confusion, rushed out of the inn, and boarded the bus, each of us blaming the other for oversleeping. When we reached the station, we had to run to the platform, our luggage banging at our sides like extra wings. I kept hissing at Susie to hurry.

"Just give me that," I said.

"I can carry it."

"Just give it to me."

We boarded the train and started walking through the cars, looking for seats. There were none.

"I told you we should have bought reserved seats," I said. Susie had bought the cheaper, unreserved tickets.

"Well, next time you buy the tickets, then."

"I will."

At the next stop, some passengers got off and two seats opened up. Susie sat slouching away from me, her body pulled in and sullen. Watching her page through the documents one of the doctors had given her, I felt the trip somehow had been a waste. In America, I had written a poem on a hibakusha, but confronted both by this modern and healed city, and by the museum displays, their images charged with horror and cliché, the weight of something I couldn't even begin to comprehend, I felt I had no right to write about any of this. What could I possibly have to say that wasn't an instant cliché? Somehow my desire to write about it sickened me. Not everything needs to be in a poem. At the same time, I was jealous of Susie for her apparent ease in social situations here, the contacts she had made, how the trip had been more relevant to her work than to mine.

But perhaps I was merely tiring of Japan, its otherness, its many demands on my psyche. Tired of the kanji, of the garbled conversations, of the English replies to my attempts at Japanese. Tired of constantly getting lost, constantly misunderstanding where to board or get off a train, which corner to turn at. Tired of the sameness of the food, the underlying Japaneseness of its preparation, and the lack of butter or cream sauce, tomatoes, the array of Greek, Szechuan, Mexican, and Italian available in the States. Tired of the movies and television programs in Japanese. Tired of feeling stupid, out of place. I needed a scapegoat, and Tokyo was too close, was now my home. Susie and this trip could serve as a safety valve for my frustrations. My choice of targets kept me from slipping into what I felt was unpermissible: longing to return to the States, to my "real" home.

I slept most of the way. It was a fitful sleep, though, the kind that happens whenever you've eaten the wrong food or your soul is not right. The images in my dreams seemed jumbled, sometimes sexual. I was in a café watching a Caucasian woman talk to a Japanese man. She was aware I was watching her. That was part of her message to me. She knew I was married. That I could not have her. And then I was running down the river walk, past the skeletal dome, toward the peace garden. I was trying to get to the museum. But no matter how hard I ran, the museum kept receding farther and farther into the distance. I could hear Susie calling me. Then I was walking along a beach. The sky was gray, misty, and the waves came in, in huge rushing rollers. The wind tore at the palm trees, and everything looked deserted and out of season, cold, icy cold. I knew I was lost. That it would take hours to get back to where I wanted to go. And then I heard Susie's voice again. She was calling me. I knew I was supposed to be awake. I opened my eyes, felt the train slowing beneath me. We were back in Tokyo.

4

My responses to Hiroshima fell into certain neatly carved grooves—anti-nuclear politics, questions of racism and the dropping of the bomb, outrage at the militarism of the United States, the only nation that has used the bomb. Walking past the displays, I'd felt both moved and morally numbed, accused both by my response and my inability to respond.

All the while, I kept flashing on the images from *Hiroshima, Mon Amour,* the skin of the lovers and the skin of the bomb victims. From adolescence on, I seem to have always been aware of my skin. But it was more than the color of my skin that occupied me. I also suffer from eczema, a condition that is both hereditary— my skin is abnormally dry—and psychological: my eczema flares up during times of stress.

When I was a very young child, my eczema was often so bad that I would wake in the morning with my sheets bloodied and huge scabs glaring from my forearms. In the crook of my arm, the skin would rub against itself, moisten and then dry into scales, bringing forth a maddening itch which took on monstrous proportions during the night. Even today, the sheets I sleep in are flecked by tiny drops of blood, as if tiny insects had bit me throughout my dreams.

My parents were understandably desperate for a solution. They needed to prevent me somehow from scratching myself. Eventually, a nightly ritual was devised: I would throw out my arms to the side, spread in an automatic imitation of Christ—such melodrama!—and then one of my parents, or perhaps even both, would tie my wrists with cloth bands to the slats of my baby crib. I seemed to do this willingly each night, without hesitation, expecting my bondage.

Perhaps this is crazy, but I sometimes wonder whether this scratching, this seeming desire to scrape away my skin, might somehow have been connected with what the world around us was telling me, silently, about race. Was my condition a way of speaking about what no one in my family ever talked about—the desire to shed the color of our skin?

In high school, my eczema flared up often under the pressures from school. I constantly feared I might not ace the next test, might not maintain my standing as a top student. Caught in this fear, common among Asian-American students, I was like a compulsive gambler who knows that at the next roll of the dice all the goods he has so precariously garnered may, in an instant, be ripped away from him. Sometimes the eczema extended beyond my arms to my neck and back, where the skin would crack and blister, like burns, to a lobster red. This unseemly sight did not do much for my self-image.

It's my senior year, on the basketball team. I am sitting against the wall of the gym, looking out on the fluorescent-lighted court, watching the first string run through the plays, plays which even now I could diagram. There's the smell of dust and sweat, a smell so sharp that it hurts my nostrils. Coach Schnurr whistles, stops the play. The players gather round. It's time now for free throws. As I head toward the canvas bag of basketballs, I hear Guttman call over, too lazy to get his own ball, "Hey, Muraslime, throw me a ball." The words refer to the patch of eczema glaring at my neck. And even though I must have felt a tremendous rage swelling up inside me, I obey him, throw the ball without saying a word. Having no tools to stop those words, I take them in.

Or perhaps by now I don't even notice the insult, have become so inured to it I merely take it as fun, a sign of belonging, the way a spurned lover might take any sign of anger or spite from the beloved and, by the deceptions of the weak, turn it into an act of attention.

He was a Jew. He should have known better the power of the word.

After we returned from Hiroshima, for the first time I started to think of where my father was on the day the war ended. By then he had been released from the camp in Jerome, Arkansas, for more than a year and was going to Western Michigan University in Kalamazoo, living with the family of a professor.

Probably my father is both pleased and anxious about this precarious new freedom. Perhaps he has looked through the pages of *Life* or *Time,* has seen the cartoons depicting the Japanese: they are lice, vermin, tiny thoraxes with huge heads attached, a buck-tooth smile and squinty eyes behind thick glasses; they are small, slant-eyed rats squirming under the huge boot of a G.I. giant smashing down with unfathomable power. Perhaps he has seen the way some of his classmates look at him, casting glances sideways in history or English or as he passes in the halls. Perhaps they whisper loud enough for him to hear. Perhaps not. (Is he imagining this? Or am I?) I know he does not date in college. There are no other Nisei, none of his kind. Does he admit to himself his desire for the white girls in his classes? Or is the sexual conflict inside him too dangerous to acknowledge?

It is the year the war has ended, the summer between his junior and senior years. August, a few days after Hiroshima and Nagasaki. A holiday has been declared, men sweep women up in their arms in the middle of streets and kiss them, and the women, abandoned for a moment, respond; firecrackers, streamers, confetti, all the trappings of a carnival whirl around intersections and squares throughout the country. People sport the smiles and laughter of peace, as if the muscles, clenched like a fist for so long, have moved on to another task, all brightness, promise, and plenty.

On August 15, 1945, my father is sitting on the steps of a house in Kalamazoo, Michigan. He hears the swooping sirens of the fire trucks from the center of town, the high-school band blaring "Stars and Stripes Forever," the tooting of horns, loudspeakers issuing speeches. He sees in his mind the street filled with banners and flags, the men with faces bright and beet-red from joy and drink, the women yanking their children by the wrist, dabbing their eyes with handkerchiefs. A squirrel comes chittering across the lawn, rears on its haunches, begging as usual for a handout. My father picks up a stone from the dirt, pulls back his arm, and then drops the stone to his feet. A voice rises inside him, insistent and restless, a twitch in his muscles, an urge to move, go somewhere, do something. "It won't always be like this," he remembers his teacher in the camps saying. "After the war you will be free again and back in American society. But for your own sakes, try to be not one, but two hundred percent American . . ."

I am American, he says to himself. I am glad we won. The light through the leaves is bright, blinding. The heat immense, oppressive. The sounds all over town joyous. He repeats his mantra over and over. He learns to believe it.

My father never slept with a white woman; never, I think, slept with anyone but my mother. Still, I know he must have thought of crossing that line, must have been aware it was there to cross.

One fall afternoon, I am home from eighth grade, with a slight fever. My mother is out shopping. For some reason, I start rummaging in my parents' closet, pushing back the pumps and flats, all lined in a row on the rack, unzipping the garment bags. (What am I looking for? Years later, my therapist will tell me that news travels quickly and silently in families; no one has to speak of it.)

From beneath a stack of folded sweaters, I pull a *Playboy* magazine. I start moving through the pages, the ads for albums and liquor, cartoons, the interview with Albert Schweitzer, with photos of the great man in pith helmet and bow tie, his famous walrus mustache. And then the foldout undoes itself, flowing before me with its glossy shine.

I have seen a *Playboy* someone brought into the locker room at school. But now I am alone, in my parents' bedroom. I worry about when my mother is coming back, I forget she is gone. I am entranced by the woman's breasts, the aureoles seem large as my fists. She is blond, eighteen, a U.C.L.A. coed. She leans against a screen, half her body exposed to the camera.

And so, like many other American boys, I discover my sexuality in the presence of a picture. And, like many other American boys, I do not think of the color of the woman's skin. Of course, if she were black or brown or yellow . . . but she is white, her beauty self-evident. I sense somehow that she must be more beautiful than Asian women, more prestigious. But the forbidden quality of sex overpowers any thought of race. I do not wonder why my father looks at these pictures, these women who are not my mother. The sensations of pleasure, of momentary possession and shame, flood over me quickly, easily, sliding through my body.

A few minutes later, I pick up the magazine, slip it back in the garment bag beneath the sweaters.

My mother, I remember, never touched me. In that way we were very Japanese. Or very puritan. In fact, I don't remember playing with her. When Saturdays came, I ran instead to the room of my aunt Miwako, who lived with us. She was the maiden aunt, the one who had time. She took me to movies, the zoo, bought me ice cream, candy.

The strongest childhood memory I have of conversing with my mother has her standing at the stove, cutting carrots or celery, letting slices slip into the pot of stew. I am sitting at the table, saying the multiplication table. I get frustrated every time I miss one; there is pleasure only in getting every one right. It is not a game, it is a performance. And it must be perfect. I look up and see her there, the steam rising in her face, her hair pulled behind her head, her slightly hooked nose freckled, not yet beginning to show the spots of age. The bones of her cheeks are angular, almost Spanish rather than Japanese. I know now she was beautiful, but I did not think so then. The distance between us, about ten feet, seems right, comfortable.

I don't know what she said to my father when she found I had gotten into his *Playboys*. I only know that later my father summoned me to the kitchen table and gave me a lecture that would serve as a model for the ones to come all through my adolescence, whenever she discovered pornography in my room. I see my father in his T-shirt and tortoiseshell glasses; his hair is shiny, brushed off his forehead. He is a little older than I am now. Some part of me must know he is uncomfortable, but I am only aware that some knot I can't untie is growing in my stomach, its strands tightening, engorging, twisting together.

He does not say much. He tells me, simply, "You will burn yourself out." I should stay away from girls; he can have the magazine because he is an adult, I must wait till I'm seventeen, eighteen—years away. And then he hands me a pamphlet from the AMA, where he works. "If you have any questions after you read this . . ."

I have no questions.

Later, I do manage to observe technically my father's ban on dates. After all, I am going to a Jewish high school; most of the girls are not allowed to date "goyim." They can hardly pass me off to their parents as David Steinberg. And I am awkward, socially backward, more adept in the classroom or on the basketball court than at a dance. Once, in senior year, Laurie Brandt, she of the long legs, does agree to go out with me, but at the end of the second date, at her doorstep, she bursts into tears. "I can't go out with you," she says, "my dad found out you weren't Jewish." I am dumbfounded. It feels like my fate. I do not go to homecoming or prom.

At nineteen—a late age for that period of "free love"—I lose my virginity to an upper-class woman at college. It is brief, joyless, done mainly because neither of us sees a reason not to. I feel relieved, the deed is done. But it does not wash away the feelings of inadequacy, the barriers I feel are there because of my looks. Is it my race or my own features? I cannot separate them; the matter is too hazy, too fraught with complications.

After this slow start, I break my father's ban with a vengeance. Steadily, surely, even after I meet Susie at the age of twenty, I come to woman after woman. My desires seem limitless. I take my father at his word. I begin to burn myself out.

VII

"*The Jap gardener pulled up a weed and sneered at it, the way Jap gardeners do.*"

—Raymond Chandler,
Farewell, My Lovely

"*The evacuees who were sent to Arkansas had been astonished to find they were regarded as white by the whites and colored by the blacks. The whites insisted the Japanese-Americans sit in front of the bus, drink from the white man's fountain and use the white man's rest rooms even though suspecting their loyalty to the nation. And the blacks embarrassed many a Nisei when they urged: 'Us colored folks has got to stick together.'*

If there was no middle ground in the South's polarized society of black and white, in the rest of the country after the war, a Nisei could live as a yellow-skinned American without upsetting too many people, and he also discovered it was not particularly difficult to be accepted into the white man's world."

—Bill Hosokawa,
Nisei: The Quiet Americans

1

Ono's dog barked in his cage. I walked past, a bit nervous. I was late as usual, though by now I knew that training, or keiko, didn't always start on time, unlike most scheduled events in Japan. The dark back yard was mainly dirt and a few jade bushes. The air was just above freezing. I could see my breath. Ono's studio was an aluminum building shaped like a hangar, the space open as a barn, the floors wooden and bare. When I opened the door, I was surprised to find two Caucasian women sitting on the old tattered brown couch. The other students lounged about in leotards and sweats, slow and lazy as lizards.

Lisl was a dancer, Gisela, an artist; both were German. Lisl was haughty, with a prominent nose and sunken cheekbones like an Aryan aristocrat, sandy orange hair, a pale complexion, yet darkened by a gray that gave her face a certain harshness; large woolen leggings crawled up her calves beneath her long dark skirt. She wore a ski sweater with dark-brown zigzags, a necklace of beads. She exuded darkness, heaviness, like a gypsy.

Gisela, the artist, was dressed in a loose blue-black suit, a white blouse, dark nylon stockings; the clothes hid her body, any hint of a figure. She was more beautiful than her friend, softer, her skin translucent, without blemish; soft rouge on her cheeks, bright-red lipstick, eyes made up in a blue-gray, the mascara nearly too heavy. She looked English, but something in the way her nose turned up slightly betrayed what was German. No, it was her eyes, the slight curve at their edges, an Eastern European slant, a hint of Asia.

She smiled at me. I smiled back. I was pretending, or

trying to pretend, that I was Japanese, that I was part of the group, not a visitor, not a gaijin.

Ono gathered the students, who rose up like baby birds to the call of their mother. Gisela interpreted for her friend. When we began dancing, I was aware of her eyes on me, of the gaze of her friend.

For my solo, I slipped on a kimono backward and started from a crouch, my body balled tight as a fist, a knot slowly loosening. Moving through images in my mind, as Ono had instructed, I saw a paper uncrumpling, a larva emerging from the sac of mucus which has kept it alive. Unraveling my limbs, I rose on my haunches. Because the back of the kimono was covering the front of my body, I could lift the thick padded silk off the floor like a giant set of wings, stretching upward, like a sail going up, a kite taking off. My hands were above my head, my legs were unbending, my arms reached to the ceiling. I arched on my toes, higher and higher, my body slowly pulling out its bulk, becoming thinner.

As I was bending backward, I felt Ono behind me, slowly stroking the air above me with a paper flower, a withered white daisy; with his head cocked to one side, he looked at me sadly, gently, his face descending. I fell back toward him, brushed his arm. Ono stepped aside. And then I was whirling in circles over and over, wider and wider, then tighter, swifter, until I collapsed, falling flat on my back, writhing.

From the speakers, there was the sound of rain, a train whistle rising, fading in the night. Blackness. The sound of rain.

I realized that for the past five minutes I had been unaware of Gisela's presence, unaware of her watching.

After the session was over, as the students collapsed about the table like punctured balloons, Gisela, the lighter, more beautiful one, asked me where I was from. I asked if she was a dancer. She shook her head, said she'd just come to watch. She asked where I was living—it turned out we both lived in Mejiro—and then mentioned something about going back together. I hesitated, since normally I rode home with one of the Japanese, a photographer.

But as the two women were leaving, I asked them to wait and rushed back to change. After a hurried *"Oyasumi nasai,"*

I ducked out the door with them, feeling as if I'd slighted the photographer.

They were the first Germans I had talked to in my life.

Outside, the night air slapped us with cold. Our breaths left little ghosts floating before our mouths. Down the hill sparkled the lights of Yokohama and its suburbs. The small street, actually more of a path winding down the hill, was deserted. I asked Lisl, the cool, impassive dancer, the one less beautiful: "Did you come to Japan to study with anyone?"

"Oh no, I don't study with anyone," she answered. "I have my own company. And then I do my own solos. Butoh is nice, and I like the sensei, but I have my own style. I'm in an Indian dance troupe. I give concerts here sometimes, and in India. But I don't want to study with anyone . . .

"Most of the sensei's students are too imitative. There's only one, you know, the tall one, I like the way he moves. Last time I was here, I watched him, we moved together. Tonight I was just too tired, too cold. I didn't feel like dancing. Just watching . . ."

"I like the sensei," Gisela said. "He's such a sweet man."

The conversation turned to their late arrival. Ono had expected them at six and they came at eight. I explained that he probably wanted to show them some videos; that's what he had done when I had come early.

"Oh yes, I've done that," Lisl said. "You go early, and he shows you the videos, and then you have dinner with his wife." She turned to Gisela. "I like his wife, don't you? Anyway, it's rather nice. He's got this routine down. It is a routine. And then he hopes you'll write about him and gives you clippings like those"—pointing to the clippings Gisela had in her hand.

I had a troubling thought: Maybe Ono-san isn't the master I think he is, maybe he's just this nice old man who dances well, but nothing special. And maybe he's just a self-promoter.

But why would someone his age have to promote himself? He had a pension, a large house by Japanese standards, and even a huge studio. When I had asked Reiko how Ono made a living and whether I should pay him for the class, she answered, "He doesn't need anything. The class is free. It's part of his philosophy."

When I went to Ono's the first time, I worried about what sort of gift to bring. Almost any social visit in Japan requires that you present your host with a gift—fruit, flowers, dessert, candy—carefully wrapped by the shop clerks. I felt extremely grateful for being allowed to visit Ono, and when I was late, I worried about imposing on him. Being on time in Japan means being on time. I assumed an eighty-year-old artist who had practiced his craft for so many years had things to teach me. Was I merely being naïve?

We emerged from the tunnel beneath the rails, passed the noodle stand, its windows boarded, its awning closed. Lights from the little bars that guard the station spilled onto the narrow street before us. On the platform, waiting for the train, I felt embarrassed that we were speaking in English. As do most Europeans, they had the power of more than one tongue. Like most Americans, I was a monoglot, despite my burgeoning Japanese. Graceless as a truck, hopelessly provincial.

They asked what my writing was like.

"Mostly I write about other people, Japanese-Americans, the relocation camps, my family. The hibakusha. I taught a group of Vietnamese refugees at a university, and a couple of poems are based on their stories. For some reason, a lot of ghosts show up in my poems. Perhaps that's why I like studying with Ono."

"Will we get to see your poems?" Gisela asked.

The train was deserted and bright, a rumbling slash in the dark. Gisela told me that she knew by the way I moved I was not Japanese.

"What did you think?" Lisl asked.

"Oh, I don't know. Perhaps Chinese. But then I thought no, not Chinese."

I asked Gisela a question. She misunderstood. "I liked the last thing you did. That was quite wonderful. Starting small, getting larger, going in circles and collapsing. But before that you were terrible. Not very Butoh-like at all."

"Yes," the dancer Lisl murmured, "you were terrible before that."

"No, I don't mean that. I don't pretend to be a dancer.

I wanted to know what in my body movements made you think I wasn't Japanese."

"Oh," said Gisela. "I guess it was that you met my eyes. You returned my gaze. That was very un-Japanese."

2

Okinaka, my Noh sensei, was a curious blend of old and new. He had studied Noh since he was six. His great-grandfather had taught Fenollosa, whose notes Pound used to translate Noh into English. But Okinaka's father, a famous Noh actor, died when the boy was thirteen; this left a gap which no one could fill, since his father was his teacher too. Okinaka went to an international high school, became fluent in English, and, according to a fellow student I met once at his house, the teenage Okinaka partied with the best of them and was known for his love of rock and roll and practical jokes. He decided he did not want to be a Noh performer. Perhaps he'd study philosophy and teach in a university or take a degree in English literature.

But after college, he decided to go back to Noh. Everything else seemed too foreign, a divagation. Noh was the life he grew up with, it was what he knew.

Still, he had had certain difficulties. He never found a teacher after his father. Perhaps it was pride, perhaps it was the inability to admit that loss. He studied his father's movements on film transferred to videotape.

"See," he said, when he showed me the tape once, "this is where the angel sees her own home up in heaven. Look at how restricted his movements are. This should suggest the distance of infinity. Of course, if I did that, it would mean nothing, it would be useless. He was fifty-five years old at the time. If I started out that way, I would have nothing to pull in when I grew older."

Without a teacher, he had a hard time moving up in the

Noh world, which works like a guild. Also, he had taken a Lebanese wife, someone he had met at the international school. It marked him as different. The Noh world was rife with gossip and did not tolerate much diversity.

The International House people had arranged for Daniel and me to take lessons. For Daniel, who was a mime, the lessons were just part of his training. I was in love with Noh, its steady ritual slowness, its otherworldly chants, the way it took you into another consciousness. Butoh had certain roots in Noh, and I found the contrast between the avant-garde and the traditional intriguing.

Though he was in his early thirties, Okinaka's manner was serious, intense. His face and body were long and angular like Daniel's. He moved with strength, but sometimes talked with a certain hesitancy. Was it merely that he was speaking English to us, or did he feel sure only on stage, in that world he had known since childhood, which his family had dwelt in for generations? And yet he had a sophistication that came from his education. He talked about Nietzsche and Heidegger and their relation to Japanese thought; he was familiar with Mozart, Motown, the music of India and Bali.

We had our lessons in the house of a woman who had been a friend of Okinaka's father. The room we practiced in had mirrors, a floor of bare boards, a shoji door. As tradition dictated, there were no windows.

The first day he talked to us about holding the fan. "It's not just a matter of grabbing the fan here," he said. "If I hold it with too strong a grip, I will completely ruin my movement. You must not hold it too tight."

I took the fan from him, held it at my side, my arms slightly bowed. Then I raised it in front of me, as slowly as I could, to just above shoulder height.

Okinaka frowned. "I took lessons in sword fighting. My sensei once said that I should hold the sword before me in such a way that if a butterfly landed at the tip, the sword would dip down."

I tried again. He shook his head and smiled. "It will take time. My grandfather told me that he only learned how to hold the fan when he was sixty."

After Daniel and I practiced some more, Okinaka stopped us. "You're still using too much strength. You have to learn to control your hand and your arm, all your movements, without pushing." He turned to me. "How much do you weigh?"

"About a hundred and seventy pounds."

"Well, you are heavier than I." He then put his arm in front of him. "I want you to push against my arm, see if you can move it."

I pushed, pushed as hard as I could. His arm might have wavered, but it didn't move back.

"You have to let your arm relax, to move it very softly. I have this exercise for you to do, it will help you learn what I am talking about."

He then proceeded to position us, with our feet shoulder-width apart, our knees slightly bent in a crouch, and our arms out in front, bent in a semicircle.

"This is the position for standing meditation. It's very easy to meditate sitting down, it takes more concentration to meditate standing up. I want to see how long you can hold this. I will come back in fifteen minutes."

After five minutes, our knees were shaking. After ten, I felt I was going to collapse, as if my muscles were on fire. I had a brief blasphemous thought that this hardly seemed worth the ten thousand yen (sixty dollars) we were paying for the lesson. I didn't know what Daniel thought of the exercise, but it was clear I lacked Japanese discipline, the desire for precision.

By the time Okinaka returned, I was sitting on the floor.

A few days after this lesson, I read an article in the English-language newspaper about an anthropological dig in northern Honshu. Apparently, the researchers had begun to uncover evidence that the emperors may have descended from Koreans. Having invaded and conquered Korea, having used the Koreans for slave labor both before and during World War II, having denied their descendants citizenship unless they took on Japanese names, having for centuries insisted on the purity of race and nation, the Japanese wanted none of this connection with the Koreans. The dig was closed, the offending evidence—pottery? shards of a ledger? jewelry?—hidden away. The official explanation was that the funds for the project had dried up.

Early on, Okinaka displayed a related attitude about race. He always expected more from me than from Daniel, a mime trained in movement. "You have Japanese genes," Okinaka would tell me. "You are Japanese in your blood. You should understand these things." My ingrained American outlook rebelled at this. Blood had nothing to do with ability; blood was a racist, a fascist notion.

I said none of this to Okinaka. I was a Japanese pupil, nodding, obedient. As I had from that first meeting with Miura, the head of the Bunkacho, I assented to the play of *honne* and *tatemae.*

Honne and tatemae are two fundamental concepts of Japanese society. Tatemae is the face you show the world, the social self that gives the expected and appropriate answers. Honne is the private self, the feelings and thoughts you keep in abeyance and let out only on certain carefully chosen occasions. In the workings of Japanese society these two concepts can be more complicated than my simple definition indicates. For one thing, an American is likely to view this division as one between telling and not telling the truth. Our preference, at least in comparison to the Japanese, is for bluntness and honesty, for telling it the way it is. Speak your mind, America, says the Donahue commercial. In contrast, Japanese society runs more on tatemae than ours, and the concept does not involve the moral judgment we associate with the division between telling or not telling the truth. Tatemae is neither lying nor selling out; it is doing what is appropriate and proper, what everyone expects. Without tatamae, society would cease to function. Honne is not more true than tatemae; it is simply another way of approaching the world.

The division between these two concepts is blurred by the ways they play themselves out in Japanese society. For instance, the extent to which Japanese workers are expected to be subordinate to their bosses would repel most Americans. If you go golfing with your boss, it is your job to make sure he wins, while not making it too obvious you're losing on purpose. Otherwise, your boss will lose face. Yet the boss, on some level, knows that this is what is expected, knows what you are doing. In a way, then, there is no lie at all; it is merely a ritual. When you go drinking with your boss, however, the humble, assenting demeanor you have at the office or on the links can, under the effect of the booze, be taken off. The Japanese have a rule that whatever a person does or says while drunk will be forgiven; in a sense, it's off the record. This is one reason why Japanese workers all go out drinking after work: it allows them to blow off steam in ways that they cannot during the day, and this escape valve is doubly valuable in a society where rules are everywhere and rigidly enforced. If you tell your boss he's a jerk while you are drunk, if you blurt out something unmentionable, everyone knows that this behavior is an expected part of the drinking ritual. What appears to an American as honne actually has its component of tatemae.

Not surprisingly, in such a society, polite superficial conversation can often have intricate, subtle, hidden undertones. A wash of information may be being conveyed under the guise of pleasant amenities. Yet listeners who are not attuned to those undertones, who lack the cultural second sense to read the slight, slight shifts of meaning and tone, may find themselves hopelessly confused. Or, at other times, completely outraged.

This is what makes encounters between Japanese and Americans so troublesome. If during the trade talks the Japanese say that they will do something or that they are thinking a matter over, this does not necessarily mean they will do it. It may mean the exact opposite. In order to be polite and allow both parties to save face, they will make vague concessions, vague, apparent agreements. But these statements have no bearing on their actual behavior. The Americans, who don't recognize the function of tatemae, take the Japanese at their word. When the Japanese don't do what they seem to have agreed to, the Americans are enraged and characterize the Japanese as sneaky and duplicitous or, at the least, inscrutable.

The Japanese, on the other hand, have trouble understanding the American belief in the primacy of private feelings. When Nakasone spoke before a group of Japanese politicians about how America's average I.Q. had been lowered by blacks and other minorities—except, of course, the Japanese-Americans—he believed, like any politician, that he was speaking off the record. But he also did not think Americans would take his views so seriously. They were meant for a private group and were to be considered totally separate from his public persona, his performance of tatemae.

3

In one of my poems, there is a line about my father: "He worked too hard to be white, he beat his son." Of course, it is more complicated than that.

I know that his father, my grandfather, would chase my father around the yard in L.A., brandishing a two-by-four. Whenever my father referred to this, his manner was surprisingly casual. The beatings were no different from the long distances he had to walk to school or the work he performed in his father's nursery. They were simply proof that my father's childhood was harsher than mine.

Sometimes I try to picture my father running from my grandfather, as he holds his weapon aloft. At a certain moment, the board comes down on flesh, whacks the sweaty, T-shirted back of the young boy, knocking him forward, a flat, dull driving pain, the wind rushing from his lungs, a dizziness of fear, panic, and perhaps relief erupting from his stumbling body. The next blow is harder, more solid; the thought rises in my father that he cannot go on, this can't be happening, each blow softened only by the fact that there is one less to go, it will somehow end.

But when I try to imagine my father squirming in his father's grip, in all likelihood it is not my father I am seeing but myself, as my father hovers over me in my room, having read the note from my teacher or having heard from my mother: I've been bad, have talked too much in class. He grabs my toy whip from the floor, the one modeled after Zorro's. The whip comes down; I do not go limp, I scramble about. The room is small, he catches me and hauls me on his lap.

Somehow, behind these acts of fathers and sons lies the backdrop of race and relocation.

As the war went on, the internees at the Jerome, Arkansas, relocation were given weekend passes. They could travel to Little Rock to eat at a restaurant or watch a movie. My grandfather or grandmother did not go on these trips, only their children. The children spoke English, were enamored of Hollywood's stars.

It is summer 1943. On a dust-dry country road, my father waits for the bus with other young Nisei. Behind them, like a bad dream, the fences of barbed wire, the rifle towers, the gates, the barracks filled with mothers, fathers, and bawling babies, with aging bachelors, with newlyweds. Down the ridge they can see the sharecropper shacks, more ramshackle than any of the barracks, with gaps in the walls and weatherbeaten, cracked boards. Rougher, looser than his older brother Ken—less Japanese—my father and his friends jostle and joke, talk about the baseball game yesterday, about Carol Hiyama or Judy Endo. These boys frighten some of the Issei in camp. They play cards behind the barracks, smoke cigarettes, curse in English.

When the bus comes, it is nearly empty. They take their seats in the front, behind an old white woman with a pillbox hat, her purse planted in her lap. Behind them, the anonymous faces of a few Negroes, a couple of men in overalls, a mother and her child with pigtails. There's never a question for my father of sitting in the back.

It is the same at the lunch counter where they order hamburgers and malts. Perhaps they notice the stares of the whites around them, but most likely they are too engrossed in their own conversation, in teasing Tosh about his crush on Carol, to notice where the Negroes are sitting. Later, these boys will sit below the balcony, below the section for Negroes. The faces of Cary Grant and Katharine Hepburn flow off the screen, borne on light, enlarged by glamour and celluloid, becoming part of my father's dreams.

Two years later, he's in college, away from the camps, entering the Episcopalian church with Professor Bigelow and his family. It is a sunny fall morning; the leaves, splashes of red and yellow and orange, swirl down to the street, crackling on the walk. The church is white, spired, clean in the sunlight. My father has no suit. He's wearing a white shirt, a tie. It is his first time inside this church.

Had my grandfather been a fervent Buddhist, things might have turned out differently. But my grandfather was too much a man of this world. Sharing with most Japanese a passive attitude toward religion, he had grown away from Buddha and the Shinto gods during his time in America. My father is an empty vessel, waiting to be filled.

As he ambles along with the Bigelows, he's a little stiff, a bit nervous, not knowing what to do. Inside, he's greeted by streams of light from great stained-glass windows: Christ in the garden of Gethsemane, kneeling in prayer, with the cross of his destruction in the distance; the disciples gathered around him, questioning, listening; the fish and bread of life laid out in jagged triangles; the haggard bearded man stretched out on the cross, eyes closed, giving up the ghost. What strikes my father more, the beautiful colors or this progression toward suffering? The light or the dark?

He notices in front of the benches a little platform that swings down, cushioned green leather. Just as the children enter the pew, they suddenly kneel down, facing straight ahead toward the altar; Mrs. Bigelow and the professor do the same. My father wonders what he should do. Self-conscious, he does the best he can with a halfway gesture, the way seventh-graders in our parish years later used to bow. The professor smiles and tries to reassure him, but my father, watching the altar boy light the candles on the altar, hearing the organ and the voices of the choir, is again wondering what to do. As the service continues and the members in the pews rise up to speak in unison, kneel, rise, kneel, over and over at exactly the right time, my father is disoriented. He feels a slight ache in his back, is thankful at least for the cushioned platform.

"This is the body and blood which is shed for you and the New Testament. Take this and drink. Do this often in remembrance of me."

Thank God, he thinks, I understand the words. And in all of this there is a music that takes over my father, something beyond sense, beyond God or Christ. What attracts him is a sense of belonging, of crossing some line, a way out of the Buddhist temples and streets of L.A., something he first felt in the radios and comic books, the very language that poured from his mouth, in the games of mumblety-peg, marbles, and baseball, in the pledge he recited in school each morning. Something that wasn't foreign, that did not keep him out.

He will convert, he will take up the cross, he will bring us to church all through my childhood, up until the time we move from our middle-class home in Morton Grove to our upper-class one in Northbrook, a time when he is finally a vice-president, when religion is no longer needed. By then I will be estranged from the church, an atheist, wondering what brought him to think a white man must be God.

Growing up, I had the usual complaints of most Asian kids about their hard-driving parents. There were never enough excellents, enough hundreds on tests; there were always errors I'd made on the field, tackles I missed. When I was seven, my father took me to the sidewalk on Lake Shore Drive. He pushed me off on my bike, screamed, "Pedal, pedal," and quickly became disgusted when I fell, yelling that I didn't listen to him. Ten years later, when I learned to drive, it was the same; sitting beside me in our Buick, he slammed on some imaginary brake in front of him and shook my arm. A terrible teacher, he always ended up screaming and shouting, muttering about my lack of concentration, my refusal to perform.

Perhaps the problem was how I took all this. I believed whatever it was that reddened his face, that clenched it so tight, that coiled his fist into a tight ball, must have come from me. I must have created this force, it was what I deserved. I was simply unable to brush it off.

Years later, when I confronted my infidelities, my own harangues at Susie, it seemed difficult—no, almost impossible—to take my sexuality and the rage it contained and connect it with my father and his rage. The equation did not compute.

I see my father now as a successful executive, writing speeches for other executives, writing videos, public-relations campaigns, giving speeches at conventions and meetings, splicing bits of information with familiar corn-pone jokes. I see him at evening striding down the fairway in back of his house, shading his eyes as his drive soars into the sun, the tiny white ball disappearing in the last blaze of orange light, the first crickets of evening, gnats scribbling their mad circles around his head. His body looks ten years younger, hardened by weights, by Nautilus, though it has begun to stoop just a touch, to descend toward earth. He is sixty, he is content, the fairway stretches out before him, he wants no other life than this. He has no problems with identity, with the past or race. He has been freed from history.

And I am still his son.

4

After climbing the stairs of Gisela's apartment complex, I banged on the metal door. It opened like an envelope. She was smiling, her face lit by the bulb on the balcony. She was as beautiful as I remembered; no, not quite beautiful, the bones a bit too sharp. Her face seemed unattached to her body, hidden again beneath a dark, loose-flowing dress, like a woman in mourning.

I entered, holding a folder of my poems awkwardly at my side like wilted flowers. I had given few people my work in Japan. It was too much of a strain, and most of them didn't read English well enough. I told myself Gisela had asked to see my work.

She lived well. Her apartment was larger than mine—a six-tatami-mat bedroom, a small kitchen, a fair-sized living room. At one end of the living room was a large drawing of blue egg tempura and flecks of gold sand against a black background. The picture was titled *Moon Hill.* The rooms were airy, devoid of clutter, vaguely European, though the low tables were Japanese. In the living room were two more paintings: another moon hill and an abstract design of brown sand, with the edges cut in rounded jags. "I don't know whether that one is a painting or not," she said. "I'll have to wait."

I admired her bookcase, shelves of Bashō, *The Tale of Genji, Confessions of a Mask, Some Prefer Nettles,* collections of Chinese poetry, a book on clinical linguistics, art books, Sartre, Joyce, Goethe.

What was I reading? she asked. My favorite authors? I mentioned Lévi-Strauss. *"Tristes Tropiques,"* she said, correcting my pronunciation. "Oh, that's rather basic. You should read some of the others." Walter Benjamin. "Oh, that's good." Czeslaw Milosz, whom, thank God, she didn't know. Edmond Jabes.

"Jabes," she said. "Jabes."

Trying to read the way her face wrinkled and registered my litany, I suddenly felt uncultured, untraveled.

She talked about Berlin in the sixties, the demonstrations. There was so much going on, she said. The first German commune. Sleeping in a room with dozens of bodies, coming back at night, crawling over the sleeping bodies, the sleeping couples, the couples making love. Drugs, staying up for days, marching in the streets.

And then, at nineteen, she left all that, went to live in London, stayed with an older couple. The husband was a barrister. They had a house in Kensington and a country house. She was treated like a daughter; she polished her English, went to plays.

She talked of her shows in Italy, Düsseldorf, Berlin, Tokyo. In London, she met a sheik who took her to Teheran. It was another world. Trips in the desert, riding on jeeps, the windblown sand digging in her hair. Bedouin tents. Women in veils; markets where flies the size of your thumb buzzed about unknown vegetables, slabs of meat.

"But India was where I really thought, We think

Europe is the center of the world, it has all this great culture, this great history, and here it's just this little speck, there's this whole continent swarming with people for whom Germany means nothing . . ." She looked at me. "You really should travel. I'm surprised you haven't gone anywhere before."

Her life seemed loose, shifting, without boundaries or worries about definitions, and as her story went on, I didn't say what I was thinking, didn't talk of the past that I felt suddenly was much too provincial—high-school football games, driving around the cloverleafs on a Friday night, Burger King, shooting baskets under a single light in the gym. Middle-class Midwestern suburban life seemed so silly and protected, almost comical against the backdrop of Europe and her travels. I could not see that my past contained its own exotic aura. Or perhaps I sensed she would never understand that aura, or that it would be impossible for me to convey it. After all, I'd spent so many years trying to escape it, to forget where I'd come from. That was part of my fascination with Europe, with writers like Lévi-Strauss, Milosz, Barthes.

I caught her eye and smiled. She smiled back. Reaching for the exotic, I talked about my grandparents from Shingu, my other grandparents from Kotchi, began repeating a speech I'd already given too often in Japan. But what did my grandparents really mean to me? Both grandmothers died before I was ever conscious, both widowed grandfathers left for Japan.

"It's been wonderful here," I said, eliding my doubts, "melding with the crowds . . ."

Her hand glided across the table to pick up her cigarettes. The movement startled me. Smoke curled around her head, slid out in a slow, diffuse stream.

I placed my hand on the table near the ashtray. When she flicked her cigarette there, I was aware of the distance between our hands, the flakes of ash.

She told me her family was Prussian. I nodded, but had no real idea what that meant. It was like some magical kingdom in an old movie.

"My grandfather owned a large amount of land in Prussia, he was like a count. I rode horses there . . . My father died when

I was thirteen and my mother sold the land. I've never forgiven her. She's still living off it."

"What does she do?"

"My mother? Oh, she goes to concerts, museums, restaurants. She has dinner with her friends."

Gisela would have loved to go back to Prussia, but couldn't.

"It must be so strong for you here, making that connection," she said. Suddenly she got up. "I was supposed to go see a flamenco dancer tonight. Should I call my friend? It wasn't anything definite."

As she dialed I was afraid she'd say she had to go.

She talked on the phone in Japanese with a fluency I marveled at. I could tell that the friend on the other end was being difficult, would not let her hang up. Finally, Gisela was off the phone.

I felt as if I had won some small victory. I asked more questions. It's my way of winning people over, showing my interest, satisfying my own curiosity, keeping myself politely in the background. Over and over, in childhood, my mother had repeated, "David, you think too much of yourself." Was this admonition in part Japanese? Perhaps I'd somehow imbibed the Japanese practice of avoiding obligation by not talking about oneself; when other people talked, they became indebted to me.

She said her father had directed films in Berlin during the war. Everyone was starving, it was a difficult time. Then he met her mother and they left the country.

How did her father feel about the Nazis? I wondered but did not ask. Did he support them? I didn't want to mention what might be difficult, what might upset her. That was not part of seduction, of winning her over.

But *was* I seducing her? Looking back, I realize I was playing a game with myself, setting up an imaginary line which I would approach but would not cross. The game was getting as close as I could and having her make the move over the line, or so some part of me hoped. Yet the confusion and general discomfort I felt with her also seemed to come from a sense of danger or uncertainty, an inability to decipher her words and actions. She was speaking in English, and yet the conversation kept moving into places, pockets of knowledge I'd been unaware of, had never penetrated. I couldn't fill in the background behind her lines. The way she both held herself back and smiled at me frustrated me, kept me from moving the conversation into a looser tone, something more friendly, jocular, less vaguely sexual.

At times, she looked like Diane Keaton in *Annie Hall*, warm, sweet, a bit disheveled in her beauty, but all filtered through the impassiveness, the distance I associated with Germans. I tried to imagine the body beneath her loose-fitting clothes, the pale white flesh. But it was her face that drew me toward her, as I shifted just a little to the table. The hardness at the mouth, the soft smooth texture of the skin. How she tilted her head downward, so that she was constantly looking up at me as if waiting for a question. When would I ask it?

I was aware I still had not mentioned my wife.

What I was not aware of, at least consciously, was how she was trying to impress me, how she was winning this game of names and culture.

When I mentioned Elias Canetti, she remarked, "I love *Auto-da-Fé*. I read it on the Trans-Siberian, along with *Ulysses.*" She talked about the endless hours of the ride, how you're not allowed to leave the train, how venders come up to the windows selling pastries and drinks, how the vast forests and plains of Siberia crawl by, the tenseness at the checkpoints. She urged me to try to travel back to the States through Russia on the train, and I murmured that I wanted to do so, all the while knowing I would not.

She mentioned reading *The Tale of Genji* on the train to her teaching job at Tsukuba and began praising the poetic license of the Waley translation over the more literal Seidensticker translation. She talked of reading the original Japanese. I could barely read a menu.

"You know, I met Canetti. He's a marvelous man. Very gentle and humble."

Though I found her remark gratifying, having met too many writers who were not the marvelous beings implied by the voices in their books, I began to wonder, What am I doing, citing these Europeans as heroes, trying to write like them? What am I doing with this woman? Fighting off these doubts, I showed her my extended poem on the Italian poet and director Pasolini. She read the English easily.

"I like this first section," she said. "But why Pasolini?"

"Because he was both a film director and poet. A Marxist, a structuralist critic. A homosexual and lapsed Catholic. He wrote political and literary criticism; he reveled in being an intellectual and yet felt most at home prowling the slums of Rome."

She came across a poem which mentioned Bertolucci.

"Do you know Bertolucci?"

"No," I answered, wondering at the question.

"He's a pimp. He's a friend of mine; he came to Tokyo. But really, he's a pimp."

5

One discovery I made in Japan was that after years of sexual relations with only white women, of knowing I would marry a white woman, of shunning Asian-American women, I suddenly found Japanese women attractive. Part of this flowed from my joy in being part of the visual majority for the first time. Day after day, in Shinjuku, in Shibuya, in Roppongi station, they rushed past me like a rainstorm, the cool placid surface of their faces, registering for me a new beauty. Suppose I had grown up there, what kind of woman would I have married?

For years, in the States, each beautiful white woman had seemed a mark of my exclusion. The stereotype of Asian women is of a doll-like submissiveness and a mysterious exotic sensuality, qualities which make them attractive to Caucasian men who have trouble accepting women as equals. As an Asian male, I was placed in a category of neutered sexuality, where beauty, power, and admiration were out of the question, where normalcy and acceptance were forbidden. None of the women I saw on television, in the movies, or read about in books dreamed of a lover like me.

But for me, the sexuality of Japanese women did not call up this baggage of history. They knew nothing of Fu Manchu or Charlie Chan. I looked at the women, I found them beautiful, but there was no charge, no feeling of being excluded, being singled out. They were not forbidden to me. There was no taboo. In their eyes, I was neither strange, nor feminine, nor dark, nor exotic, nor irrelevant: I looked like their brothers, their fathers, their husbands, their lovers. Perfectly normal.

Sometimes I talked with Susie about these feelings, but given the course of our relationship, sex was a subject we often entered warily. There had been too many difficulties, and they had started quite early.

I am twenty-one, my father's age at his conversion that year the war ended, the year of Hiroshima and Nagasaki. A senior, I've been going with Susie since last September. It is fall, the year of Haiphong Harbor, the secret bombing raids on Cambodia, the marches on campuses, the lines of candles held out in some small protest. This is the year my father and I argue, over and over on the phone, about my decision not to go to law school, to become a writer.

At this time, Susie and I are one of the certified couples on this small campus. She is beautiful, with long brown hair, a pale Wasp face, like Ali MacGraw. She wears peasant blouses, jeans— the uniform of the times. She is two years younger, and the men in her class, when they see me with her, envy my upper-class status.

But I am restless, uncertain, aware of powers growing inside me over which I have no control, which manifest themselves in conversations with women on campus, looks when we pass on the lawns, a sense something is there that I could have if I pursued it. I know something has changed since high school. Without knowing how, I have gained this knowledge—I can create desire, I can make them want me. Even while I fear they will shun me, even though the small voices still echo inside me, the voices of difference, of the years without power, I find the conversations drifting toward sex, toward fidelity, toward jealousy, toward Blake's Nobodaddy and issues of property. These words tumble from me, I listen, listen and question, and the women begin to reveal themselves, to let down their guard. A second, a minute, an hour before they do, I know this is happening. I can use this knowledge.

So one night, as if it were an experiment, as if it were the most natural thing to do, as if it were all in the spirit of the age, I tell Susie I want to be open. I want to sleep some nights in our room, some nights with others. We are sitting in the campus forum, drinking coffee, books—Yeats, Darwin, *The Prince*—strewn around us, the other booths filled with debates about the war, some professor, the symbolism in *Death in Venice*. Smoke drifts up from the booth behind her, as if from the top of her head. She stares at me. She doesn't know what to say.

A few hours after this conversation, we are in the basement of a dorm on South Campus, in one of the coed washrooms. The washroom is empty. I am staring at one of the gray doors to the stalls, listening to Susie retch up more than a pint of vodka. Her coughs come from deep in her gut, she muffles her sobs. Go away, she is saying, I don't want you to see me like this.

She sprawls on the cold concrete, her cheek nestled on the porcelain, and she waits for the heaving to begin again. When she emerges, her face will still be red, tight, wet. She will look haggard, years older, she will not want to see me. She knows what has happened. She has given in.

Last night, writing about all this, I started to weep. I felt enormous pity for her, for my father too, for the mutable and wasteful stupidity of human beings, their capacity for suffering, the puniness of their dreams. In this sadness, I felt joy too. Something was shouting inside me, like those poems of D. H. Lawrence's, that miraculous voice: "Look, look, we have come through."

6

Saturday. Noon. A gray and gritty Tokyo day. As I stood at the entrance of the shopping mall, beneath the giant Alta video screen, the crowds bubbled in and out of the Shinjuku station, hundreds on hundreds of black bobbing heads. They wore winter colors, black, gray, blue; coats like mine of thick wool. They clutched bags from Isetan and Seibu, filled with shirts, dresses, cassettes, packets of makeup, the pale powders of Shiseido. The people near me looked around, poking their heads back and forth. They were meeting a friend, a lover; most of them were young, wearing the loose baggy cuts forbidden to office girls and sarariman. I looked up. Michael Jackson moonwalked across the giant screen: the gospel of video, only without the sound. Across the street, the trains rattled past, making their endless circles of the city.

I was there to meet Yuri Kageyama. Saito, a young man who had translated my poems from an anthology of Asian-American poets, had arranged our meeting. Saito said Yuri was my age, had been born in Japan, of Japanese parents, but had spent much of her childhood in America. She was a poet and had lived in San Francisco for the last ten years.

Across the boulevard, a Japanese woman strode straight toward me, wearing a dark coat, a black skirt, a black jacket, black stockings, and long silver earrings. Her hair was permed, her face small, oval, a dimple like mine on her right cheek. Her lipstick was bright coral.

"Are you David Mura?" she asked.

"How did you know me?"

"Well, you said you'd be wearing a black coat and carrying a black shoulder bag."

"I wondered if you could pick me out as an American."

In many ways, Yuri looked like most of the Japanese women around us, but she possessed a flash that somehow wasn't present in the others. Perhaps it was her lipstick, or the energy of her small frame. Young Japanese women seemed to fold into themselves when they greeted each other. It wasn't just the gesture of bowing, it was the way their bodies always seemed to be stepping backward as they talked or giggled. Yuri had looked me straight in the eye and thrust out her hand in greeting. Her eyes and smile carried a wry, suspicious air. "Be forewarned," they said. "Nothing gets past me." Certain minority women in America have this toughness, this unwillingness to waste time with bullshit. Sometimes it's strength, sometimes bitterness, sometimes both. With Yuri I couldn't yet tell.

She suggested a tempura restaurant nearby. Walking among the Japanese crowds, we talked in English. But I didn't feel self-conscious as I sometimes did with Susie. Yuri and I both belonged, and did not; we shared a dual privilege. Even our clothing matched; I was also dressed in a black coat, black pants, white shirt.

The walls of the restaurant and the booths were paneled in pine. There was a tatami room in back. We sat in a booth. Yuri ordered in Japanese. I wondered if it seemed strange to the waitress that the woman was ordering, or that we were speaking English to each other. By this time, I could read enough kanji to get by on basic menus, and I could order for myself. Still, I was relieved to let Yuri order.

I asked why she had come back to Japan.

She said that she had gotten tired of the petty squabbling among the Japanese-American writers. Too many had too narrow a definition of what Japanese-American writing should be. "Everybody's written their barbed-wire relocation-camp poem," she said. "But if you stray from that in any way, you've sold out. You can't just write a love poem or a poem about a flower."

She mentioned that after she wrote an article criticizing Japanese-American poetry, other Asian-American writers treated her like a traitor.

"I wanted to see what it would be like to come back here to Japan, to raise my son here. And Gordon"—her husband—"was having a hard time making it as a jazz musician. It seemed the right time to leave."

We talked about life in San Francisco and the West Coast Japanese-Americans. I began to feel the presence of a community I never knew existed. Despite Yuri's criticisms, I was fascinated by Asian-American literary politics.

"Back in the Twin Cities, I'm the only Asian-American writer I know. It's the land of Scandos, Lutheran, and lutefisk. The big minority there is Irish Catholic." That wasn't much different from the suburbs of Chicago where I grew up, I told her. "My high school was almost all Jewish, and many of the girls couldn't go out with me because I wasn't Jewish."

Nodding, she told me that many Sansei males she knew in San Francisco felt insecure about their sexuality—they just didn't feel attractive.

"And then, of course, they see white boys picking up on the Asian women . . ."

Still, Yuri didn't always feel sympathy for the Sansei males. Many of them held traditionally Japanese chauvinistic values. They often felt that Japanese women, with their dashi legs— short and thick like a Japanese radish—square hips, and small breasts, lacked the beauty and glamour of white women. I felt pangs of self-recognition, and yet I was also relieved to know other Sansei men had similar uncertainties about their identity.

As Yuri and I talked, I thought how ironic it was that I had had to come to Japan before I could learn how other Japanese-Americans in my generation were dealing with their background. Oh, I had read Japanese-American novels and poetry, but they sometimes felt distant, almost mythical, unconnected to my experience in the white Midwest. Certainly Yuri had her biases, but she didn't try to hide them. I felt an easy camaraderie with her. I knew she had praised my work in an article in the San Francisco *Poetry Flash.* And something in our sensibilities resonated with each other. I admired her willingness to speak out, to stand apart from the group.

The poems she showed me that afternoon confirmed that we were mining the same territory. It wasn't just that they dealt

frankly with sexual matters, or that her father appeared to have a
temper like my father's down to the occasional violence of his rages.
No, there was a plunge beyond the acceptable and well-mannered,
a sense of sexuality as destructive and violent, as representing a dark
limit of human relations where rage reveals itself; a sense conveyed
by images which left both the reader and the writer hovering on
the edge of shame, anger, obsession. In one of her prose poems,
a Sansei woman makes love to a member of a Chinatown gang. She
is cheating on her boring, middle-class schoolteacher boyfriend,
who is a Sansei. And yet, in the end, the Chinatown gang member
fails to satisfy her. She sees his body as too smooth, too feminine,
his equipment too small: *He thrusts on and on, quickly, rhythmically,
on and on, able in his smallness—a limp worm-like finger of an organ, with
shrunken wrinkled hairless bags for testicles—to reach deep only on rare
occasions, just rubbing forever . . .*

"I just got so angry about hearing about dashi legs," she
said, "that I wanted to write something in retaliation."

"Well, yes, it does that." I felt angry, but whether at Yuri
or at the woman in the poem or about the whole issue of race and
sex, I didn't know. And yet I also felt relieved by the poem. Perhaps
my sexual feelings weren't mine alone. "Do you think many Sansei
women feel this way?" I asked.

"I don't know. Obviously, we're all affected by those
images. The trick is to take apart all those definitions of masculine
and feminine."

"But most people don't even want to talk about these
images, to see what's really inside them."

I showed her a passage from my poem on Pasolini, which
originally came from a poem I was writing about Mishima:

> *Once he shoved me down like a drowning girl,
> and the bristles of his beard brushed my spine,
> and his fingers slipped through my sphincter's flower,
> formed a fist which ground it open, dug
> for organs hidden like diamonds. Feeling
> myself pound, twist and plead, jammed round his wrists,
> I stared past the boundary where beauty starts.*

(So I, turning my head in the gap, like a screw
driving from my mother into the world, burst
out, soundly and beautifully, horrified and blue.)

Yuri looked up. "Yes, I see," she said. "Have you written much poetry since you've been here?"

"Not much. I've worked some on the poem about Pasolini, but mainly I've been keeping a journal. I sometimes worry that I've lost the feel for poetry, or perhaps I'm just learning how to write about myself."

I repeated Wilde's statement about needing a mask to tell all. I talked about the mask of Noh and the Kabuki whiteface, the whiteface of Butoh. I talked about Pasolini's life, his varied interests. And I wondered why I knew Yuri and I were going to be friends and nothing more. No complications, nothing like the way I felt with Gisela. I felt more like Yuri was a sister, part of my family.

We emerged from the restaurant into the early dark. Neon flashed down the street, a welter of theaters, restaurants, Pachinko parlors, strip shows. We passed the Mister Donut all lit up in pastels, a re-creation of the American fifties, down to the jukebox with Elvis and Buddy Holly. A woman passed who had my mother's slightly hooked nose and high cheekbones. I could smell the burnt shoyu from the mochi stand near the station. We entered amid the flow of crowds. And I thought how, to those around us, we probably looked like just another Japanese couple. I felt pleased by this, and saddened. At the ticket booth, when we went our separate ways, I waved to Yuri and walked up to my platform, these thoughts in English shuttling in my brain, silently marking me off from the others around me.

VIII

"Would you like your daughter to marry a Japanese?"

—*Grizzly Bear*
magazine (circa 1925)

"Go someplace where there isn't another Jap within a thousand miles. Marry a white girl or an Italian or even a Chinese. Anything but a Japanese. After a few generations of that, you've got the thing beat."

—John Okada,
No-No Boy

1

The February air was clear, the day white. Along the main street near the station, the shops spilled out their goods. Racks of shoes, pottery, towels, magazines; bins of oranges, apples, bananas, signs with kanji, photographs of sushi. A plastic, life-size Colonel Sanders, like a bizarre, transformed Buddha. Schoolchildren in caps and uniforms, carrying their satchels, housewives with baskets on their arms, students in oversized suits, black skirts and blouses; the tinkle of bicycle bells before and behind me. Over the walks, there were awnings of blue corrugated metal. Enclosed in their shadows, fluid as drops in a stream, the crowds moved on. Here and there, bright plastic streamers fluttered on lampposts. An old woman in a kimono paused to look at a window. The rubbery smell of udon wafted from a doorway.

As Susie and I walked to the train, I worried we might meet Gisela, then brushed the thought away. She was in Tsukuba, teaching. Besides, Susie and I were late as always. I was off to a luncheon of Japanese academics to hear Anthony Thwaite, a British poet, speak. After that, I was going to a performance of Noh. She was going to the National Center for Pediatrics Research to meet the head of the center, and then to her tea ceremony class. As Susie handed me the tickets, I thought, She knows nothing. And then: But nothing has happened.

Near the end of the train platform, several pigeons waddled like pudgy businessmen. A small boy was crying into the knees of his mother. My train came first. Susie was headed in the opposite direction. "Let's meet in Shinjuku for dinner," she said. I waved as the door closed, her face shuttling down the windows of the car, like a series of cards, a film in slow motion. And then she vanished. Hanging on a strap, swaying back and forth with the train, I opened my book. *Swann's Way.* I was nearing the part where Swann's passion is starting to reveal the cracks in his psyche, where his self will crumble.

The train was passing the tall buildings that circle the city, where sarariman hunched, like potters, over papers and figures, columns of kanji. Their shirts were white, their hair thick and black, like mine. Young women in uniform handed them papers, bent over their desks, talked in high nasal voices. A vast empire of wealth produced and processed. A world without wives. In the narrow winding alleys, below the tracks, the bars were closed; unlit pink-and-blue neon signs stood at the doors like tiny robot sentries; behind the bar counters, the owners set up glasses, swept, opened the doors a moment for the stale air to flow out; the daylight thrust in like a finger, pointing to the darkness where the stools waited. In a few hours, the narrow, dim rooms would be jammed, filled with shouts and music, bodies heated by sake, bourbon, and sho-chu. The streets would explode with neon; crowds like waves would ebb across the massive intersections. And I would be lost among them, looking for my wife.

2

In the years when Susie and I lived together before we were married, I had a number of lovers. I never hid their existence from her. To justify myself, I wanted her to do the same. It was freedom and equality by fiat; like a newly empowered government, I banished the idea of possession, proclaimed a communal vision where sex was a fluid, vascillating energy, a utopia without property. I cajoled, I whined, I shouted and raged. Our arguments grew fiercer; my depressions ranker; her despair deeper. I slept ten, fourteen, seventeen hours a day. I'd go out at night and come home drunk, high, angry, weeping. She told herself she had to get out, she had to get out. Every day she woke to see me lying there, comatose, sleeping off the drugs, the smell of another body, one more night. She would look at the light pouring through the window—leaves, bare branches, rain, snow—she would not know what time of year it was, how old she was, where it was going, if it would ever end. She thought she was crazy, I was crazy. While I slept, she sat on the couch and wrote out short, abrupt sentences about her need to leave. She would speak of this to no one.

All those years, what a slow dissolution, what a show we put on. She worked in the Health Department, then entered premed, then med school, trying to bind together a life that kept splitting in two. The everyday pleasures of shopping, of fixing meals, of studying the bonds of carbon, the phylum of the beasts; the life of tea with friends in cafés, parties, plays—it was all coming apart in a shadowy netherworld: the hidden bonds between us, private plays, private parties, other shoppings of pleasure.

It was madness. One day, suddenly she saw this. It was a doubt that would not go away. After eight years, she asked for help. And found herself sitting in a room, on the floor, before another woman. The therapist wore a long burgundy dress, had salt-and-pepper hair. Her job was to do nothing at first but listen to Susie tell her tale and ask for help. Later would come the instruction, the necessary changes.

And then I was there, beside Susie, talking to this woman, laughing nervously, not knowing what to say.

"We cannot go on," said the woman in the burgundy dress. "We cannot go on if you do not stop."

I couldn't believe it. I sat there looking at the woman in the burgundy dress, at Susie. I sat there and thought I could never close that door, never sit alone in a room with only one woman, sit there the rest of my life, touching only her, sleeping beside only her. Impossible. Monstrous. Frightening.

I sat there and said, No, no, no. I sat there and looked at the light.

3

The play was *Dojoji,* a special Noh performance. On the bare
floor, the masked dancer robed in green and gold glided in circles, never lifting his feet between steps, only his toes rising at
the end of each stride, like a sigh. The beat of the drums grew
faster, a gasp for breath. His mask was gold, the twisted features
of a demon. Behind him the great cedar painted on the back of
the Noh stage spread its stillness. The dancer turned, pounded
his feet in time to the drums; the drummers, in measure, shouted
out calls: the taiko drummer's short and abrupt, the *otsuzumi*
drummer's high and long, almost a yodel. The flute flew up and
down like a leaf in a whirlwind. Seated to the side of the stage
on their knees, like a row of candles, the chorus droned,
chanted.

Gisela followed in the *utai* (song) book, moving her fingers down the columns of characters. I couldn't have kept my place
without her guidance. I felt embarrassed, aware of her hand, the
fingers small and pudgy, a pale white. From time to time I looked
at her. At times she looked back. I felt her body beside me like a
weight pushing me down.

Above the stage hung a huge bell. The demon snake had
to be captured by the monks of this temple. The dancer was crossing back and forth on the stage; members of the chorus held the
rope from which the bell was suspended. The bell weighs several
hundred pounds. So much of Noh is hypnotic, a somnolent slowness, tension created by what is held back. Now, in contrast, the
speed was violent, chaotic, the drumming and flute and chanting
were wild, beyond control.

The rope was released, the bell dropped like a safe, the
dancer leaped, disappeared in the bell. Silence. Then a single drum
call, long, starting low and moving to falsetto. The other drums and

the flute joined in. Now the procession from the stage. Encased in darkness, the demon was gone.

We ate at an eel restaurant near the train station. We sat in a wooden booth, beneath a line of boards advertising the menu. Gisela ordered for us both. The waitress brought back lacquer bowls filled with rice, strips of grilled eel laid across the top. I poured Gisela tea, started to discuss the Japanese. "But where does the energy that they don't spend in abstract analysis go?"

"Or does abstract analysis take place in the culture in a way we don't recognize?"

We shared the intimacy of foreigners, the power to stand above the culture and observe, criticize. The sense of minds clicking into each other, the give and recognition of intelligence. A laugh of delight.

Momentarily she let down her shield. "There was this time when I was six, I remember the day, I see this girl brushing her long, thin hair, making it into . . . what do you call it in English?"

"Braids?"

"Yes, braids. Anyway, I decided that day that there were things about my mother I didn't like. Later I came to accept them. That there was nothing I could do." She blew out a puff of smoke. Leaned back. Languorous, tense. "When I'm in Europe, I call my mother once a day. I'm a good daughter. I know she's expecting me to call."

I wanted to ask more about this mother, to trade secrets about families and the past, the way Americans do. But she had already said, "Germans always want to know everything about you the first night they meet you. There's no mystery. The Japanese aren't like that."

Later, in her apartment, the room was cold, damp; the heater glowed by the table, its bars like the neon on the streets. I felt rooted to the floor, like a tiny idol in a temple. She smiled often, almost as if we were sharing some joke. We drank cups of tea, the rough-hewn porcelain giving up ghosts of mist. The distance between us seemed to close and open like a ventricle. I kept wanting to reach out, to take her hand, to bend toward her body. I sat in silence. Susie was with Takako Inada, visiting a medical center in Nagoya.

The telephone rang. Gisela answered it and had a conversation in Japanese. She put down the phone, went to the door, returned with a box. "Chocolates," she said. "He left them at the door." It was the friend again. A ten-minute conversation filled with *"isogashii"*—busy, and *"osoku ni natte"*—it's late. The stereo repeated softly, *"Like a bridge over troubled water / I will . . ."* Sounds of the crowd in the background of the Simon and Garfunkel concert. She hung up, returned. "He kept asking if he could come over, and I said I was working. Are you really working? he kept asking. Is someone there? I told him no, I'm working . . ." A slight conspiracy is set up, the shared knowledge of her lie, the secret she is keeping.

"It's really pathetic. I don't know what to do . . ."

Now they were singing, *"Counting the cars on the New Jersey Turnpike. They've all come to look for America . . ."*

"We're in this group that studies Noh together. I told him three years ago I wasn't interested. Then he went away to Germany for a while. He came back, I still told him no. So he got married. I feel sorry for his wife. She's German. When they got married, I really tried to make friends with her, but when we met she was so cold . . ."

I thought of my wife, whom I still hadn't mentioned, how it felt in the old days when she and one of my girlfriends met.

"Well, you weren't very angry with him on the phone." I talked of how the relationship between any two people becomes a system they both maintain. "In a way, what you're doing is supporting his delusion."

She ignored my remarks, went on speaking of the Noh group, the art world she had entered.

"Oh, they accept me. But I'm not taken quite seriously. Or maybe I am. I don't know. It's always Gisela-chan this, Gisela-chan that." Language one uses with an intimate friend, a lover, a child. "Gisela-chan, Gisela-chan. And then they laugh. I'm usually the only woman. We go out after gallery openings, first to one bar and then to the next. We drink. The wives never come." The phone rang again. She ignored it.

"I don't understand it," she said, meaning her effect on men. She'd meet someone at an opening, an embassy gathering, a party, and he'd fling himself at her foolishly, make extravagant, absurd statements.

I felt the undertow, some hint of a game I didn't quite understand. I thought of the film *Hiroshima, Mon Amour,* about the Japanese married man chasing the French woman through the city. But perhaps I was making this up, perhaps the game was merely a chimera I was creating.

Gisela rose, unplugged the phone, then sat back down beside me. I took a sip of tea and saw my other hand fall, rest casually on the knee hidden by her skirt. It was like watching a stone drop down a well. Waiting for the sound. Before it touched her, I lifted the hand, poured myself another cup of tea.

"Lisl and I aren't all that close," Gisela said. "She's funny. She's so critical at times. She just says what she thinks. I've been in Japan so long I'm not used to that. The other day at this concert she was criticizing me for being too passive. And then she criticized me when I said I didn't like being touched."

Yes. She will not be touched.

She showed me pictures of her paintings. "I did these in Berlin." They were of naked figures, skeletons, skulls, but only in blurred, soft outline, nothing grotesque or sharp. The figures were dark, Germanic, but with none of the clichés that come with the Nazi Grand Guignol. The music on the stereo was a Noh flute, slow, moaning and mysterious, rising to a piercing screech, like the cry of a ghost, the squeal of metal, then descending quickly into silence, a low, breathy drone. "I suppose I did my best work there. I like how Japan has changed me. I'm more *yasashii,* I've lost that angst. I like the light here, the landscape. But I worked more in Berlin, I did more paintings."

I thought of how I liked the Berlin paintings better than the moon hills, of how I liked the softness she had acquired, of how she might use it and strengthen the darkness in these figures. I kept thinking about this because I wanted to pretend I could be useful to her, that somehow I could change what was happening between us into something more benign.

4

It is the summer before I will go away to college, the summer of James Taylor, the summer I will ponder all summer long the possibilities of girls I have not met, the possibilities of life outside my parents' house, the freedom of staying out all night, of having girls stay all night; I, who have hardly kissed a girl or felt her breast. It is August, I'll be going to school in two weeks. My hair is getting longer, beginning to fall over the tops of my ears. Although I am not conscious of my plans for this hair, my father is. One day he declares, "You think you're going to go away to school and let your hair grow. Well, you're not."

He takes me downstairs to the basement, sits me on the white vinyl kitchen chair, fastens with a safety pin the old sheet around my upper body, takes out the clippers, the scissors, and begins his work. All the while, fury, frustration are growing inside me. I can't speak, I know there is nothing I can do. He is not Delilah; he needs no guile, no sleeping lover. A puppet plopped in his chair, I clack my teeth. Nothing comes out.

I watch strand after black strand fall on the white cloth. It's only hair, but what I feel is some horror of the irretrievable. And still he does not stop. The whirr of the clippers. More cuts. He pushes my head to one side, then the other; he tells me to move the chair back. I pick it up, move a few inches backward, bring it down.

A shout of pain. A hand whacks across my head, a flat hot ringing in my ears, and immediately again, a fist to my arm, duller; the pain less hot, and ringing, deeper, more solid. "You idiot, you did that on purpose." He grips my arm, the fingers squeezing back the pain I've given him—the chair has landed on his foot. I have deliberately tried to harm him.

Even now, I can't decide. I thought at the time the chair was an accident. Some part of me wants to believe it was an accident. I was helpless, I couldn't fight back.

And then it is seven, eight years later, one afternoon in my twenties, the bathroom of the apartment Susie and I shared on the Native American side of town, just at that time we were beginning to leave the age of hippies, of long, straight hair. She has a sort of shower cap on, a shower cap with tiny holes through which I pull with a hook strands of hair, which I am soaking with foam. The dye will make the hair blonder, streak it, give it a cheapness she will hate and I will want more of. It is a sign that she loves me.

As we do this, she is nervous, laughing. I am reassuring her. I too am tense, but I can't show this to her. We make jokes about Angie Dickinson, truck-stop pickups. I am careful, clumsy, as I let the foam spread with a hiss from an aerosol can. As she sits in that chair, a sheet spread over her body, I ask her to move her chair. She does so. I continue, with no hint, no glimmer of recognition. Not until this morning, staring out at the gray sky over the houses of St. Paul, the winter smoke curling above the green shingled roofs, rising through the barren branches at my window, not until it is years later, after the therapy, after the recovery, after the dipping a thousand times into the stream of memory, will I see it. When it no longer matters, and that past is now long ago.

5

A week after going to see *Dojoji,* I went with Gisela to an art exhibit at the German consulate. The exhibit was in the consulate foyer, a huge room encased by glass. When we arrived, there was already a crowd of Japanese and gaijin, all with drinks in their hands. German, Japanese, English, a babble of voices.

"The woman is an amateur," Gisela said. "Oh, her work sells, but it's terrible. I go only because her husband has been kind to me. He works at the consulate. He's older than her, but charming, amusing." The pictures looked like the colors at the end of a broken kaleidoscope or the broken shards of multicolored dinner plates. I had no way to judge them. I deferred to Gisela, who bent her head slightly downward as she drank from her wineglass, her eyes looking up at me, holding mine, smiling.

Several times, people mistook me for her lover. They told her this in German, and she told me what she said, that it wasn't so. And then she laughed.

Later, she turned to me and remarked, "You have the face for a Genji." Then: "No, it is almost feminine, like Genji's, but rounder, less lean, less defined." We were in Roppongi, at a Vietnamese restaurant which was owned by a Japanese in a white suit. He had invited some Germans, and a gay American potter who'd lived in Kyoto for years. As dish after dish arrived, ordered by our host, the potter talked of arriving in Kyoto when Americans were scarce, of the consistency of the clay, the quality of the kilns, of his shop, his shows. The sake was poured, his face grew redder, his laughter louder, his speech slow. It was like watching someone fall overboard, swimming for a while, caught in the wake's bubbling foam. Then the ship growing distant, the sea opening beneath him, his body going under, like a deep breath.

For a while, Gisela showed mild interest, then was bored. "I'd rather it was just the two of us," she whispered.

Our host was also drunk. He kept coming over to Gisela, talking to her in Japanese, bending toward her. "He's just invited me to an opening," she said. "He's very rich. He owns a gallery."

It was much later that night, when I left sometime around three, that I felt something change. "I don't understand you," she said. "That look, what did it mean?"

A few days afterward, Susie and I were on the futon in the tatami room, with the shoji closed and only a small shaded bulb for light.

"You haven't told her you're married?" Her eyes seemed

wide and narrow at once, her face pointed. I could feel myself drawing back. Our shadows, thrown by the light, were enlarged on the shoji and the white walls. "What did you think you were doing?"

I think of certain moments, moments when I could have said something. "It just never came up."

"I don't believe that. And neither do you."

I try to laugh, to smile. Know I should not. Each movement, each remark annoys her, brings on the expected litany. It is and is not like facing my father and his anger.

"Don't expect me to make it easier for you. Of course, there's no excuse. It's as if you've learned nothing these past few years . . ."

I bend my head down, push my hands through my hair, stare at the tatami, the patterns of straw. I fold my hands on my lap. Some blow is coming. I know it. Behind me the electric heater hums, its heat brushing my back.

"You need to deal with this by yourself, I'm not going to help, I'm not going to make it easier for you . . ."

My last meeting with Gisela was tense, strained, a series of miscues created by me. Or so she chose to think.

We had just been to an art gallery in Roppongi. We caught a taxi below the Tokyo Tower, its girders all lit up, spearing the dark. Suddenly she revealed that she had a husband and they were separated. Perhaps it was the wine from the reception. Her husband had been teaching in America, had taken one of his students as a lover. A *"petite affaire,"* she called it. "It didn't bother me. These things happen all the time." He was brilliant, a linguist, spoke six languages. "I'll show you his book when we get to my apartment."

I pictured him as tall, arrogant, an Aryan blond in a dark turtleneck, long hair, a jutting chin. There had been no photos of him in the apartment.

She kept talking of his brilliance, the way some other woman might talk of her husband's wealth. He had taught in Japan

for a couple of years, they had come here together. And then he
went to the States.

"Now he expects me to follow him there. Just like that."
We were passing the pink neon of the Almond Coffee Shop, the
Roppongi station, the highway on girders up above us, above the
congestion. Neon splashed everywhere, crowds of dark-garbed
bodies, black hair. I looked at her face.

"No, I'm not angry. I have a life here, I teach. I'm not
ready to go back to Europe, much less go to America. I was there
once before, I don't need to go back." She paused. "He just expects
me to leave my life here. I told him if he wants to come here and
teach, that's fine." Now the taxi was threading through the narrow
alleys of our neighborhood, white concrete houses behind gray
concrete block walls. Jade trees, bikes, street signs, vending machines glowing in front of small shops. "Why would I be jealous?"

We got off at the subway station near her house. We
started walking and found ourselves beneath a great red *torii*
(arch), lit by spotlights. Stones crinkled beneath our feet. Down the
hill, the winding alleys, the traffic of Tokyo, a ceaseless hum. I
decided now was the moment to tell her. As always with her, I was
wrong.

"Why did you say that, the way you did, that you were
married?" she asked. "Why would it matter to me? You made a
point of it. You didn't have to do that."

The temple was closed, the golden doors locked. We
walked back down the steps. In the alleys, the smell of the gutters
crept up. We passed a small playground with the shadows of swings,
bars, skeleton constructions. We sat down on a bench there. It was
too cold. We started walking toward her apartment.

"I don't want to have a *petite affaire. . . .* You're so
strange," she said. "Really, I don't understand you."

I watched her face, looked down to the dark expanse of
her coat, the dark folds of the skirt. We had reached the steps of
her building.

"I'm not angry. I just don't think I like you. How could
you say a thing like that?"

I said Americans want to know more, to leave less beneath the surface.

"No, it's not American," she said. "It's not that at all. I have never known anyone like you. The way you act." She turned and walked up the steps.

6

The swiftness of the train was like a dream. Encased, flying through the countryside, in two hours I would arrive in Kyoto, several hundred miles away. In fall, farmers in cone-shaped straw hats, fastened by kerchiefs tied at the chin, would be bending up and down in the fields. Baggy blue pants, quilted *happi* coats, a T-shirt underneath. Picking up sheaths of rice, moving next to fields of black ash, small fires burning near a ditch. But it was still winter, almost spring. The fields were empty. Dark, spotted with stubble, they were incredibly tiny, no bigger than one or two football fields. A vanishing way of life, supported by government subsidies. A life I would not have had even had I been born here.

I kept trying to shake away the words of our argument, Susie's face, her finger pointing, her sharp movements, the distance between us. I thought of how, just before we married, I felt as if I were closing a door forever, as if I were going to be trapped in a room with no escape. Then the door closed, and I didn't look back, didn't even hear it shut. When we argued, I had this sudden surge: it's okay, we're married, it will work out. The room expanded. The fear had left.

I knew then that because of our past we could not allow the small deceptions that over time grow larger and larger and become shifting fault lines, imperceptible, unconscious, until the ground falls apart, and the cracks, irreparable, deeper than anyone realized, are revealed.

Now I had broken that promise.

I looked out the window, tried to recover the ordinary. As the train passed through the mountains, covered with small pines and trees, I realized I had no vocabulary to describe what I saw: the vegetation was alien, leaves in fern-like patterns, narrower, more regular. The same with the architecture: the uniform, cramped forms I could not name. I thought of Susie, of Gisela, of my own stupidity. The small towns and winter fields whipped by.

When I arrived in Kyoto, I checked into a cheap *minshuku* (inn) and called Susie. Our talk was mechanical, brief. I had told her that I wanted to see the famous fire festival in Kurama, a town just outside of Kyoto. Reiko had recommended it. In truth, I had simply wanted to get away from Tokyo, from all my confusion. I went to bed early, spent the next day wandering through Nijo Castle, past the pale-gold panels with tigers and giant cedars. I walked across the floorboards that gave little squeaks—the nightingale floors designed to warn the soldiers inside of intruders. White sand gardens with tiny bonsai pines, gray and black volcanic rocks. Scores of schoolchildren, tourists with Nikons. If Susie were with me, the schoolchildren would be shouting out, "Haro, haro," and the college boys with their Nikons would be asking her to stand beside them for a picture. She would soon get irritated, feeling like a monkey in cage, a trained seal. We would argue, or I would soothe her. I walked for hours. The day seemed endless.

When evening came, I waited half an hour in line for the train to the festival. The sun had disappeared over the mountains, leaving only a rim of flame over the rounded, dark-green peaks. Boredom. Darkness floated up the mountains toward the last bits of light.

I kept asking why I had come.

A one-street village of small wooden houses, Kurama was snuggled into the side of a mountain. The mountain loomed above the town like a huge black wall. All up and down the asphalt main street there were small torches and braziers burning.

Suddenly a group of men marched up, clad in happi coats, white headbands with blue polka dots, white cloth shoulder pads, and loincloths, their buttocks bared. On the pads they carried a twelve-foot-long cone of wood, the end of which was a bright splash of flames, spewing up smoke. What they were chanting—*"Sei rei, sei yo"*—I didn't understand. I was later told it meant "Long dead ancestors, rest in peace."

From time to time, when the fire got too large, the men would put down the torch and someone would take a cup of water from one of the buckets or barrels along the street and douse the flames a bit. Then they would pick up the torch and begin marching and chanting again, the smoke completely engulfing the carrier closest to the top. I felt as if I had just stepped into another, older Japan. A peasant Japan. One closer to the Japan my grandfather knew.

Above the street, people on balconies leaned over and waved, shouted to the men bearing the torches, the flames at the end almost the size of a man. As each torch passed, more and more of the crowd began to pick up the chant: *"Sei rei, sei yo."* Some of the bearers stopped, took a swig of sake, more and more drunk. Torches weaved back and forth, coming right up to the faces of the onlookers, the flames threatening to fall upon them. The drunken torch men kept chanting, unaware they were wavering, endangering the crowd. The small boys with them looked frightened, delighted. Dogs barked and circled at their heels. The torches moved on.

I looked up the mountain slope, the dark mountain wall rising and melding with the sky. Sharp shadows of pines jutting up in the dark. Suddenly I felt tired and wanted to be away from this crowding and shouting, the denseness of Japan. Somehow I felt I had ruined everything, not just the weeks it would take Susie and me to get over it, not just the weeks when the face of Gisela would slowly recede, the presence in our room at night, the space between us. No, the mark was deeper, longer, more permanent.

And yet some part of me kept repeating, Nothing happened, nothing happened, as if that were an answer.

A torch swept by, flared in my face. I coughed, pulled back. Drums started to beat and the chanting grew even louder. One of the torch crews hurled its torch on a large pile of sticks in the middle of the street. Another crew tossed its torch in. Another, another; the flames heaping, bubbling, jetting higher and higher. Smoke everywhere, dense as fog.

And then through the flames, on the other side of the square, a face leapt out. A white face. I knew it, knew she would follow me. I ducked under a crowd rope, ignoring the policeman, and started scrambling past the burning sticks to the other side.

The air above the street curved and melted; the houses, when I looked across the square, seemed to billow with flames as the torches lined up down the street, like huge birthday candles, waiting to be tossed into the bonfire. I was nauseous from the smoke, entranced by the flames.

Of course, the face I had seen in the crowd wasn't Susie's. She was back in Tokyo. The woman didn't even look like Susie, though she was white. I felt foolish, relieved. The strength left my body, tiredness set in. My legs ached.

Flashbulbs popped around me, heat pulsed toward me in a solid wall, hotter and hotter, sparks, ashes, flames. Small children sitting on their fathers' shoulders rubbed their eyes, as if about to cry. The din and drums, the destruction of the flames, were deafening. I turned, made my way through the crowd, to the steps that lead up the mountain. The air was suddenly cooler; ahead of me, away from the flames, everything seemed darker. I started up the steps.

It was a slow climb. The only sound was a small ditch of water trickling beside me in the dark. After passing beneath a thick oak torii, I came upon a stone well with copper cups. As I scooped the water up, I could see the stars flickering in the blackness of the pool. The cup splashed through them. I poured the water over my hands; another scoop, and I drank. The water was cold, bitter as iron. The stars in the pool reappeared.

I knew then it was all over. I had passed some test. Perhaps of my own devising, of my own stupidity, but I had passed. If I had passed badly, I would recover. I had been granted a gift. I stood there in the darkness.

At the top of the mountain was a shrine, small and shabby, made of plain wood. I shook the brass bell which hung before the entrance. It made a tiny rattle, like the shifting of sands. I clapped twice, bowed, and looked into the shadows of the shrine, at the lacquered table and the little box and bowls inside. I asked blessings on the spirits of my grandparents. It felt foolish and right, more fitting than prayers inside a church, more naturally my home.

Something settled inside me. I had come on a journey. Gisela was not part of it, she was a roadblock I'd set up. My relationship with Susie, my writing, that was the center of my life. Did there need to be something more?

I spent a long while at the top of that mountain, wandering through the pines and cedars, the trunks that rose forty, fifty, sixty feet over my head. In the thick dark, amid the smell of the needles, I felt a sense of uncanniness, of whatever was Japanese inside me, suddenly palpable and present in the wind that flowed around my body, in the memory of the torches, their intense heat. It was so familiar, so familial, that peace. I knew the way back. I could return to Tokyo.

PART
TWO

PART
TWO

I

"What makes power hold good, what makes it accepted, is simply the fact that it doesn't only weigh on us as a force that says no, but that it reverses and produces things, it induces pleasure, forms knowledge, produces discourse. It needs to be considered as a productive network which runs through the whole social body, much more than as a negative instance whose function is repression."

—Michel Foucault,
"Truth and Power"

"When you know the masks as well as we do, they come to seem like the faces of real women."
—Fumiko Enchi,
Masks

1

At the end of February, almost out of season, a last snowfall. At evening, it dusts the city in whiteness, spots the black umbrellas bobbing down the avenues, vanishes in the thick black hair of shop girls, in the short-cropped cuts of sarariman. The tires of taxis slosh through the flakes, darken them to slush. The great crowds rushing through the stations emerge to a night that is muffled, less jangling than the normal pace of the city. The lights in the alley-sized streets flash on the crystals, which then vanish in the shadows. For a moment, quietness settles.

Romping like children, Susie and I build a snowman in the vacant lot in front of our house. Empty space in Tokyo—a minor miracle. She is laughing and singing "Frosty the Snowman." I grumble about the cold, how my part of the snowman, the second ball, is refusing to grow. It is crumbling apart each time I pat it.

"Whose idea was this anyway?" I lack her patience to pack the snow down after each roll. The ball stays loose, collapses like a delicate, failed soufflé.

We put two olives in the head for eyes. The one olive pit sticking out at the nose makes the snowman look like a snow bird, so we attach tiny wings. Susie exclaims that that the snowman has the webbed neck of Turner's syndrome, the stunted limbs of a Thalidomide baby, the weird eyes of chromosomal breakage.

"Never make a snowman with a doctor," she says.

We debate and give up on the idea of using dried lotus roots for hair. I am glad she is so happy, that the tension between us has lifted. Just as we finish, a woman passes, walking her dog, and laughs, *"yuki dharama"*—*yuki* for snow and *dharama,* the little red round-bellied gods you see at Buddhist temples and cemeteries.

Later, after it snows some more, we look out the door, and the snowman or snow bird has taken on a more peaceful demeanor, the rough edges smoothed out into a primitive abstract figure, featureless as any enterer of Nirvana might be.

Sipping tea on the floor in the kitchen, the nabe bowl before us emptied of its stew of shrimp, soy sauce, and vegetables, we watch Japanese television. I can, aided by the visual messages, understand the dialogue of the more stereotypical programs. I forget I am listening to Japanese. On one program, a young American is staying with a Japanese family. Standing in the living room, towering over the others, he looks bloated, pasty, pale. Accepted by the family, he elicits the help of the father in smoothing over his engagement with a young Japanese woman. Still, this young American, his whiteness, seems an aberration, almost a joke. I am seeing the reverse of the Asian stereotypes in *Sixteen Candles* or *Gung Ho* or *Valentine's Day*. In my revengeful delight, I understand how much loneliness and anger I felt in America.

Susie finds the exchange student both funny and annoying. She is almost as angered by Asian stereotypes as I am and shares some of my resentment toward American culture. And yet she is who she is.

"How is this picture of the foreign exchange students any different from the one in *Sixteen Candles?*" she asks.

"For one thing, the Japanese woman he's becoming engaged to isn't seen as a freak."

"How do you know? You can barely follow the dialogue."

"You can see it. Look how the father treats him."

Arguments on culture, on race, discussions of distance, the histories between us. Trying to negotiate the space that is marriage. In our two small rooms, we sit watching television; later, I am at the computer, Susie behind me, huddled in bed, the red coils of the heater humming beside her. Photographs of Butoh dancers, prints by Utamaro, tacky tourist watercolors and postcards from Tono, Kamakura, Kurama, on the walls. The pottery in the kitchen, cheap, newly bought, rough-hewn with charm. The TV set and washer picked up on the street, the tables from secondhand furniture stores.

We are nearly midway through my stay. At times a sense of severing comes over me, as if I can hear the ties to my old life breaking, the way one can hear telephone wires snapping in the cold or ice buckling. Something is coming apart. There's a loss of balance, a floating, as if I were adrift at sea, out of sight of land for so long that the sight of land, once thought to be so reassuring, so absorbing, seems frightening and strange, an impossibility. I had started the year thinking I would return at its end to the comforts of America. Now America seems distant, distasteful, no longer my home. And yet I cannot stay here in Japan. Or can I? And if I were to leave, I'd rather go on to other parts of Asia, and then to Europe. Susie feels less certain. At times she longs for home.

Who are my friends? An architect and publisher of a dance magazine; a student in music composition; an artist who runs a snack bar; a photographer who teaches at a radical school each Thursday and is writing an article on the uses of violence; a high-school English teacher; a Noh musician; a translator in a trading company; my Japanese teacher, who's the wife of a section chief at Mitsubishi. They speak English in varying degrees, and each conversation is full of confusions and mistranslations. At times the results are comic. A woman in Susie's tea ceremony asked, *"Sun de imasu ka?"*—Where do you live?—and Susie in confusion replied, *"Shin de imasu ka?"*—Am I dead? Later she told the woman that she was drinking sake (wine) rather than seki (cough medicine) for her cold.

"She must have thought I was a lush." Susie laughed.

At other times, the language intervenes in more difficult ways, in questions that are not understood or can never be asked since to a Japanese they would seem either rude, irrelevant, or unanswerable. I think that Reiko mentioned something a few weeks back about taking a trip to Shingu, my grandfather's hometown, with Haruki. But she's said nothing about it since.

"Should we ask her about this?" I asked Mrs. Hayashi.

Maybe these friends are impolite, Mrs. Hayashi suggested.

I don't know what to make of this. Reiko has been so kind to me. It ought to feel natural simply to ask about this. But it doesn't. Somehow it would interrupt the flow of our friendship. I fear appearing the crude American. I let it go.

Eleven 'Clock comes on, with its silly wisecracking hosts and games. Young women in bathing suits run across the stage and, using a rope, pull themselves up a greased incline. At the top they put on underwear and slide back down. "I'd be furious if it weren't so silly," says Susie, as she turns off the set. "But of course, that makes it even more infuriating."

We open the closets, pull out the futon, roll it out on the tan tatami mats. Beside it are a book of Japanese vocabulary, tapes of dialogues, my Noh recital. I write, listening now to the sounds of the Noh *Kan,* the taiko, otsuzumi, the *kotsuzumi,* an instrument which I learned to play just last week.

Susie climbs into the futon beside me, her body steaming from her bath. She asks me to hand her her book on shiatsu. I pick up a familiar novel, with descriptions of dinner parties with a Margaux on the sideboard, smoked trout, a cassoulet, and the sounds of the words are strange to me, the food foreign. Rather than *The American Poetry Review,* or the latest minimalist fiction, I read *The Tale of Genji, The Tales of Heike, The Tales of Ise,* the theories of Zeami, who weaves an aesthetic around hana (flower) in a discourse that seems bafflingly vague, self-contained, intuitive, and circuitous, that lacks the specificity, directness, or linear logic of Aristotle's *Poetics.* I study poems of Buddhist doctrine, Noh plays about Gods, feudal *daimyos* (lords), and princesses, stories of lovers in tiny inns, temple monks, fishermen, merchant daughters in Osaka. All of them say the form is empty, the self decentered, the substance you learned in the West is absent here.

As I fall asleep, I think of sleeping in a bed two feet above the ground. The idea seems awkward, surreal. I think of my grandfather, his emigration. Of a circle closing. When will I return to the place he was born?

The next morning, the snow had melted to mush in the streets, our sculpture to a small mound. There was the sound of dripping from the eaves, with an occasional plop when a big glob fell, and the scrape-scrape of women cleaning off the street in front of their houses. Susie was meeting Takako Inada for lunch. Then she was going to accompany Takako through her day and pick up Takako's children from day care.

"I think she's going to do it," said Susie. "I've finally convinced her that Kei-chan and Haito-chan aren't going to go crazy if she divorces her husband."

"You're the devil in her ear."

"Get serious. She told me she's been supporting her husband for several years. He wanted to leave his job at the *kaisha* (company), to stop being a sarariman, so she agreed to finance him in setting up a business. Only the business still hasn't taken off. She's going to be better off financially after the divorce."

Near noon, I went to a take-out sushi shop on Mejiro Avenue and had some maguro, ika, and futomaki. I asked for *koora,* but was told they had none. I settled for a Kirin cider. At least I'd finally learned to pronounce Coca-Cola in Japanese. Japanese is an unaccented language, but I'd had difficulty eliminating the accent in words borrowed from English. I also couldn't quite pronounce the Japanese *r,* which is approximately halfway between the English *r* and the English *l.* I'd already given up on using the *reshito* for *receipt* and found that *ryoshusho,* the Japanese word, was easier to pronounce.

I walked a few doors up to Renoir, one of the half dozen coffee shops along the avenue on the way to the station. Its decor was white, stark; the clientele mainly college students from the nearby university. They wore white shirts, oversized black sweaters, dark pants and skirts. They'd adapted the style of the American fifties, a time of innocence, frivolity and prosperity, safe from the problems of crime and race, the decay of the city.

I ordered a *bienna koohi* (Vienna coffee), scones with whipped cream and marmalade. I was reading Fumiko Enchi's *The Waiting Years.* I was going to see her in a week, and I was worried about how the meeting would go. She was eighty years old and was in the hospital for cancer. The interview would take place there. I was surprised that she had agreed to see me. She was the leading

Japanese woman novelist. The other novelists I'd tried to see had all said they were too busy. I lacked the credentials, wasn't writing a dissertation on their work.

When I left the coffee shop, the afternoon sunlight had melted all the snow, the air had warmed. I passed the stationery shop, the pottery shop, the Kentucky Fried Chicken, the Chinese restaurant, the French restaurant where we went for paella. Around me schoolchildren in their blue uniforms giggled; women on bicycles carried their groceries home, a child sometimes strapped to the seat in the back. Young men in the local 7-Eleven browsed through *manga* (comic books). The young women beside them were reading *Sassy, My Life, Elle.* We often stopped at the 7-Eleven on our way home late at night, picked up some instant curry rice, a bento of teriyaki chicken or sushi. I realized again how much I would miss this country, how I felt I was dwelling in some protective womb, this world of faces that looked like mine.

When I got home, I went up on the roof. I'd been meaning to do this since Okubo, the real-estate man, had shown us our apartment. As I stepped onto the gravelly surface, the skyline of Tokyo hit me on all sides—the shopping center of Ikebukuro, with its thrust of skyscrapers, a little to the left; then to the right, Shinjuku, and beyond that Shibuya, the ring of centers along the Yamanote-sen line. All my travels through the city had been by train or subway. My sense of the city was from the ground, winding through small streets, looking for this shop or that class, or trying to choose a restaurant. I felt as if I'd just climbed up from a system of tunnels, was suddenly seeing sunlight and distance, with a new sense of space and vertical heights.

I could see dozens of apartment buildings within a block, and dozens of balconies with clotheslines. Tiny walkways ran between the buildings. No yards, though here and there a single pine or a large jade plant fronted a building. The balconies indicated that each apartment was about twelve feet wide, rabbit hutch after rabbit hutch. The scene had an Asian sense of space. Inside, the apartments were cluttered with goods, the people well fed, the refrigerators full.

Down below, I heard the *yaki-mo* man and his loud-

speaker recorder blaring out his selling song. Yaki-mo were mountain potatoes roasted in charcoal (most apartments, like ours, did
not have an oven). His song, a folk tune, seemed ear-splitting and
obnoxious, rather than charming and quaint.

The skyline suddenly reminded me of the panoramas at
the beginning of cop shows. Television gave no sense of Tokyo
space. Either the small rooms looked large on the tiny sets, or the
streets, seen one at a time, lacked the curves and dead ends, the
layout which was designed in feudal times to ward off invaders and
which gave the city its labyrinthian feel.

So, I thought, this is where I live. I've become one of
them, an anthill dweller, a member of the hive.

2

On a late afternoon in March, the huge shadow of the Ikebukuro
Seibu fell out over the crowds leaving the station. On the walks
were old men and women with wizened faces, kerchiefs or caps,
their clothes a soft pale blue. Shoe boxes and rags laid out before
them. Sarariman stood with their feet propped on the boxes, fin-
gering a toothpick, a cigarette. The shoppers joggled by, laden with
bags. We passed the Mister Donut, a Pachinko parlor, an electron-
ics store, the cameras and recorders layered in tiers, the prices on
little tags beside them.

"You remember the number?" Susie asked.

"Of course."

"Oh, don't go off in a huff. I just don't want to go through
that again."

I was going into the Ikebukuro branch of our bank to use
the cash machine. I knew she was right. Two days after we had built
the snowman, I tried to use our card in a bank in Shinjuku. I'd
forgotten our code number, but since I couldn't read the kanji, I
didn't realize that was why the machine wasn't working. I thought

I hadn't pressed the right buttons. On the third try, the machine ate my card. I felt like an idiot. We were nearing the end of the month and short on cash. We had to borrow from Daniel and then ask Hasegawa, from International House, to arrange for a new card.

This time I emerged from the bank triumphant. "Here it is. Your sugar daddy provides."

All through our stay in Japan I enjoyed being the one who was providing our income. Back in the States, there'd been many years when Susie had made more than I did, and we assumed that after she finished her medical training, this would certainly be the case. She had trouble adjusting to our changed situation in Japan, and she thought about going back to the States more often than I did. Lately, especially after visiting Takako at her clinic, Susie would talk of how she missed being a doctor, how not working was beginning to unsettle her.

I stopped at a shop window to admire a sports coat. A mother passed by with her daughter, in her navy schoolgirl uniform. The girl's hair was cut in bangs. Like me, she kept stopping to look in the windows. Her mother yanked her along.

"Takako keeps telling her children that their father's away on business trips," Susie was saying. "I told her there's got to be a point when she tells them the truth."

"Well, she's finally told him she wants a divorce. She told his in-laws too. That's a start."

"She still thinks she's a freak, that there's no one else who feels like her."

"It's hard to tell, though, what people actually feel here. You can't assume they want the same things Americans want or think the same way."

"Of course not. But I think things are just beginning to change. Did you see in the paper that the Socialist Party just elected a woman as its head?"

We walked into Seibu and took the escalator to the great depato market. It was so familiar by now, the sections for pickles, for sushi and sashimi, for pre-made teriyaki, breads and pastries, little balls of chicken on a skewer, prepared European dishes—boeuf Bourguignon or chicken Kiev, curries, teas, wines, and beer.

"How much do you think we need for the party?" Susie asked.

"I want to make sure we have enough." It was an old argument, the Jewish mother in me versus the parsimonious puritan in her.

"We've got some teriyaki *kushi,* some sashimi, and we're going to do a nabe. And then there's the pickles, simbei, and desserto."

"I just thought it would be nice to have some sushi too. And a little lamb."

"Do you see how much we're spending for this meal?"

I handed over the ten-thousand-yen bill (about sixty dollars). The woman behind the counter in her white coat wrapped up the meat, handed it back with a *"Doomo arrigato"* and a smile. Like many of the Japanese, her teeth were bad.

"Why don't you get the liquor."

"Oh yes, Sahib."

"You know how everyone drinks."

"Kirin?"

"Hai. Ii okusan, ne."

"Baka."

"Nan da?"

"You heard what I said," she called back as she disappeared in the crowd.

"Taxi drivers, bus drivers, *ne.* There are some such persons who are women in the United States," Akiko said, looking at Susie, who nodded. "But there are almost none in Japan. We're far more limited." Akiko brushed her hair to the side. Her cheekbones were high, her face narrow, her eyes a bit too close together. You noticed her freckles, the intenseness of her gaze, the rapid hand movements, the back-and-forth motion of the cigarette to her mouth.

Suddenly the conversation in our tiny tatami room shifted back into Japanese. At the end of the table, Matsuo tapped his cigarette against the ashtray, jabbed it in the air. I took a sip of Kirin and leaned back against the shoji. This was one of the first times we'd had anybody over to our house and I was pleased with the way things were going. The words came too fast for me to translate— *kaisha . . . kakumei . . . nihon no bai . . .* with a splattering of English words—truck driver . . . construction . . .

Akiko and Matsuo seemed to disagree, were feinting back and forth.

"It's going too fast for me," I said, and asked Ken to translate. He smiled. "Well, I don't know if I can review it all."

In the background, I could hear Setsuko, Ken's wife, and Susie in the kitchen. "Are you going to have a baby?" Setsuko asked.

"I hope so," said Susie.

Suddenly I found the whole scene hysterical, and burst into laughter. Perhaps it was the absurdity of trying to deal with my limited Japanese, or simply the delight of having guests in our *apaato.*

". . . time for revolution," translated Matsuo, "but people always say it's not time."

Setsuko popped her head in and made some joke about *kakumei* (revolution) and everyone laughed, even me, who understood nothing but still found everything hysterical.

I had met these people in various ways. Ken and Akiko had been introduced to me by Saito, the translator. Saito worked in a modest job at a small trading company. Earnest, without the ability or desire for irony, he always seemed a bit distracted or confused, especially in groups of people. He wore wire-rim glasses and had terrible teeth. He spoke halting but fluent English, was avidly interested in Japanese-Americans, and seemed to see me as more important than I was. I sometimes felt that I was some sort of prize he was showing off. On the other hand, he had been very kind to me, introducing me to a number of people, including me in the activities of his friends.

Ken Uchida was a Sansei who had married Setsuko, a Japanese woman, while working for a Lutheran missionary organization. As part of his job, he had spent time dealing with Japanese leftists who were involved with activists in various Asian countries. He had been monitoring the activities of the churches in Korea and knew quite a bit about the political situation there. He was intelligent, with a scholarly manner, and Japan seemed to have brought out a certain confidence in him, as if he had finally found his area of study.

Akiko was a high-school English teacher. She and Saito were part of the group Ken had been dealing with. The group held English classes once a week, and I had met Akiko when I was invited by Saito to speak there. Akiko's English was more aggressive and swifter than that of any Japanese I'd met, man or woman. Her favorite authors were Faulkner and Fitzgerald, her favorite word "despise." She was a bit older than the rest of us, and more bitter. Her life as an independent woman in Japan had not been easy. She lacked Reiko's ability to shift in and out of roles, to act like a proper Japanese without being at all self-conscious about what that implied about the situation of women. In this way, Akiko was more American.

And then there was Matsuo. I had met him one night in a Shinjuku jazz house. He'd been there with John, the American scholar we'd talked to at the party after Ono's performance. When I asked Matsuo what he did for a living, he answered, "I get high." He had a preference for dated jazz, rock, beat, and black idioms, and persisted in calling his apartment "my pad." After refusing several times to tell me what he did for a living, he finally said, "For bread I do commercial photography; for my spirit, I do creative photography." His commercial photography consisted of liquor ads for Suntory, fashion shots for Maru-Maru and other department stores; his recent creative photography documented the Theater of the Deaf. Many of the shots were of their hands as they acted. We started talking photography, authors— Sontag, Benjamin, Brecht, Herbert Marcuse—and the Japanese left; he told me stories of his travels in America, recited his own poetry and lines by Allen Ginsberg and Bob Dylan, listed the deceptions of Nakasone and the Liberal Democratic Party. When the night ended around five and we stumbled out into the gray

Tokyo morning toward the first trains, I knew we'd become friends.

"Yeah, yeah, yeah," Akiko said and, interrupting Matsuo, launched into another stream of Japanese. Matsuo didn't seem angry, just serious, anxious to pursue where she was going. It was nothing sexual, the disparity in their looks and style precluded that. Akiko could pass as a housewife or the schoolteacher she was, and she was handsome, if not quite classically pretty. Matsuo was thin, wore glasses, jeans, and a baseball cap, and, with his long hair falling behind his ears, looked like a washed-out refugee from the sixties. His teeth stuck out.

Matsuo began talking about the farmers at Narita airport and the recent political demonstrations there. The farmers had begun the demonstrations even before the airport was built. The government had compensated the farmers for the land, but most Japanese believed that the compensation was not equitable. The taking of the land destroyed the farmers' way of life, even if they could find employment elsewhere. The enlarged airport would also displace more farmers, and most Japanese had at the least mixed feelings about the new construction.

"There's going to be a demonstration in a few weeks," Matsuo said. "Would you like to go?"

Sure, I said. The prospect seemed harmless, marching up and down with a sign in front of the airport. Of course, as with much of what happened in Japan, my preconceptions would turn out to be completely wrong.

"I met some of the farmers with a white friend of mine," said Ken. "It was quite revealing. I was barely fluent at the time; my friend had been working with them for years, spoke impeccable Japanese. But later one of the farmers said to my friend, " 'You know, we feel closer to Uchida-san than to you. He has the same blood.' "

"The Japanese people are not ready for a revolution," said Akiko. "It's a very repressive society."

Ken gave as an example the Japanese treatment of Koreans: "It's not like in America, it's very difficult for them to become citizens. They have to renounce their Korean names, to give up their cultural background completely. Many go along with this because they can't get certain jobs otherwise.''

"How did they get here?" I asked.

"Many of their parents were brought to Japan as slave labor.''

"There's also the Ainu," said Matsuo. The Ainu were the original natives of Japan.

"Yes," said Ken, "they're virtually wiped out. You just see some of them in Hokkaido in the tourist sites. It's like certain Indian reservations in America. They've made the Ainu into living relics, exoticized them in trinkets, postcards, and wood carvings sold in shops.''

I felt somewhat chagrined. I was so in love with Japan, I didn't want to hear anything negative about the country.

"The Japanese see themselves as superior to other Asians," Ken continued. "That's why they don't have any qualms about dealing with Marcos. Or South Africa.''

I wondered what Matsuo and Akiko thought of Ken's criticisms. They seemed to agree with them.

"But why haven't I heard any Japanese talk about all this?" I asked.

"It's their dirty secret," said Ken. "Like racism in America.''

At this point, Akiko and Matsuo launched into Japanese, and I totally lost the thread of the conversation. When things turned back again to English, Akiko was talking about a feminist writer who had criticized racism and agism among feminists.

"Are you talking about Simone de Beauvoir?" asked Susie, who had just returned to the table with the skewers of teriyaki. In a few moments, it would be my turn to get out the sushi and prepare the lamb.

"Ah, no, no, no, no," said Akiko.

"What does Beauvoir say about that?" asked Matsuo.

"She's critical of all the radical movements for ignoring old people.''

"Not from the start," Akiko observed, "but when she . . ."

"When she got older," said Susie. Everyone laughed.

"This writer is really quite radical. She doesn't believe in the family."

"How so?" asked Susie.

"She rejects being called mother or grandmother. She despises it. Her anger toward agism is very, very attractive to me, but far more dangerous than feminism."

"But being a grandmother is very different from being a wife," said Susie. "Being a wife implies being a servant, but grandmother doesn't imply the same degree of servitude."

"She doesn't like wife, because it's something taken for granted. She denies being called grandmother or mother. All these terms are from the family," said Akiko.

"But historically grandmother and grandfather were respectful terms."

"But she wants to be called just a woman. She just likes woman."

"Just like a woman . . ." Ken sang.

"Yah, yah, yah," said Akiko, brushing it aside as everyone laughed.

The conversation branched off again. Ken, Matsuo, and I began talking about the film *The Ballad of Narayama* and its depiction of an ancient peasant custom in which old people were left to die on a mountainside.

"When you first started talking," Susie was saying to Akiko, "I was unhappy because one of the mistakes I think American feminists made was to reject their roles as mother, because that's one of the most exciting things . . ."

Overhearing this, I decided against joining their conversation. Of course, I knew that Susie wanted children. I just couldn't decide exactly how I felt. I wondered how long I could keep from confronting this question by agreeing to forgo birth control, making a vague acquiescence to Susie's wishes.

3

The hospital where I met Fumiko Enchi was on the other side of town. The day I went there was gray and rainy. Hasegawa-san, my contact at International House, came along to translate. We had to take two different trains and a bus before a long walk through the streaming wet streets.

As with most Japanese hospitals and institutions in general, the building was dimly lit and distinctly unattractive. The pale graying walls, old furniture, and dark linoleum floors were all in sharp contrast to the contemporary stylishness and electronic wizardry of Japanese stores. The Japanese don't ascribe to Western notions that a pleasant environment will help people recover. Much of the basic care in Japanese hospitals is performed by relatives, and there's a sense that illness is something to be kept hidden within the family, a stain not to be acknowledged before outsiders.

I was grateful for the chance to see Enchi, especially considering her condition. Over eighty, she lay on the bed the whole time we were talking, which was to be kept to half an hour. Her face was tiny, too small for her small body. Hasegawa, my translator, wasn't quite prepared for the questions I wanted to ask. Because Enchi's voice was soft, difficult to hear, and the interview brief, the final transcript wasn't very substantial. She kept admonishing me to study in detail the Meiji era if I wanted to understand her novels. But what I remember most is the image of a frail old woman in a white robe, IV in arm, lying on her side and whispering, smiling from time to time, patiently answering the questions of this Japanese man who could speak no Japanese.

I did manage to ask a few questions about *Onna-men* [*Masks*], the first novel of hers translated into English, and *Onna-zaka* [*The Waiting Years*]. *Onna-zaka* is a novel based on the life of Enchi's maternal grandmother in the Meiji era, when the neo-

Confucian code required wives to submit completely to the will of their husbands. Tomo, the wife of a bureaucrat, is married to a man who not only is indifferent to her but forces her to arrange his love affairs and to share the household with his mistress; later, after tiring of this first mistress, he adds another. When Tomo first discovers her husband's indifference to her, she feels tormented both spiritually and physically. But instead of expressing this, her features are described as possessing the "tranquility of a Noh mask." When I asked Enchi about this passage, she said, "For women, *hyojo* [facial expression or expression in outward ways] means a lot, as you can see by thinking about Rokujo in *Genji*. Once a woman acquires her own hyojo, that hyojo conflicts with the pressures that come from daily life . . . there is a philosophical contradiction and struggle between what a woman wants and how she acts, which gives her a unique power to become a wraith." Though many Japanese protest that Japanese women are happy in their roles, Enchi implies that their anger goes underground and is expressed mainly through the figure of the demonness or wraith. Only out of nature, in the supernatural, can the woman express her true feelings. At the end of *Onna-zaka,* Tomo's niece delivers Tomo's deathbed speech as if she is possessed by Tomo's spirit, and Shirakawa, Tomo's husband, reacts as to a ghost.

"To make one's wife and mistress live together in a house was considered a natural thing to do for a successful man in the Meiji era," Enchi said. "In that time, women had to kill their 'self' in order to survive . . . Their inner intellect . . . was often directed to religion—especially Jodo Shinshu Buddhism." In many ways, things are quite different in present-day Japan. As Enchi pointed out to me, "Tomo was a smart woman, and if the time had been now, she would have gotten rid of her husband and changed the situation by herself."

Still, as my Japanese teacher Mrs. Hayashi had told me, most Japanese women, even today, would probably try to "endure" or "preserve" if they found out their husband was having an affair. Perhaps this has more to do with concern for their children than fear of their husbands. Was there a hidden anger waiting to be acknowledged, expressed, and resolved? In her novels, Enchi had explored the precursors to women like Takako Inada, Akiko, and Doi, the new head of the Socialist Party. But this new world was one Susie seemed to see more clearly than I could. The women we met found in her an outlet for secrets they would not tell another Japanese.

During much of the interview, Enchi lay on her side; at one point, she even turned over toward the wall, so that I could not see her face. The room grew darker by the moment. We could hear the rain splattering out the window. The smell of cooking, of smoke, wafted in. At times, I felt I was at a séance, a scene from her novel *Onna-men,* with its exploration of the occult and Noh, the links between the expressionless depths of the Noh masks and the mystery of women. I was in the presence of another ghost, someone from my grandparents' era. Much of what she said alluded to a world that no longer existed, that I couldn't begin to fathom. She grew tired, pale. The time was up. I thanked her profusely, in my accent-ridden Japanese, bowed over and over, and a few minutes later emerged into the rain and neon and traffic that seemed so distant from her world.

In my early twenties, during the summers, I sometimes visited my aunt, whose small house in Stamford looks out on Long Island Sound and is wedged in between the larger mansions of rich businessmen and executives. The foundation of my aunt's house was once a playhouse for the children of the next-door mansion, and even though many additions have been made, the house retained for me an air of childhood fantasy. After I first read *The Great Gatsby,* I sometimes imagined my aunt's house as the carriage house in which Nick Carraway resides, next to the mansion of the fabled, mysterious Mr. Gatsby.

But it was more than my aunt's house which entranced

me. My aunt and her roommate, who was an artist and an illustrator of children's books, lived a life informed by New York City, where my aunt worked as a manager for a Japanese restaurant, a life filled with talk of Broadway shows, ballet, and the opera. When she was younger, my aunt had worked for a Broadway producer, had met Katharine Hepburn, had watched Eugene O'Neill direct *The Iceman Cometh.* She had gone to parties in the Village where people like Jackson Pollock, Frank O'Hara, and e.e. cummings appeared.

From classical records to Japanese pottery and prints, from children's books to various Japanese foods, my aunt's house was filled with objects exotic to me, that embodied some alternative to my parents' all-American suburbia of bridge, golf, and television. She was the only person in my family with books like Robert Lowell's *Lord Weary's Castle* and W. C. Williams's *Paterson* in her bookcase. Her roommate, Baye, was Japanese, and their house was the one place where I heard Japanese spoken with any frequency.

So: In this archetypical scene I am setting, I am sitting after dinner with my aunt Ruth and Baye and Susie. I am asking my aunt about her childhood, about my grandparents. I ask because my father never talks of the past, nor does my mother. At home, when I have tried to bring up the subject of the camps, my father has simply said, "I had fun in the camps. Back in L.A., after school, I had to work in my father's nursery. In the camps I could go out and play baseball." My mother replies that she does not remember, she was too young, it wasn't all that important. Only my aunt will talk about the camps, about the past, about her parents. On these visits, I listen to story after story. Sometimes they are humorous, such as the time she was on a pass from camp and was walking through the town of Jerome, Arkansas, and some ladies on a porch, drinking mint juleps, called out to her, "Dear, are you Anna May Wong? You look like Anna May Wong."

Other stories invoked generational differences, such as the time my aunt asked my grandfather to sign the loyalty oaths. She believed the Nisei needed to prove they were good Americans, she wanted to believe she could be a part of the country. My grandfather looked at her and said, "When they let me out of here, then I'll sign up," and walked away.

In my mind, these stories took on a legendary quality. Japanese are not necessarily known for their oral tradition, and though my aunt was an adequate storyteller, I don't think I was impressed by the way she told these stories. No, I loved them because they were a clear link to the past that my parents had not provided. Just as importantly, the stories had a certain romantic cast. They pictured my grandfather as a certified character, a somewhat lazy and fun-loving man, who liked to gamble, smoke cigars, and play the Japanese biwa, who wrote haiku until a stroke kept him from holding a brush ever again. He cried when this happened, and he went upstairs and stayed in his room for a week. In making this legend, I choose to ignore my father's resentment of the work his father made him do, or the scene in the back yard with my grandfather brandishing the board like a weapon above my father's head.

In my aunt's stories, my grandmother was pictured as a seer, a ghostlike creature with an eye for the future and the other world. In one of these stories, it's the thirties, their time of prosperity before the war, when they lived in a small house in west L.A. (today, a freeway runs through it). I see my grandmother shaking my grandfather awake. It is just before dawn, the light in the room is blue as a flame. He waves her away. He's naturally a late sleeper, and perhaps he was down in Japan Town the night before, playing hana or poker, drinking sake with his cronies. But my grandmother keeps shaking him. Even in the cool before day, she is sweating, her eyes and face muscles squeezed tight, as if she has just taken a bite of a lemon. "What is it now?" he asks.

"You mustn't go out today," she says.

"Why? Just let me sleep."

"No, listen to me," and she tells him of her dream. Like a pitcher knocked from the table, it spills about chaotically, it makes no sense. Images of blood, of broken glass, of his face in pain.

"*Bakka rashii,*" he mutters. She is a worrier, he thinks, always has been, has never embraced the world as he has, has never learned English, never ventures far from the confines of their neighborhood and the other Japanese families that surround them like a cocoon, like cotton batting.

He leaves for the day, ignoring her pleas, drives off in his shiny silver Packard, bought with who knows what funds. He has the tastes and work habits of a rich man's son.

Now she wakes my father, who is ten at the time. Instructs him to go to the temple. Gives him change to place in the box there. Tells him to light a stick of incense, to give prayers to the Buddha. He must save his father. They must pray for him.

My father comes back. Two hours later, she sends him to the temple again. And later, again. Again.

It is getting dark now, the sky is beginning to take on the colors of fire and blood. Farther west, like a red-hot coin fresh from a forge, the sun is dipping into the cooling waters.

Her husband still has not appeared. One, two, three hours. Finally, just before midnight, a sound of steps on the porch. She rushes to the door.

She sees the bandages first, the shock of white cloth wrapped around his forehead. He is angry, wincing from pain. She can see a pinkness beginning to seep through the cloth. He has had an accident, his car has been totaled.

"Don't ever," he says, "don't ever tell me your dreams again."

Several years later, during the war, they are in the relocation camp at Jerome. A summer that seems swimming in dampness, the heat seeps up from the swamps nearby, films the air, pours out of their bodies. Mosquitoes, fireflies, tiny gnats, moths hover at the screens until the lights are turned off. In barrack after barrack, the families are cramped together, with clothes for partitions, with paper-thin boards. They hear each other's snores, the arguments between husband and wife, fathers and sons, mothers and daughters; they hear the sound of love cries, of a baby bawling. There's the smell of shoyu, wafts from the benjo downwind. Outside, in the rifle towers, the privates are bored. One tosses a cigarette over the edge. It falls, scattering flakes of ash, tiny red sparks.

Suddenly my grandmother wakes screaming. She has seen it, her sister's house in Tokyo. It started with a whooshing sound, then the wailing of sirens. Streaks of light through the sky, boom after boom reverberating. House after house catching on fire. My grandmother sees it all, the flames peeling the paper walls like skin,

the pine and cedar boards rippling with flames, her sister trapped
in a ring of white heat, succumbing to the smoke, fainting.

And then my grandfather is holding her, yanking her back
and forth, trying to understand what she is saying. It is like holding
an infant wakened in the night; it is like holding a ghost.

Near the end of the war, more than a year later, she
receives a letter detailing her dream, her sister's death.

The night my aunt told me this story was the night her
roommate, Baye, told me about living in Tokyo during the war. I
had known Baye since I was a child—she was almost a second
aunt—but she had never talked much to me about the past. Spurred
perhaps by my aunt's story, I started to ask Baye questions. I knew
she had had a baby during the war, that she had married a man with
tuberculosis, against her family's wishes, but I wanted to know
more.

"I remember once we were walking in the hills," said
Baye. She was sipping tea near the picture window, which looked
out on the blackness of the waters below, the sound of the tide
moving out. Her hair is salt and pepper, in a bowl cut; her body
is small, beginning to bend at the shoulders. She has the hopping,
quick movements of a sprite, a pixie, though she can also possess
the petulance of a youngest daughter. "I was pregnant, and we had
this apple, because I was pregnant. And I was so happy. We halved
the apple and ate it, and it was the most delicious apple I have ever
tasted. I think that was the most happiest moment of my life."

And then she told me of the time when the firebombs
came. She could hear the sirens going off. Her husband roused her.
Part of their house was already on fire. He and the maid would try
to douse the flames. She was to take the baby to the shelters.

"So I picked up the baby in my blanket and I went out the
door. But I was so panicked, I ran around the house. I could see
the firebombs falling down the street. I went back to the door and
opened it. My husband asked me why I wasn't going to the shelter.
I didn't know. It was like a dream. I ran around the house again
and came back. And then again."

Baye was laughing as she told me this. She couldn't believe how silly she had been, she said.

"And then I was running through the streets. And the bombs were falling in front of me, and it was almost as light as day. They looked like light bulbs, one after the other, falling from the sky. All of the houses were in flames. I jumped to the side of the road, into this ditch, and it was wet at the bottom. The blanket was wet too, the baby had gone shi-shi, and I realized I'd forgotten her diapers. I was so angry, diapers were such a luxury, they were almost as precious as gold, and now they were probably lost in the fire. I was so wet and tired, and I wanted to die, to just give up and lie there in that ditch. But then I felt this sucking at my breast. The baby was trying to eat. And I thought, Well, if she can do that, if she wants to live, I guess I can."

When Baye finished, my aunt Ruth said, "You know, I've lived with you for fifteen years and I never heard that story." My aunt, Susie, and I were all aware that both Baye's husband and child had died of tuberculosis before the end of the war.

I don't remember if this was the night my aunt Ruth told me about how my grandmother had once suspected that my grandfather was cheating on her. I recall that my aunt mentioned something about a white woman named Evelyn, and how my aunt didn't know if she was the one my grandmother suspected. At any rate, when my grandmother had that premonitory dream, she woke up my grandfather with a knife blade pressed to his throat. "If you ever . . ." she said, and left the sentence unfinished, as Japanese often do.

My grandmother, my aunt, her roommate, Baye, the dreams and secrets of women, how the past is or is not handed down— Onto all of this I was now adding the layers of Japan, of Enchi, her fascination with Noh, its masks and ghosts', adding the ways Susie and I moved through the world of Japanese women, the ways our marriage was changing, moving in directions that, if they sometimes troubled us, deepened our understanding of who the other was, who the other was not. What did it mean for our marriage? In Japan, after Gisela, I recalled my grandmother and the knife blade in a different light. But then all my aunt's stories somehow meant more in Japan, assumed their place in a past, a culture that was unimaginably different from Susie's Wasp background, her

Mayflower ancestors, the seventeenth-century graves in Sandwich, Massachusetts.

What can be shared in a marriage? What cannot? There is a knowledge that cuts if you let it. We ask our partners to be and not be us, to give in to our fears and warn us. We think we know everything about their lives, but we can imagine nothing, they are strangers beyond our comprehension. Back and forth, the river of Japan eddied through our lives, creating, disturbing our dreams. Sleep with me here, now, in this small room.

5

One day near the end of winter, a friend of Susie's father took us to the American Club for brunch. The rooms there were large as in a temple; the furniture wide, solid, plush. In the huge dining room, trays and trays of food were laid on the tables: scrambled eggs, eggs Benedict, slices of lamb, ham, bacon, sausage, roast pork, two types of potatoes, juices, fruit, waffles, quiches. Sitting at the tables were dozens of American families who had been transferred over by Honeywell, 3M, Bank of America, IBM. Though there were some Japanese guests and members, the language was English, the atmosphere American, the viewpoint colonial. Here the displaced families could retreat from the strangeness and difficulty of Tokyo. Here they could pretend they were back in America.

Susie had grown so accustomed to Japan that this display of America seemed boring. But my negative reaction ran deeper: I felt alienated, displaced, suddenly angry.

Three years before, when I visited San Francisco and found so many Asians, I thought, Who are these people who look like me? What are they doing here? Now, at this club, in a group where the whites were in the majority, I asked, Who are these people who don't look like me? What are they doing here? The white members thought I was Japanese until I spoke, and this increased my identification with the coat checker and the waiters. One woman in a polyester pants suit said to me, "Thank God, you don't speak with an accent." My countrywoman, I thought. I looked at the white faces and read there a sense of privilege, a view of the world unaware of its blinders.

Later, walking home, Susie and I argued: not so much about my anger toward America as my refusal to judge the Japanese. When it comes to being ethnocentric, she said, the Japanese at times seem to have Americans beat.

We were passing through Shinjuku station, threading through the crowds. Here and there, vagrants, their faces grimy, their beards thick stubble, their clothes so soiled they seemed iridescent, propped themselves against the walls or napped inside cardboard boxes, their feet sticking out at the ends like those of bodies at a morgue. Dressed in suits and ties, in crisp dark dresses and heels—no American casualness—the shoppers, like us, walked on.

I admitted Susie was right. Their ethnocentrism was more than the practice of emperor worship and its idea that all Japanese are descended from the Sun God. On one level, there is a cultural preoccupation with anything Japanese which often excludes the concerns of events and people beyond the borders of Japan. This is the attitude which makes Japanese complain that the novelist Kobo Abe doesn't write about Japanese subjects. Takako Inada told Susie that when she went around collecting money for Amnesty International, everyone wondered why they should care about the internal affairs of other countries; they kept asking her why she didn't collect for Japanese causes. But beneath this self-preoccupation or, in part, as a result of it, Japanese racial attitudes have a much darker side. As Ken and Matsuo had pointed out, in dealing with Marcos or South Africa, the Japanese businesses and government seem to have fewer qualms than their American counterparts; most Japanese identify with the whites in South Africa rather than with the blacks. The treatment of people of Korean ancestry in Japan is rife with prejudice and reflects the Japanese sense of their own racial superiority. Such beliefs have a direct link to the history of atrocities that the Japanese have perpetrated in Asia during this century and their refusal to acknowledge those atrocities in their history books or the public consciousness. A greater number of Chinese, almost five million, were killed by the Japanese than the number of dead in Hiroshima and Nagasaki; the average Japanese, though, is much more cognizant of the latter atrocities than the former.

And yet none of this seemed to truly engage my anger the way America's history of race relations did.

"Perhaps that means you're still an American at heart," said Susie.

No, there's more to it than that, I told her as we got off the train. My alienation in the American Club reminded me how I felt when we went to movie theaters in St. Paul, when I would turn around and realize that no one in the crowd looked like me. How did I get here? I'd ask myself, and then bury that thought.

But what about the Japanese? Susie asked. Isn't there some reason you want them to be perfect?

"That's ridiculous. For one thing, I know less about the atrocities and faults of Japan."

"Stop being so dense. Think about why it's so much fun here. We're away from American news, American problems. We have the freedom that comes from being a gaijin, we're not bound by Japanese rules. And at the same time, we can pretend we're not really Americans, that we don't have some responsibility for what happens in Nicaragua, El Salvador, Lebanon, or wherever Reagan's sending his troops this week. If you can pretend you're Japanese and say the Japanese are perfect, then maybe, just maybe, you can lay down your American burdens. But that's ridiculous. You just don't get off that easily."

I spread out my arms. "Okay, okay. Nail me down. I'm an American. Let me redeem the sins of the world." I looked down the road and could see, among the crowd of Japanese and the racks of magazines and shoes lining the walk, the glowing white statue of Colonel Sanders.

"Look, there's the father. Or is that the Holy Ghost? Oh, Father, forgive me, I am an American. I have forgotten thy herbs and spices, thy old Kentucky home, thy stubby little beard and red-bulbed nose. Let me kiss that nose . . ."

I felt the whack of Susie's purse. "Violence! Oh, God, yes," I blurted. "I have an American wife."

And then I ran to make sure I wasn't hit again.

II

"The violence of the Zengakuren does not precede its own regulation, but is born simultaneously with it: it is immediately a sign: expressing nothing (neither hatred nor indignation nor any moral idea), it does away with itself all the more surely in a transitive goal (to besiege and capture a town hall, to open a barbed-wire barrier) . . ."

—Roland Barthes, *The Empire of Signs*

"Someone must have been telling lies about Joseph K., for without having done anything wrong he was arrested one fine morning."

—Franz Kafka, *The Trial*

1

It's early Sunday, the brief span of emptiness before the city, as always, explodes like a carnival. A few lazy-eyed schoolboys stroll out the Harajuku station gates. A young couple walks by slowly, their heads together. My jaws ache from Butoh training last night, from forming the mouth of a horse, a demon. I'm worried. I'm a little late. Jesus, this is a country where the average late train is only thirty seconds slow. In a few hours, the lane before me will be a sea of black bobbing heads, young kids with clothes by Cerutti, Miyake, Kenzo, bought with their parents' money. Each weekend, they flock to the park near the Meiji shrine. Dressed like bobby-soxers, they dance in circles—this is a country of groups, no one dances alone—to rock-and-roll golden oldies.

Matsuo's at the entrance, waving, smiling. He's wearing jeans, a sweatshirt, a blue Puma cap, out of which stringy strands of hair droop to his shoulders. His eyes are hidden under tinted glasses. He holds up his hand to slap me five and smiles. "Ready to go, man?"

After about a five-minute walk from the train station, we reach the edge of the park, where our group of thirty or forty is milling about the vans. The group seems to be in their late twenties and early thirties. Unlike most Tokyoites, they are dressed casually, the men in jeans and sweatshirts, the women plain-looking, almost like schoolmarms in ill-fitting sweaters and plaid pants. They seem to belong to the section in *Glamour* where those who have broken the fashion code are pictured with their eyes blacked out like criminals. In a sports coat and dress slacks, I feel out of place, more in tune with the young college kids preparing to dance the day away.

Matsuo introduces me to Kimiko, the leader of the group.

With glasses and a short-cropped bowl haircut, she looks like my
aunt Miwako. She smiles, I perform my little Japanese greeting:
"Hajimemashite" and *"Doozo yoroshiku"* ("It's the first time,"
"Pleased to meet you"). Kimiko explains that the group is going
to protect me, to keep me, the American, from being arrested.
Matsuo's worried that if I'm arrested, my fellowship might be
revoked. Or my visa won't get renewed, I'll never get back into the
country. He tells me it's illegal for foreigners to participate in
political activities. I'm a bit nervous. I haven't heard of this law
before.

One of the demonstrators is a man who had polio, and
Matsuo and I have to haul him into the van. He is heavy and limp,
like someone who's been knocked out; his head jerks back and
forth; he smiles at us and our awkwardness. On the long ride home
after the demonstration, he will point out each bar we pass: *"Biru
o nomitai yo"*—I want a drink—until the joke becomes a refrain to
celebrate the day.

The leader, K., gives instructions, most of which concern
me. At the airport, the riot police will search the van for Molotov
cocktails and weapons. I can pass as Japanese, but I must not speak.
Matsuo asks for my passport and any other possessions that will
identify me. As I hand him my wallet, Enchi's *Masks,* and a small
notebook, I recall that Susie insisted I check three times for my
passport before I left the apartment: I could be arrested if I didn't
have it. I argued with her: she was being paranoid. Now having the
passport could get me in trouble.

More than an hour later, fifteen minutes from the airport,
Matsuo nudges me. We're slowing to a rest stop. Someone hands
me a cold mask, sign of the famed hysterical Japanese hygiene; you
see people wearing them in the streets, like surgeons on parade.
Next I'm handed a blue nylon parka with a hood. A white terry-
cloth golf hat. Gloves. A pair of sunglasses.

Battle dress, says Matsuo. It will prevent you from being
recognized in photographs. The gloves will protect you if you fall
on the ground. All through the bus, people put on their uniforms.
I do the same.

I descend awkwardly from the bus. I feel as if I'm going

to rob a 7-Eleven store. If the Japanese police don't arrest me, the fashion police will. The ordinary Japanese stare at me. Everything looks dark, far away. I'm one of the group, I feel the solidarity created by the stares of those outside the group. But in the washroom, staring at my image, all I can think is that I look like the invisible man: with the hood, golf hat, mask, and sunglasses, I have no face. Oh, H. G. Wells.

I burst out laughing at my reflection.

To become part of a group, one loses individuality. But that is a Western way of expressing this process and presupposes an emphasis on individuality missing among the Japanese. Becoming part of a group entails too a loss of privacy. What Westerners find most oppressive in Japan—even more than the conformity—is the way public space predominates. The Japanese regard themselves as one huge family, and in a family there are no secrets. It's not just physical space which is cramped in Japan but also psychic space.

Becoming part of the tribe of invisible radicals appealed to me. It was a totally new way of rejecting my American background. And I could do this without consequences. I was playacting, donning a role I could doff as easily as taking off the mask and cap, the sunglasses and hooded windbreaker.

I wasn't going to a political protest. I was attending a masquerade.

2

At the tollbooth, plainclothes police take pictures of the buses. The tension inside the van increases. Five minutes later there's a roadblock, a riot policeman waving his hands. He looks like a reptile in his gray gear: a huge helmet, a plastic protective visor, plastic guards on his arms extending over his hands (like a catcher's shin-guards), a nightstick, a whistle, heavy black boots. Clumps of police stand about the van, primitive warriors armed for battle.

The door rips open. Visor up, he peers inside at our masked figures, shoves back the wheelchair of the man with polio. I stare ahead, then out the window. Act nonchalant, I tell myself. No one says a word.

The door slams. He waves us on.

When we stop by the side of the road near some woods, the airport is nowhere in sight. We tramp into a small clearing.

It's like a picnic. A row of foodstands with bento, noodles, octopus balls, mochi, cuttlefish, ice chests of beer and soft drinks. Protestors crowd around them. Farther on, in the middle of the clearing, hundreds of others sit in the mud. Banners stretch over them; each group has planted a flag in its midst. Some groups are identified by the helmets their members wear—red, black, white.

Except for the Japan National Railway Union workers, who are dressed in their uniforms, everyone wears a mask, a cap, dark glasses. There are hundreds of invisible people.

At the head of the clearing is a stage with huge woofers above it. Other speeches pour forth from speakers mounted on a van in back of the clearing.

We're barraged with sound, another example of how Japanese culture eschews a center of focus. The Japanese mode of perception is more amorphous, more intuitive than that of Westerners, fluid not fixed—in Noh, the shout-shrieks of the drum calls are sounded simultaneously with chants of classical poetry; in Bunraku there are two areas of focus, the puppets on the stage, the storyteller and the singers on the side, and you cannot look at both at once; on Japanese TV, writing often flows across the bottom of the screen, and this writing has nothing to do with the picture; screens can now be divided into three, four pictures, one for each station. And on a more general level, there's simply Tokyo life with its overstimulus and chaos, assaults from all sides by neon, crowds, music, barkers, loudspeakers, video screens.

I know little about the demonstration, only that the farmers around Narita have protested the building of the airport and the issue has become a rallying point for the Japanese left. Now the authorities are planning to expand the airport and take even more of the farmers' land; according to the left, the airport would then

be used for military purposes. Talking with Matsuo, I've come to
feel that the demonstration itself is more important to him than the
issues. "It's like the university intellectuals," he says. "You can do
so much theory that you lose touch with practice."

   The speeches are all the same: We must smash the airport,
stop the plan to expand, down with Nakasone, we must stick together. Over and over speakers shout, *"Minasan"* (everyone). As
in all Japanese group process, every contingent gets a speaker—the
red helmets (students), the black, the white, the Japanese National
Railway, people from Okinawa, from Hokkaido, from Kyushu, the
farmers, the farmers' wives, the lawyers who defend demonstrators,
the assistants to the lawyers . . .

3

I'm pissed. The leader is worried about me and won't let me go
anywhere without Matsuo. Matsuo even has to accompany me to
the john. I feel as if I'm in second grade ("Use the buddy system,
children"). As we walk to the protable toilets, which were brought
here especially for the demonstration, Matsuo tells me the helmeted groups are the fighters who will try to break through the
police lines.

   "The black helmets are the most crazy. The anarchists."
Pause. "I used to be one of them."

   He shows me a scar on his forehead from the blow of a
billy club. It's like a permanent dent. There's another on his arm.

   "I got this in a bar in Berkeley. A guy asked me if I was
Japanese and said, 'I'll forget Pearl Harbor if you'll forget about
Hiroshima.' And I said, 'No waaaay, man.' He took out his knife
and attacked me. Then the police came and asked me if I wanted
him arrested. 'No,' I said, 'it's over, everything's cool.' "

   Then Matsuo smiles like Puck, the imp of chaos. During
his college days, he was expelled because he took a picture of the

university president, blew it up, then pasted it on the concrete between the gates of the university. In the morning, every student who entered stepped on the president's face.

Behind their masks, caps, hoods, and sunglasses, all the demonstrators look androgynous. Then one of the white helmets takes off her helmet. I witness how deep Japanese etiquette runs, even among radicals. She laughs, and even though she's wearing a mask, she brings her hand up to cover her mouth—maintaining the gesture of feminine politeness despite her radical garb. In medieval times, it was impolite for women to show their teeth, which were blacked out—the gesture had sexual implications—and this custom of women hiding their mouths when they laugh persists.

The speeches go on. Two, three hours. I've got no notebook, no book. I'm getting bored, very, very bored.

Matsuo asks if I'm bored.

"Oh no, no, really, this is interesting." I think of the lines by John Berryman: ". . . my mother told me as a boy/(repeatedly) 'Ever to confess you're bored/means you have no/Inner Resources.' I conclude now I have no/inner resources." Four, five hours.

After five and a half hours, there's a loud whirring. I look up. Like angry bees, helicopters are circling the clearing. The group leader stands, raises her hand. Great, something's going to happen. We march fifteen paces; the leader motions for us to squat (it's too muddy to sit). After fifteen minutes of squatting, my legs ache. I remember high-school gym teachers forcing students to squat in the corner, never allowing them to rise or rest their legs.

I am not having fun.

More speeches. More circling helicopters, their whirling drone closer and louder.

Suddenly a truck drives up, clears a path through the crowd. Probably a garbage truck, I think. But then the back of the truck rears up like a horse, dumps a pile of loose stones. The white helmets rush up as if it were money and begin putting the rocks in little satchels or boxes. People clap and cheer like children. The speeches on the stage continue to spill out, a Japanese version of

Chinese water torture. The red helmets march up, each member gripping a wooden or steel pole. I'm surprised to see the last members are carrying plastic Kirin beer cases of Molotov cocktails.

"I thought they searched all the cars coming in here," I ask Matsuo.

"They probably hid them somewhere near here days or even weeks ago."

Whatever violence occurs at this demonstration, it's not going to be spontaneous. It's not like the demonstrations I participated in at college. There most of the protesters were pacifists, and if violence occurred, it was usually caused by the police losing control, going berserk. Here, the helmeted groups are clearly armed for battle. They expect to attack the police, not simply react.

Everything has been orchestrated, impeccably planned.

Suddenly there's a noxious smell in the air. Tear gas. Matsuo keeps repeating, Don't rub your eyes. Just let them water. Small explosions between the helicopters overhead. More tear gas. Explosions in the distance.

I feel frustrated at not being able to wander around. I look back. Through the crowd, two hundred yards away, beyond a wooden fence at the edge of the park, I can see students running, a few riot police, a few clubs swinging, scuffles. As the tear gas increases, I realize how the cold mask acts as protection. Up above, the helicopters are moving lower, in tighter circles, louder and louder.

A report from the platform: Several groups have already encountered the police. Realizing I'm in a battle, I think of Civil War films where something is happening over the ridge or in the next valley, some crucial encounter that may decide the fate of the entire campaign, but no one knows how the fight is going, we're all anxiously awaiting the next report.

Finally we begin marching. My group is mainly women, children, and the handicapped, and I find myself hoping there will be no violence. Cowards die a hundred deaths and live to tell about them. Out of the park and past a field, a small clump of houses. The tear gas increases. My eyes begin to sting, I start to cough. My legs ache from an hour of squatting, my mind is numb from hours of boring speeches, my hands and shoes dirty from the mud, my stomach growling with hunger. I think again, I'm not having fun, really, this is not fun.

And yet, as the tear gas fades behind us, I find I like being part of the group. With my invisible man outfit, headed for the airport, I'm doing something a hakujin, a white person, could never do. One giant step for the radical Japanese left, one small step for an American Sansei.

We march down a road lined mostly with fields: rice, carrots, spinach, tea. A few houses. Almost no one sees us except for an occasional bicycle rider or car driver. At one point, an old man pulls away from a group of women restraining him and tries to stop the line of protestors. Everyone marches around him.

After a half hour, a plane takes off over the trees. I wonder if we're ever going to get to the airport gates. Everyone is chanting, over and over, *"Kuu-ko—fun-sai, nik-ki—soo-shi"*—"Smash the airport, stop the second plan." As I chant through the gauze mask, not quite knowing what I am saying, I feel somewhat ridiculous, as if engaging in an act of bad faith. Occasionally, as dusk comes on, I take off the dark glasses and realize the whole day has had the quality of a surrealistic dream, in part because everything was darker than normal.

Matsuo pokes me. A pickup truck rumbles past; there are wounded protestors in the back, slumped over each other, holding their arms or faces, marred by gashes. Blood drips down their cheeks, dries on their arms.

"Kuu-ko—fun-sai, nik-ki—soo-shi."

I am hungry, tired, bored. Despite my initial nervousness about my own safety, I want to see something happen.

We march through dusk into night. Suddenly I see lights ahead. We're finally at the airport, we're going to make our showing, to confront the riot police. My body tenses. My eyes search the darkness ahead.

But no, a hundred yards down the road our group stops before a large one-story wooden warehouse. The protest, says Matsuo, is over.

I feel like Peggy Lee—Is that all there is? And then: Oh shit, we're going to have to walk back to the vans. And then: I can't wait till I get home and eat, I can't wait to take a bath.

So much for my revolutionary fervor.

Matsuo asks me if I want to "pee-pee." We go inside, past picnic benches covered with checkered tablecloths; some women and men are cooking *kare raisu* (curry rice) at a stove. There are containers of hot water for tea, cups and plates on dusty shelves next to the wall. A color television set faces a group of chairs, and Matsuo explains that there is always some spot like this for people to rest and eat after a protest. The news comes on. Everyone starts shouting. The man trying to turn up the sound becomes so nervous he turns it off, bringing forth loud jeers.

And there on the screen is the demonstration I've missed. A group of red-helmeted students march up to the shields of the riot police, pause, begin pummeling them with their poles. A riot policeman is writhing on the ground; two students take turns hitting him with their poles. Everyone cheers. A Molotov cocktail explodes at the feet of some riot police, and they are engulfed in flames. Each image flashes across the screen with an immediacy, a clarity that the whole day has seemed to lack. Where did all this happen? How, why, did I miss it?

And then the news is over, someone changes the channel, people disperse. As we leave the warehouse, we pass a young man with a huge gash opened beneath his eye, right over the cheekbone. See, Matsuo says, what the riot police did. I stop, stare in fascination at the wound, the cheek's raw exposed meat, half an inch deep.

To my great relief, we don't have to walk back to where the march started. The leaders have planned ahead; the buses are waiting in a parking lot about a quarter mile away. It's 7:30. Our group waits an hour for members who have fought with the riot police. I wonder why some people chose to participate in the violence and others didn't. Matsuo explains that if a person has a family to support, he or she can't afford to lose a job. Generally the college students do the fighting.

Matsuo says that he has no strong moral convictions against violence. Something must be done, somebody must say something. The Japanese people would pay no attention if there were no violence. He seems unable to see that the use of violence might be counter to the aims of the political movement. His personal reasons for not participating are less rhetorical. During the sixties, he participated in a number of riots, but after college, he fell into a deep depression.

"A couple of my friends died in the riots," he says. "And one was blinded. Afterward, I just didn't feel like fighting."

Matsuo's face is calm, resigned. He tells me that he started to drink a lot, did not work, and instead sat around the house all day listening to records. His wife, whom he has since divorced, supported him.

I don't ask if this was partly the cause of their divorce. He has already revealed more to me than most Japanese I have met.

A few days later Matsuo will send me a poem, which begins:

> *before dawn I received a letter*
> *from a friend who died 15 years ago*
>
> *but I can't decipher his message*
> *written on black paper with black ink . . .*

In the dark back of the van, Matsuo talks about his father, who worked as a television cameraman, was once a Communist, and who died several years ago. Matsuo and his father often had violent political arguments, not so much about their aims, but about the means to achieve them. Matsuo's father was against the violent tactics of the *Zengakuren,* the Japanese student radicals. I tell Matsuo of my political battles with my father, who has always voted for Republicans from Eisenhower to Reagan. During the Vietnam War, when I registered as a C.O., my father almost disowned me. Of course, we also argued over the length of my hair, but I don't tell Matsuo about the scene just before I went to college, when my father insisted on cutting my hair. Somehow that is too painful.

Instead, I talk about how I learned not to discuss politics with my father. Both of us accepted that perhaps there'd be no winner in our battles, realized it might be better to get along than to prove a point.

Fathers and sons. Certain battles do cross cultures.

4

The causes of the protestors' violence were, of course, multiple, and I'm sure I didn't understand all of them. Obviously there was a long tradition of how such protests were supposed to be carried out, and as with much else in Japan, tradition did not need to be explained or justified in the way it does in the West. The culture had developed for centuries in relative isolation, had a solidity difficult for Westerners to imagine. We constantly search for psychological causes and believe that violence must arise spontaneously, must shoot out like a rocket from the combustion of the moment, an instantaneous release spurred by a history of mounting tension.

When I talked to Mrs. Hayashi about the protestors, she immediately expressed her disapproval. "They are not," she said, "true Japanese." She implied they were a bit crazy, a nuisance. The majority of Japanese were opposed to the tactics of the demonstrators, though they sympathize with the farmers.

The violence of the protestors began to make more sense if I viewed them not as independent subjects who define themselves but as those who are defined by others. By the definition of Japanese society, the protestors were outlaws, and so they acted like outlaws. Faced with a charge of guilt, they acted so that the charge would fit them.

Even in Japan I was attracted to the outlaws, those whom the rest of society pronounced as bad.

And in a crazy way, I see this too as part of my legacy,

the legacy of the relocation camps. For I admired the fact that the
protestors were doing something, were not sinking back into *sho
ga nai* (it can't be helped) passivity. In contrast, the Japanese-
Americans confronted with the power of the U.S. military and
government at the start of World War II did not protest. The
Issei, many of whom did not speak English and who were not
citizens, had few resources or legal recourses. Many of the Nisei
were too young and lacked the position or knowledge to mount a
protest.

One of the few key legal challenges to the relocation
orders was that of Fred Korematsu, a Nisei nursery owner in
Oakland. Korematsu refused to obey the evacuation orders and
was arrested, convicted, placed on probation for five years, and
finally sent to a relocation camp. In 1953, Korematsu's case went
to the Supreme Court, which ruled that the army had not violated
Korematsu's constitutional rights: the evacuation orders were justified by the war as "proper security measures . . . the urgency of
the situation demanded that all citizens of Japanese ancestry be
segregated."

In the early 1980s, Korematsu's case entered again the
labyrinth of the courts. For almost half a century he has been
fighting to prove himself innocent of a nonexistent crime, a crime
which required no act but his birth, his very identity. It is hard not
to see in this a situation worthy of Kafka's heroes.

Many Nisei faced with this accusation acted as if it were
true. And it was: they were Japanese. Of course, many Nisei also
argued that being of Japanese ancestry was not a crime. But who
decides what is a crime? As Kafka knew, that job is not for every-
man, is not for K. It is the function of the law.

But in what ways did the Nisei act as if they were guilty?
Some went to the camps demonstrating their rage, others directed
it inward. In the recent hearings on the redress for the relocation
camps, one man described how he screamed obscenities at the
guards and dared them to shoot him when he arrived at the horse
stables where the Japanese-Americans were first housed. With these
actions, he showed his desire to be destroyed, to be punished for

his weakness. For if he had been shot or bayoneted because of his actions, his punishment would have a cause for which he was responsible. By association, then, the punishment of the relocation would also make sense.

But most of the Nisei went quietly. Like my father or my aunt, many were eager to prove they were true-blue Americans. Many Nisei later joined the army and fought heroically, like my uncle in the 442nd in Europe. Others served as translators for the troops in the Pacific. If, when my uncle came back from the war, he couldn't rent an apartment, the attitude of *sho ga nai* took over. Like my uncle, my aunt, my father, most Nisei tried to imitate white middle-class America, to work hard and keep quiet. They became engineers, dentists, teachers, reporters. They bought houses, put their children through college.

And by their quiet obedience, by their decision not to protest, by their willingness to fight in the service, by their efforts to educate themselves, by their hard work, the Nisei did, as the history books tell it, become part of America. As the back of one of these texts proclaims: "In the years since World War II the Nisei have achieved remarkable social, economic, and political progress—the successful realization of their destiny—and the closing chapters of this book document the current acceptance of Americans of Japanese ancestry." But such a view wraps things up too neatly and hides the rough edges, the doubts and lingering bitterness, whatever would not make the Nisei an American success story, a paean to patriotism.

By assimilating, the Nisei shed what had made them guilty: their Japaneseness. Did they see this shedding as an admission of guilt? I don't think so.

Paradoxically, Japanese beliefs helped the Nisei assimilate. For instance, their forbearance in the face of their punishment was part of the spirit of *gaman,* the willingness to endure. Their assimilation was an acting out of a Japanese proverb which reinforces the group: The nail that sticks up gets hammered down. Assimilation was a way of not sticking up.

Is it any wonder that the next generation would inherit, instead of Japaneseness, a sense of shame?

5

A week after the demonstration, Matsuo sent me a newspaper clipping, signing it: "Hope your eyes are O.K. By & to whom did our tears flow? See you soon." The report read:

> *Narita, Chiba Pref.—At least 241 radical leftists opposing New Tokyo International Airport were arrested Sunday as they clashed with riot police, hurling Molotov cocktails and rocks, during a march near the airport here. The demonstrators were armed with steel pipes and wooden staves.*
>
> *Police responded with water cannons and tear gas. Fifty-three policemen were injured and window glass of private houses and stores in the neighborhood were smashed, police reported.*
>
> *Simultaneous "guerrilla" activities by the militant leftists, including Chukakuha (Middle Core Faction) members, occurred at the Sanrizuka area here shortly after a national rally sponsored by the Anti-Airport Federation was held at Sanrizuka Park in protest against the second phase of work on the development of the airport.*

A truck disguised as a fire engine and apparently loaded with flammable material burst into flames in front of a maintenance building in the airport compound shortly after 5:30 P.M. The fire was soon brought under control, leaving no one injured. Also, a bomb was found to have been planted at Keisei Railway Company's Narita Station. And a taxi also caught fire in the airport parking lot in the evening.

A total of 9,500 riot policemen, the largest number since

the opening of the airport in 1978, were mobilized Sunday from Chiba and twenty-seven other prefectures throughout the country to guard the airport from the demonstrators.

The violent demonstration did not affect the departures and arrivals of aircraft at the airport.

6

There was a Greek restaurant near Ken's house. With a six-lane highway on concrete stilts above it, the avenue was like a tunnel. At evening, everything was bathed in shadows, leaving only the sense of sunlight hovering somewhere above. Buses crawled by, taxis moving in and out of lanes, jerky as pinballs. On the walls of the restaurant were scenes from a Greek fishing village, the buildings white, austere, the boats with a single sail, netting drying on the docks. The Greek owner, behind the zinc bar, talked with the men at the bar in Greek, talked as if to relatives, as if he had never left home. The waiters were Japanese, young, quiet, and demure, like ushers at a funeral home. Setsuko ordered: moussaka, gyros, saganaki, spanakopitta, ouzo, the dishes almost Japanese in sound. She wore a black dress and gold earrings; her lipstick was a shade of plum. Ken wore jeans, a plaid shirt.

"Actually, the area is called Sanrizuka, not Narita," Ken corrected me. "The Airport Corporation tried to buy off the farmers and split the ones who remained opposed. After a while, they were just moved out by force. One reason they resisted so stubbornly is that the land was given to repatriates following World War II—within living memory. The land was considered poor, and the farmers had to clear it themselves, build their homes and such."

"So it's not ancestral grounds," said Susie. I began to wonder how much else I had wrong.

"For the Phase II site, the corporation bulldozed all the topsoil there into huge piles of earth to prevent the farmers from farming. It's really weird to look at. There're these stretches of arid soil, and then these hills with lush grass on top. But the farmers keep coming back, they actually produced a million dollars' worth of crops one year I was there."

"What about the radicals?" I asked.

"They saw the farmers as a way of supporting a traditional Japan outside of the government. And of course, there's the anti-military angle. But the Chukakuha has been trying to gain control of the issue for years. They finally split with the farmers over the *tsubo* issue."

Ken explained that the farmers took the land that wasn't owned by the corporation and divided it up in small parcels (a *tsubo*, or 3.3 square meters) to sell to as many members of the various support groups as possible. This would increase the number of people directly involved with the land.

"The Chukaku was very opposed to the tsubo strategy. They began to hold separate rallies, which were more prone to violence, either from the *kidotai,* the riot police, or from the Chukaku. It was a Chukaku rally that you attended, not an Opposition League one."

"I'm confused," said Susie.

"Well, it gets pretty complicated, the more you look at it."

"I'm not sure I agreed with the violence of the demonstration. It wasn't like American demonstrations at all. It's weird, the whole thing reminded me of something out of Kurosawa's films, like *Ran.*"

Susie and I had seen the movie, based on *King Lear,* just a few days after I went to the demonstration. While in Shakespeare's play the actual fighting takes place off stage, the fighting in the film deserved top billing. Long after we had left the theater, the scenes of supposed horror kept recurring, like a series of brilliant paintings. Helmeted troops storm up to the king's castle: suddenly, through a trick of lighting and because the castle is on a mountain of volcanic ash, almost everything turns into black and white—the helmets, the spears, the leather chest protectors; the only color left is the brilliant red of the banners, held aloft by the soldiers, scuttling across the screen in silence, against a dark-gray background. Scene after scene of death follows, each arresting, each lyrical: the ladies in their kimonos, screaming, weeping; they sit before each other, seem to hug, when, simultaneously, each plunges a dagger into the other, in a mutual suicide. They fall slowly, eyes open wide, looking toward the ceiling. Even the warrior propped against a gate, staring in shock at his severed arm, while his body quivers and twitches, seems merely one more image to add to the scroll, another brilliant panel.

Later came still more battle scenes, the banners of yellow, of red, of blue, drifting, scrambling across green fields, along with yellow, red, and blue helmets, horses swiftly clattering, charging. Riders slowly fall off their horses, are dragged like dancers discovering new motions that the body can make.

"When I was watching the battle scenes in *Ran,*" I said, "the colors gave the battle a beauty and glamour, a look of absolute perfection. And I couldn't help but connect those lines of battle with the red and black helmets of the demonstration, with the way everything was so orchestrated. And later, when I watched TV, the students marched up to the shields of the riot police, who were also identified by their uniforms, and there was no chaotic rush of one side toward the other. No, the riot police simply stood their ground, waited until the students got in front of them. They did nothing until the first row of students, in unison, raised their clubs and brought them down on the shoulders and shields of the front row of riot police."

"But the riot police have real weapons, not the home-made crap the demonstrators use," said Ken.

"I can't believe you almost got caught in all that," Susie said.

"Okay, the battle isn't even, but that's not my point. I kept trying to figure out why the protestors didn't protest more openly, why they didn't take off the masks, why they didn't seem to question the violence of their tactics. In Kurosawa's film, it seemed that the aesthetics of the battle scenes won out over any question of morality, that the Japanese emphasis on aesthetics and the group was all a piece. And the riot had that same ritualistic quality. It's as if you don't have to think about individual ethics if you're a member of a group."

"I think you're right about it being like a ritual. The demonstrations are actually more to solidify the Chukaku than for purposes of political change. But you have to remember that they always show the violence of the students on TV, never the violence of the kidotai. There has never been a reprimand of any kidotai who have injured or killed protestors, but the government has spent years pursuing various demonstrators."

"I wonder, though, if some of the demonstrators are merely using the political issue as a pretext to take out personal frustrations," said Susie.

Ken disagreed.

"Well, you have to admit there's a certain amount of bad faith in the youthful demonstrators," said Susie. "After graduating from college, most of them will stop their political activities and become sarariman. They'll join the politically apathetic mainstream of Japanese society, completely forgetting their earlier radical activities."

"But is that any different from the yuppies in America?" asked Ken.

"Maybe the problem with Japanese politics is that there is no middle ground between apathy and violent demonstrations," I said. "No one's been able to come up with an effective method of peaceful protest, since people seem unwilling to risk their anonymity."

"That's too much of a simplification," said Ken. "The farmers have been living in what is virtually martial law for years. In a way, it *is* like a war. The kidotai function like a secret police: they tap phones, monitor all radio communications, arbitrarily block access to local roads, search and confiscate things from cars and homes, make raids without warrants. And they'll arrest or detain any foreigners who even begin to sniff around the area. I've been chased from there myself."

"You see," said Susie, "I was right to be worried."

"I was hardly in danger."

"I kept waiting all day for him to call," Susie told Ken.

"How could I have called? I was sitting in a field of mud listening to speeches I couldn't understand. And then I was getting tear-gassed. It's not as if I was out having a night on the town."

"But you liked it, didn't you?"

"I did and I didn't."

I realized that I would probably never know as much about the situation as Ken. I didn't have his contacts, or his fluency, or his dedication. And I hadn't married a Japanese woman. And yet, in recent weeks, especially after the demonstration, I'd felt more direct connection to politics than I had since the early seventies, when I marched with others at the state capital, protesting the war.

I felt as if Susie was trying to put a damper on my enthusiasm, and though I didn't want to put her into the role of the cautionary female, she seemed to be putting herself there. Fine, then. She didn't have to follow me. After all, Setsuko hardly ever joined in these discussions. I could never tell if she was bored or not.

I asked Setsuko how she and Ken had met. She was more forthcoming than many Japanese. She talked of how he seemed different from Japanese men, more deferential, less self-centered.

"He was so nice. I didn't want to become a Japanese housewife, just stay at home with the children." She worked part-time in a boutique. Ken was planning to go to grad school in the States in a year. "Still, if I'd known there were others like him, maybe I would have waited, ne. He always dressed so funny, not like you." She pointed to the sports coat I'd just bought in Harajuku. I was embarrassed. "There was that time when I saw him off to the States. We'd known each other just a few weeks, ne. Ricketts-san"—a friend of theirs who worked with the Sanrizuka farmers—"went with us, and I spent most of the time talking to him."

"My Japanese wasn't very good then."

"And you were wearing this silly fur hat and boots and a big parka coat."

"It was cold."

"But that hat looked so silly."

The waiter came up. Did we want some baklava?

"Do they have Turkish, I mean Greek, coffee? *Greek-ku kohee arimasu ka?*"

"You always do that," Susie said. "Don't you remember, the Greeks hate the Turks."

"But the waiter's Japanese," I said, after he had taken our order. "This wasn't bad. Not quite Chicago's Greek town, but it's nice for a change."

"Did we tell you about this new restaurant in Roppongi?" Setsuko asked. "All they serve is appetizers. It's combination Greek and French."

On the train home, Susie dozed with her head on my shoulder. Across from us was a young Japanese couple, the girl slumped against her boyfriend in the same position. I was reading Kafka's *The Trial*.

I began thinking about how Ken and I differed. Of course, we were both Sansei, from the Midwest, had both felt out of place in high school, and had both come to Japan to find ourselves both Japanese and not-quite Japanese. "I hate it sometimes at work when they expect me to act like a Japanese," he once said. "If a hakujin leaves at 5:30, they don't think anything of it. But they expect me to stay at work like them, to leave at 7:30 or 8. Sometimes I leave at 5, just to spite them."

And yet he and I were different. He'd become much more immersed in the culture than I had, had tied his life to it, was going to be a scholar of Japanese history. I'd adopted the fashions. Next to him, I felt slick, as if I were getting by on flash not substance. I hadn't found any niche in Japan where I was truly comfortable. As the train slipped into our station and I nudged Susie awake, I wondered if I ever would.

7

During the sixties and seventies, many Sansei joined the effort of César Chavez and the migrant farmworkers and ended up protesting against the Nisei landowners. In doing so, the Sansei were in part identifying with their Issei grandparents, whose initial position on the West Coast was much more like that of the migrant farm-workers than either the Nisei or the Sansei. Perhaps I was trying to identify with an older Japan, one less tainted by middle-class values, through the farmers at Sanrizuka. Of course, such identification was pretty passive and chimeric. But it is not one my father, for instance, would have made.

For me, and perhaps for many of my generation, one important meaning of the camps centers on the powerlessness of both the Issei and the Nisei against the government. Despite my awareness of the powers arrayed against them, some part of me believes they could have and should have fought back. What this indicates is hard for me to admit: I am ashamed of their weakness. I do not want to claim any of it as part of my heritage. It is the part of the past I would disown.

This explains why I, and many other Sansei, are more angry at the Nisei than at the Issei. Despite the obstacles in their path, the Nisei, our parents, were in some sense able to succeed in America, to enter the middle class. We love the Issei more unequivocally because they were defeated. They never recovered from the camps. They verify that the camps were horrible, represented an overwhelming power and authority that could crush the spirit.

Thus, the weakness of the Issei allows me to identify myself as one of the downtrodden, one of the powerless. And yet, as a Sansei, as one assimilated into America, with a sense of myself my parents did not possess, I can escape that powerlessness by my protests, my political engagement. Like a child, I want to have things both ways.

In the light of Kafka, the story of the camps becomes a parable, a parable whose meaning I must somehow solve.

One day, K. steps out of his door to find a notice: he must report to the authorities. Who are the authorities? He does not know, only that he must report to them. When he reports to them, they give him a number, tell him to come back tomorrow. When he comes back the next day, he is taken by bus to a train and then by train to a place with others who have been given numbers and notices. He realizes he has been imprisoned. He is no longer singular, no longer private. The communal beds, shower stalls, and toilets only confirm this, as do the barbed wire and rifle towers with guards. What is his crime? He is K. That is his crime.

My father's name was originally Katsuji Uyemura. Then Thomas Katsuji Uyemura. Then Tom Katsuji Mura. Then Tom K. Mura.

What is the job of the son of K.? To forgive his crime? To try him again?

III

"Henry went to the control station to register his family. He came home with twenty tags, all numbered 10710, tags to be attached to each piece of baggage, and one to hang from our coat lapels. From then on, we were known as family #10710."

—Monica Sone, *Nisei Daughter*

"I don't like Japan, Mommy. I want to go home to America."

—Sansei child after her first day in an evacuation center

1

April. The cherry blossoms appeared overnight. In Ueno Park, messengers from offices staked out claims early in the morning. In an eye blink, the park was filled with thousands of celebrants, sitting on blankets, pouring sake into tiny cups. Men danced, put kerchiefs on their heads, hugged trees, wandered into other parties. Their co-workers pulled them back, but the energy of these drunkards seemed boundless, irrepressible as the blossoms above them, their brief beauty. Women in kimonos appeared like apparitions. The sun poured down. All down the walkways, the cherry trees floated like pink clouds beneath a clear blue sky. Children walked by, tugging their mothers, holding pinwheels that whirled in the breeze. And then the breeze was filled with blossoms, tear-shaped and soft, whirled about in their one airy flight.

We watched the cherry blossoms one day with Reiko and her friend Moko, who worked at the national television station. I was still going to Ono's and taking Noh lessons. But I was spending more and more time with Matsuo and his friends from the Japanese left. Some were writers or translators, and we talked of Japanese-American writers, of black and Chicano writers. These Japanese knew more about these writers than I. Their interest was keener, pushed by the impulse toward the exotic, the foreign.

For Matsuo talk of politics was like a blast of fresh air, a necessary high. Benjamin on violence, Bakunin, Mao, Kim Chi Ha. The goals he spoke of were unformed, immense. Nakasone, the Self-defense Forces, were only immediate obstacles. He and his leftist friends seemed like perpetual students. They were gentle, polite. Boisterous, argumentative when drunk. We sat in dim bars, sake and shochu, bourbon and beer reddening our faces. Smoke unfurled from the fingertips around us, clung to our clothing. The music on the speakers was American rock: Janis Joplin, Van Morrison, Bob Dylan. Matsuo pushed back his glasses, sang along. He took off his cap, his long hair tumbled down. He sang louder. He was drunk. He complained about the airport, the LDP, and Reagan, then motioned to the woman behind the bar to turn up the sound.

With him weaving and leading, we wandered through the Shinjuku alleys at 3 or 4 A.M., seeking an even smaller, dingier bar. The glasses there were white with water streaks. A roach crawled up the counter. Susie shuddered and pointed. We lied and said we were too drunk to drink any more. We burst out laughing.

One Saturday, Matsuo and I went to see a film about the day laborers in Tokyo, who are organized under the yakuza. Of course, the yakuza exploited the laborers, and the film's backers expected that the film might be difficult to produce. What happened turned out to be even worse. Both the first and then the second director of the film were murdered.

The exploitation of the day laborers benefits many businesses, Matsuo told me. The police have little incentive to clear up these murders; a traditional agreement leaves a certain portion of yakuza activity untouched. "I knew the second director," said Matsuo. "We went to school together. He was always too optimistic, too trusting. He thought what happened to the first director wouldn't happen to him."

After several nights of carousing, of long political talks, I began to feel frustrated with Matsuo. We never seemed to move toward the type of intimacy I associated with friendships back in the States. Only after I had known him for months did I learn that he had a daughter. He saw her once a month; he showed no interest in my meeting her. Yet the one time he did mention her, he revealed how he differed from most other Japanese. Because she was overweight, some other children had been teasing her. He had told her it didn't matter what others thought, that he loved her and she had to learn to love herself.

It's hard to convey how amazing this advice was: very few

Japanese fathers would ever have spoken so directly about their feelings, would have placed the daughter's self inside her rather than in her obligations to the group.

Still, I wondered about how far his concern for his daughter's self really went, considering the small amount of time he spent with her. In this he wasn't very different from most Japanese fathers, whose workaholic hours leave them little time at home. But perhaps I was merely judging him by American standards. Or perhaps my criticism came from frustration. I wanted an American friendship. Matsuo did not.

And then, one night, at his girlfriend Keiko's house, the screen lifted just a bit.

2

As Matsuo launched into his argument, he waved a cigarette about, bent forward. His Puma cap was on the table, next to a glass of beer. His glasses made his eyes seem small. I could see Keiko in the kitchen, washing vegetables at the sink. Her hair was cropped short, boyish; her face was past its youth, the age of mothers on the street, but intense, concentrated, angry, resigned.

In a way, I was annoyed. I had thought this evening was to be a small party of two couples, a celebration of friendship and our first time at Keiko's house. Both Susie and I had wanted to talk with Matsuo and Keiko about childhood, marriage, relationships, things you talk about with American friends. But as Matsuo talked on about politics, we felt more and more disappointed. He didn't appear able to shift to a different mode.

"Man, there is no average Japanese," Matsuo was saying, "it's just a concept, something the social powers use to discredit radicals, to alienate us from the population."

Susie shot me a glance across the table. She knew Matsuo had promised to help Keiko with the preparations for the party.

Instead, he'd spent the afternoon writing answers to my question of how the leftists should deal with the average Japanese. I felt as if I were partly responsible for his failure to help Keiko.

Matsuo tapped a long finger of ash into the tray. As with the Japanese language, which moves in circularity, in indirect statements, vagaries, and unstated premises, he refused to be pinned down by a desire for facts. I asked about the practicality of certain Japanese leftist tactics. "It's a very difficult problem," he replied, "we're still trying to formulate an answer."

I felt like an American businessman trying to get a commitment from his Japanese counterpart. I wondered if anything was actually being said.

Susie whispered that we should give Matsuo a hint and begin setting the table and preparing the food. We made jokes about some lessons in feminism. Matsuo didn't get it, or pretended not to. He had the logic of a fanatic, the puckishness of a schoolboy who won't do chores. He had spent his passion elsewhere, there was nothing there for Keiko. Susie stayed in the kitchen. I hesitated, then returned to the table. The negotiations resumed.

Perhaps I should have expected this. I knew that night after night, in the tatami rooms of tiny restaurants and bars hidden in the mazy passageways of the city, he'd sit just like this, talking into the night with other leftists. Though sometimes Keiko went with Matsuo, most often she waited for calls that never came. Or came at two, three, four in the morning. "Keiko's going to kill me," he would tell me, and then stumble off to her apartment. It was no different for her than for the wives of sarariman. Only she had a job, her freedom, and no children. She worked at a trading company; her English was fluent and marketable. With Matsuo there was no future, only a present that never seemed to stop.

I could hear Keiko and Susie giggling in the kitchen.

"But what about more practical matters," I said, "like the position of women."

Matsuo still didn't get what I was driving at. He merely shifted gears, turned the corner, and went into a long spiel about the shop girls who bow to customers at the entrances of the stores and, in tiny, childish voices, repeat, Welcome, welcome, welcome.

Or the girls in the elevators of the Kinokuniya bookstore who, with the same childish voices, pipe out the floor numbers, fight off the hands of perverts, and live inside a steel box, going up and down hundreds of times a day. They were all waiting to get married, were given only the most menial of jobs. In the big trading companies, the women from Todai, the Harvard of Japan, were merely office girls. Their one reward for graduating from Todai is that they can then marry a Todai Honda sarariman.

"So where do you and Keiko fit in all this?" I asked. It was not a question I would normally have asked a Japanese, but I was annoyed. I wanted to pin Matsuo down.

Matsuo said he admired Keiko's intelligence, her fierce independence. And he felt that their relationship was more equal than those of traditional Japanese couples. He couldn't order her about, did not expect her to do anything for him. She traveled where she pleased, her hours were her own.

I could see what he meant. She was certainly different from the typical housewife, the women I'd seen pushing strollers down the street or in the grocery, bending over the packages of sushi, one arm reaching for the plastic-wrapped tuna, the other linked to a small child.

"But what about marriage?" I was determined not to let him off.

He said that he couldn't marry her, because his future was uncertain. "I could be arrested any moment for my political activities, I could lose my job. Keiko wouldn't be able to count on me."

I took this in part as an excuse to avoid commitment, evidence of concern for his freedom rather than Keiko's security. There was no way I could get him to see any of the contradictions in his relationship with Keiko, how convenient the relationship was for him, how much it resembled the traditional Japanese marriage.

And yet I felt uneasy about being so judgmental. I thought of his work with the Theater of the Deaf, his teaching, his feelings for the suffering of others. Even Keiko recognized something exceptional in those feelings. "I'm not like that," she said to me once. "I have to think of myself. But I admire Matsuo. He has a passion." It was her way of shrugging, *sho ga nai*—it can't be helped.

As Matsuo launched into an attack on the Japanese secret police, I looked at him and saw someone quite sad. Keiko, despite her understanding, was probably going to leave him eventually. That night I had already seen signs that she was tiring of his lack of consideration. And what of the rest of his life? He had a daughter he rarely saw. His ex-wife was still angry at him, still bitter about the years after college when he had been depressed and spent much of his days drinking. He had no brothers or sisters. His mother, to whom he was close, was old, would soon be gone. I could see him at the end of his life, living alone, like one of those divorced sarariman, in a small room crammed with books and records and papers and photographs, his long white hair and thinning body making him look more and more like an old woman, some wild witch in an abandoned village. What would he be able to show for the years? Photographs in yellowed magazines, a few obscure books, a few articles.

Perhaps such speculations tell more about me than about Matsuo, tell more about the reasons why I was not devoting my life to politics, tell more about my own selfishness, what I would not give up: marriage, children, friends, a life without loneliness, without paranoia or fear, buoyed by the small comforts of the middle class.

Writing this down, I can hear Matsuo's querulous voice: "What right have you to judge what you don't understand?"

3

By the time we were all seated around the dinner table, the two of them seemed as settled as a long-married couple, the arguments, angers, and blindnesses present and accounted for. As we plunged into the meal—plate after plate of peppers, onions, mushrooms, slices of lamb, sautéed with shoyu, rice wine, sugar, and ginger—Keiko seemed to forgive Matsuo's lack of help in the kitchen.

Afterward, the four of us lay groaning, rocking back on

the cushions. Susie began to clean up, until Keiko waved her away. She was massaging Matsuo's leg, play-punching him and pouting, then bursting into laughter.

Matsuo began to talk again about the average Japanese. I had to laugh. Matsuo was like a terrier gnawing the pants leg of the postman. He wouldn't give up till he had drawn blood. But as he spoke about the violence of the Japanese soldiers, as he described their invasions of Asia in the first half of the century, the executions in Manchuria, the rape of Nanking, I began to feel as if he was carrying things a bit too far.

"Japan is peaceful now," he said, "but it's always there, that violence."

I told him he sounded like an American racist. The Japanese couldn't be trusted, were sneaky, inscrutable. A recent article in *The New York Times Magazine* had described the rebirth of Japanese nationalism and had focused on groups on the far right. I felt that the article completely obscured the marginality of such groups and the apolitical nature of most present-day Japanese. Such distortions helped many Americans legitimize their resentment toward Japan's economic resurgence.

Though I didn't say so to Matsuo, I suspect that the main reason I found his argument troubling was that I felt much more comfortable with America-bashing than Japan-bashing.

"You don't know the Japanese," Matsuo said. "All you see is the present, not what is hidden." And to illustrate his point, Matsuo began to tell us about his uncle, who was in the Japanese Red Army during World War II.

The Japanese Army had swept through Manchuria like an arctic wind. People fled before them, but where was there to flee? One day, the troops marched into a village. Their uniforms were soiled, their faces tight, squinting in the sunlight. In the muddy street, splinters of ice were beginning to form. Matsuo's uncle said they had been fighting for days. The commander, short, imperious, with a thin pencil mustache, ordered the soldiers to assemble the villagers, and minutes later, the soldiers emerged from the dark doorways, their rifle butts pushing children, mothers, old men and women, the few fathers left. Sometimes a mother carrying an infant stumbled and fell in the mud. Two or three infants were crying out of control. The air smelled of manure, the coming cold.

A young sergeant translated the captain's orders. The captain pointed to a husband who had emerged from one house. His clothes were ragged, his beard thin, pointed, with tinges of gray. Then the captain pointed to a woman from the house next door, as she juggled the infant in her arms up and down. She stopped her cooing. The infant wailed. The woman's face was taut, her cheekbones high, angular, regal; her complexion smooth, dark as an olive. The prettiest woman in the village.

Then the order came. The man and woman were to lie down in the mud and copulate. If they didn't, the whole village would be shot.

Matsuo's uncle said he hated the captain for this. But the uncle said nothing. What could he do? At least the village would be saved.

The soldiers were ordered to make sure the villagers watched. The couple lay down in the mud, the flesh of the man's back white and pink, gleaming like a fresh-washed sheet. There were bits of straw on the ground. Infants bawled. A crow coughed on a rooftop.

And then the man and woman were scrambling for their clothes, pulling them on even as their knees still rested in the mud. Some of the soldiers continued to stare. Others turned away, as if the aftermath, the closing up of the wound, were what they were forbidden to see. Matsuo's uncle felt a tightness in his stomach, the numbness of his lips like the slight twitch of poison from consuming bits of blowfish.

Now there were new orders. The soldiers were to line up all the villagers on the east side of the street, facing the sun. Matsuo's uncle knew what was happening: they were going to be killed anyway. "No, no, no," he shouted. "What are you doing? Stop." He felt like a ghost speaking to the living.

Three soldiers rushed up to him, grappled him through the mud, away from the line of villagers, all of them squinting, shading their eyes. They could have been waving to him, seeing him off on a voyage.

Caught in the grasp of the soldiers, who spit the word *"baka"* over and over, Matsuo's uncle could see the blue of the sky, a few clumps of whiteness like fat fists of chrysanthemums. And then a rifle butt knocked him in the temple.

For three months he lived inside a tent surrounded by barbed wire, then in a corrugated tin shack which leaked long strings of water that formed another set of bars around his body. Mice scurried in the corners, then left. There was nothing for them to eat. The solitude was deafening, but not deafening enough. Though he grew quite thin, he would grow even thinner the next year, when he was captured by the Russians and sent to their prison camp in Siberia. He learned scraps of Russian, more plentiful than the food. The nights, endless and black, hunched down over him, like enormous birds. The cold was dense, arctic, an anvil pressing down. The other Japanese with him shunned him.

He told Matsuo this story years later, when Matsuo was a little boy. It was the ending of the occupation. All around them, the city of black ashes and ruin was beginning to vanish. Everywhere workers were digging underground, planting the rails that would thread the city together. The boy was skinny, buck toothed, full of energy; he ran through the streets in a white T-shirt that was beginning to tear, had streaks of dirt on his cheeks. He had been fed on food from America served at his school. Like the sound of saws, drills, and hammers all around the city, he was part of this enormous energy of rebuilding. Which the uncle could not share.

Why he told Matsuo all this seems mysterious. It must have terrified the boy. "I kept saying, No, no, no, no, how could people do this?" The boy wanted protection, he wanted delusion. Was he old enough to know?

No, said the uncle, this happened. I saw it. I was there.

And then, a few months later, the uncle killed himself. This was around the time Matsuo discovered that the labels on the crates of food from America said, FOR ANIMALS ONLY: NOT FOR HUMAN CONSUMPTION.

"But he was always proud that he had stood up to the commander," said Matsuo, "that he had said no."

And then: "You won't find stories like this in the Japanese textbooks."

Keiko, Susie, and I were silent. Miles Davis on the stereo, the winding glissando of the trumpet sliding down to a few low notes. Matsuo said the Japanese government had just won a suit which supported their banning of a textbook that said the Manchurian invasion was an invasion and not an incursion.

"The government wants to wipe out that history, keep the people from remembering. And it's succeeding. That's what kind of violence the state does." Matsuo took a drink of beer and paused. "It makes me ashamed to be Japanese . . ."

5

Matsuo and I shared an obsession with history, with moral judgments. We reacted with fury at present-day attempts to cover up what was problematical or difficult or painful in the past. Listening, I felt a special bond to him. He was somehow giving me permission to reclaim parts of the past most Americans don't want to recall, to look back without blinking, to feel as much as possible how the past resides within us.

Like Matsuo, I too have a story of an uncle and World War II. It didn't make quite the impression on me that his uncle's story made on Matsuo, but it remains one of my personal talismans from the past, something that sticks more than the dates and documents and textbook accounts of that time, the relocation camps, the 442nd, the all-Nisei division, the resettling after the war. After we returned home from Keiko's that night, I wrote down the details of this story. It consists of three successive images. There is no continuity. That has been lost.

1942, Seattle— The notice board was across the street from the Buddhist church, right next to the Nakauchi grocery, the bins of tomatoes, oranges, lettuce, and asparagus. A small crowd stood around it. One of the young men, in a tan nylon jacket, was walking away, muttering, but the rest were silent.

As my uncle moved forward, he could read CIVILIAN EXCLUSION ORDER at the top of the broadside. He saw Mr. Nakauchi, thin, balding, with wire-rimmed glasses, his grocer's apron stained by unknown produce, craning his neck at the edge of the crowd. My uncle thought of bowing, but merely smiled and nodded to the father of his girlfriend, and resumed pushing his way forward.

"All persons of Japanese descent . . ." He had heard rumors that something like this was going to happen. The scrawled messages of vandals had sprouted up since Pearl Harbor on storefronts, sidewalks, walls, and doors. Now the messages had the sting of prophecy and not just slander, and the JAPS GO HOME or KILL ALL JAPS painted sometime during the night merely echoed the headlines of newspapers on the doorsteps:

FIFTH COLUMN TREACHERY TOLD

FIFTH COLUMN PREPARED ATTACK

SECRETARY OF NAVY BLAMES 5TH COLUMN FOR ATTACK

JAP BOAT FLASHES MESSAGES ASHORE

MAP REVEALS JAP MENACE

CAPS ON JAPANESE TOMATO PLANTS POINT TO AIR BASE

No one knew if there was any truth to these headlines. Many were proven false, but others sprang up in their places, impossible to erase. When this last headline appeared, it seemed so absurd that most of my uncle's friends thought no one would believe it. His friends lacked imagination, my uncle thought, could not see that truth was no longer the question. The war, the country, had entered the realm of the fantastic; what people believed mattered more than the truth.

And here, on the bulletin board, in black and white, on paper dampened by the Seattle fog, was the truth. They were all going to have to move. The broadside didn't say where; it said only that they were to report to "control stations." Why didn't they say where? What did that mean? And what had they done?

My uncle caught himself. Looking for reasons was going to drive him crazy. He felt the muscles in his back tighten up toward his neck. He released them, then turned and began walking down the hill, heading for home.

But now, of course, home was only a word. It had been dismantled by that sign, its string of words.

At the bottom, he looked back up. Everything was shrouded in whiteness, a dampness pressing against his face. The crowd, the notice board, seemed to drift off above him, floating, vanishing.

"Japanese aliens and non-aliens"—the phrase popped into his head. *A non-alien. Is that what I am?* And he began to laugh.

1944, France— The woods were rinsed with a gray light, and the cold pressed to the ground the last bits of darkness. Up the hill, bare branches and black trunks emerged, stiff and gnarled. Here and there a clump of green fatigues, a splotch of whiteness. Mortar craters. If it were warmer, the bodies would already be beginning to bloat, to acquire their stench, but it was early December; the first few flakes of snow dusted the grass, the torn-up earth.

Holding in his belly, my uncle's hands are warm, steaming wet, gathering the cold. His head leans forward, he jerks it back, it leans forward again, he lets it fall. He can think of nothing but the pain shuddering inside him, like a small animal, driving inward, scurrying for warmth. It moves with every breath, a faithful promise, and he thinks for a second, This, this must be what childbirth is like. What a strange thought. He tries to think of the wooden tub he bathed in as a child, the waters almost boiling, his skin reddening, his face flushed with sweat, and then it's the water that's reddening, something spilling across the glittering surface, like the reflection of the sun.

When he opens his eyes, the light hurts. He can hear cannons in the distance, muffled rifle cracks, like the sound of branches cracking in the cold. Leaning his head to the ground, he stares at the mud, its small pockets of wetness. The earth shudders faintly. He looks up and sees the branches at the top of the hill forking and dividing the drifting clouds. He thinks of mochi, of pounding the rice on New Year's, of a sizzling steak. His stomach caves inward. Baka, he thinks. No last meal.

He thinks of Fukuda, their talks at night in the camps. Fukuda had argued that the Nisei needed to look past the war, which meant looking past the camps, the "Slap the Jap" slogans, the loss of their farms, their nurseries, their groceries. The Nisei needed to fight harder and better than the whites in defending their country, needed to win by blood the rights others would deny them.

Fukuda was all right. It was just that he believed too readily in the words, the patriotic rhetoric, had pushed away all doubts and questions. In his own way, he was as fierce and pig-headed as the gang of *Kibei* (Nisei who had gone to school in Japan), who pulled him behind the barracks one night in Poston and pummeled him in the dark. They were angry at America. They thought Fukuda was America.

"So why are you here?" Fukuda asked one night after they landed at Anzio. The hills were lit by flashes of artillery, a low rumble.

It was useless to answer. As if any of the syllables that his tongue and lips might mouth could capture any of it, could make sense of what he had seen on the beach, the tiny figures ahead of them, beside them, scurrying on the sand, falling on the sand, rising, not rising, as the froth of the waves pushed forward, bringing in the tide.

What time is it now? Three, four o'clock. It's starting to get dark again. Yes. Just let me sleep.

Four hundred yards away, leaping over the stream, thin strands of mist rising from its stones, two dozen soldiers move through the woods. Their bodies are sweaty, their uniforms crusted with mud, their beards dark, scratchy. Whispered shouts. Thud of boots. Jangle of rifle straps. Rustle of underbrush. Darkness bends over them. Bends over just as one of them, minutes later, bends over my uncle, who sees this white face, looming like the moon, and only when that face mutters, out of breath, the half-heard syllables, "All right . . . soldier," does my uncle know he's been rescued by Americans, he's going home.

Chicago, 1947— My uncle enters a building on the South Side, near Cottage Grove. He has looked at the papers over breakfast, the eggs, bacon, and coffee no longer a miracle to him, part of the life he is fading back into. He has left the soldier at the bottom of the hill, farther and farther behind, letting him acquire an almost mythical status. In the housing section, he's marked certain addresses. He doesn't want to stay with his sisters anymore. His parents are back in Seattle. He doesn't want to go back there. He'll make it alone.

As he walks up the stairs, he hardly notices the slight pain from his wound; it's almost vanished by now. Instead, he's thinking of what he can afford to pay. He plans to go to school on the G.I. Bill and has a job washing dishes at a country club in one of the suburbs. The door opens, and it's like a dream; he knows what will happen, sees it in the face of the man standing there in suspenders and T-shirt, a man his father's age, short, squat, his hair white and close-cropped, the veins in his face red and visible. As the words "Mr. McCormick . . ." register on that face, which does not change, which looks away from my uncle, as if somehow it was his face and not his stomach that was scarred, as if the war had somehow written some indelible message on my uncle's forehead, my uncle knows he will have to look elsewhere, that his home will never be here, a flight down from the old man. But the reticence in the way the man glances down, as if talking to his feet, and announces that there are others who've already asked to see the rooms, this reticence does not prepare my uncle for how the last phrase is spit out, something about a son, Guadalcanal, just as the door closes, soundly, firmly, with only a hint of rage.

Minutes later, waiting for the bus, smelling the slight stench of the stockyards some way off, hearing the train cars rumble half a block away, my uncle lets out his breath, muttering, *"Sho ga nai"*—it can't be helped. And this too strikes him as incredibly funny.

I'm as stupid as Fukuda, he thinks. And I'm still alive.

It was hard for me to reconcile the uncle of my story with the pharmacist of later years, jocular, beefy like a sumo wrestler. I knew the stoicism I attributed to him in the story, his refusal to believe that somehow America will accept him, his failure to imbibe the patriotic wine that made the 442nd giddy with courage, stamina, and hope, his refusal to mouth bland platitudes, all owed more to a need in me than to some real and hidden aspect of his character. I was embarrassed by the way the Nisei seemed to beg to be let into America, embarrassed because those feelings existed within me.

My uncle's story left me with Matsuo's phrase: "It makes me ashamed to be Japanese . . ."

6

In New York, just before I left for Japan, I went to see *Year of the Dragon.* The film is about a white detective investigating the Chinese gangs in New York's Chinatown. American films involving Asians appall me with a sickening regularity. I almost always leave the theater cursing racist stereotypes, sputtering in rage. I then vow to myself, as I did after seeing *Year of the Dragon,* never to see another such movie.

Of course, even as I vow this, I know I'm lying. I can see movies such as *Bachelor Party* or Clint Eastwood's *Heartbreak Ridge,* and though I am appalled by their obvious sexism, racism, homophobia, etc., I'm able on another level to give myself to the mindlessness of these movies in a way I can't do with books. And this runs true even when the movie is filled with Fu Manchu war lords or exotic Suzie Wongs or Marlon Brando houseboys. I'm both enraged and enthralled by the magic of the movies, and their capacity to enthrall always brings me back.

And so, a few months after seeing *Year of the Dragon,* I found myself with Susie in the Seibu department store in Tokyo, looking up at the movie posters, trying to decide what we should see. I was reluctant to add a yen to the coffers of Sylvester Stallone, yet I am also one of those deranged individuals guilty of seeing all four Rocky films. "It will be a cultural experience," I rationalized, "seeing the way the Japanese react, trying to read the film through their eyes." I bought the tickets. I gave in. I saw *Rambo.*

The Japanese reaction to the film was curious. In the lobby, venders were selling the usual programs that one sees at Japanese theaters, filled with pictures from the film, explanatory text, interviews, and so on. Such accoutrements attest to the Japanese interest in commentary and explanation, as well as reading in general. There were Rambo model guns on display, and Rambo gear, from camouflage clothing to toy knives. Yet despite their attraction to the military gung-ho aspect of the movie, the members of the audience were, as all Japanese audiences are, quiet and polite. They did not shout at the screen or find their emotions aroused to some sort of fighting frenzy (even at such high-energy audience events as pro-wrestling, Japanese audiences are relatively calm and quiet compared to American audiences). The Japanese audience seemed to identify with Rambo rather than with the Asian hordes he single-handedly disposed of. Of course, audiences generally identify with the protagonist, but the Japanese feel themselves superior to, and separate from, other Asians.

I felt that my peculiar status made me more aware than either the Japanese or other Americans of the multiple ways in which this film could be read. I laughed at the simplicity of the movie's version of the world even as I was disturbed by its underlying messages.

In the film, Sylvester Stallone plays John Rambo, a Vietnam vet, with a mission to free a group of POW's still in Vietnam. Rambo possesses a primitive, almost neolithic sense of a warrior. When he is dropped into the jungle, Rambo's parachute jams and catches the wing of the plane. As he is dragged and pummeled by the plane, he uses his machete-sized knife to free himself. His main weapon is a bow and arrow, whose silence allows him to penetrate the Vietnamese prison camp. Later, chased by both the Vietnamese and the Russians, he picks them off one by one, using guerrilla tactics. He merges so thoroughly with the landscape that he can step from a slab of mud on the side of a cliff, just as the clay men used to emerge from the sides of the cave in the old Flash Gordon movies.

Vietnam was, of course, a guerrilla war. Rambo, who is half Native American, becomes the impossible bridge between America and the East, cunningly shedding America's technical prowess, a prowess that was, in many ways, a liability in the Vietnam War.

At the end of the movie, this anti-technological bias comes into clear focus. Having been betrayed by the Washington bureaucrat who did not want him to find the POW's, Rambo comes into the compound which houses the bureaucrats' computers and electronic tracking devices. He fires round after round of machine-gun bullets into the equipment, all the while screaming, with his teeth flaring and his eyes wildly open, in an orgasm of destruction.

"Wasn't that last scene amazing," I said to Susie, as we rode home on the Yamanote-sen. The lights of the city flashed by, the huge King Kong at Takadanobaba, a twelve-foot couple dancing on a wedding cake. "I felt as if he was shooting not just at the computers but at the technological miracles of the new Asia. And the Russians in the movie seemed more like Nazis, and the Vietnamese kept coming after Rambo like the Japanese in old John Wayne films. They never ducked, they just came mindlessly forward. It was as if Rambo were fighting World War II and the Vietnam War all over."

"I knew you'd be pissed. Why did you want to see it?"

"You have no appreciation of trash," I replied. "It's

strange. I bet we're going to see more films like this, like *Year of the Dragon* and *The Deer Hunter.* Especially as the new tigers of Asia begin making their economic swing upward. But there're also going to be other films, films that somehow elevate Asian culture, like *The Karate Kid.*"

"*The Karate Kid?*"

"Yes. I'm serious. Look at the way the kids back home are starting to wear T-shirts with kanji. It's going to be interesting how other Japanese-Americans take to it, whether they're going to identify with this new Asia or not."

As I said this, I could feel myself being swept up, filled with a rush I couldn't quite define. I started to talk about Lévi-Strauss, about the Mbaya Indians and the ideological uses of myth.

At this point, Susie was looking out the window.

"You're not paying attention to me."

"I was just looking at that Suntory ad, the one with the woman in whiteface with her eyebrows raised wearing a metallic breastplate. It's such a riveting mixture of the old Japan and the new."

"So what? I was talking to you. Sometimes I get so pissed at you," I said *sotto voce.*

"Okay, okay. I'm sorry."

"That's not good enough. You're always tuning me out when I talk about these things."

The train was pulling into our station. We walked down the long corridor to the street, past the ads for inns in Nikko, weddings, Maru-Maru department store, the Suntory modern court lady, ghostly and hip.

"I said I'm sorry."

"Sometimes I don't think you realize how much racism affects me."

"Oh, God."

"No, you don't. You think it's something I can put on and off, that it's not there all the time. You think it's just a movie, *Rambo, Year of the Dragon,* but it's the way the whole culture looks at Asians."

"Listen, I'm the one who feels out of place here. You can talk with Matsuo for hours and he never says a word to me."

"That's not true. He was interested in your views on feminism."

"Oh sure, but it made no impact on him."

We started up the avenue, past the bank, the Kentucky Fried Chicken, the Pachinko parlor, emptied of its patrons, its neon and fluorescent bulbs dark. At the all-night corner grocery, a Japanese version of the 7-Eleven, boys stood by the magazine racks poring over manga. Their hair was manicured and collegiate, not like my long, free-falling mane. They were like younger brothers, another generation. Susie walked beside me in silence.

"So you're angry," I said.

"No, it's you who's angry."

"Look, every time I'm not getting what I want from you and *I'm* angry, I know it's because you're angry. Only you never admit you're angry." I knew we were in for a long one. It would go on like this back and forth, for one, two, God knows how many hours.

At home, the coils of the heater glowed. The one lamp threw my shadow against the far wall, where Susie was scrunched up.

"I don't know," she said. "Of course, I sympathize with you. But . . ."

"But what?"

"I'm a white liberal. I'm filled with guilt."

"So what does that mean? You act as if guilt's an excuse not to do anything."

"But what am I supposed to do?"

"Well, for one thing, you can stop acting as if racism is my problem. That's the thing with white people, they always think the race problem is there for the coloreds to solve."

"That's ridiculous. I married you, didn't I?"

"Of course, but that's not the point. You keep saying you support me, but you don't want to really talk about these issues. It makes you uncomfortable."

"It *does* make me feel uncomfortable. I don't know what to do."

"Well, figure it out, then. Jesus, remember when all the women we knew were studying feminism. After a while I finally understood I couldn't just start studying it for you or for the women we knew, I had to do it for me, for who I was."

"You were hardly a model of feminist propriety."

"Okay, I had to change. I was an asshole. And I still need to change."

"You think if you just say that, it's solved."

"At least I've stopped saying, 'It's your fight, honey, I support you.' You know, there came that point when I realized that taking in what Susan Griffin was saying in *Pornography and Silence* probably meant I'd always feel alienated from the whole society, from all the ways that the media portrays women? Well, somehow you've got to do that on race." I was still angry now, but I could see things more clearly.

"It's just that I don't have control of it," she said. "I'd like to save you from it, but I can't. And I feel as if it's my fault. And I know it's not. And I know it is."

"So you feel contradictory. We all do."

"You always seem so sure of yourself. As if you have all the answers."

"Of course I don't."

"But you act as if you do. And I get so pissed at that. You're so self-righteous. And you don't see what it's like for me here. I'm always this adjunct. This wife who tags along. And it's true, I don't care as much as you do about all this political stuff. I'm a doctor, but I'm not doing any medicine at all. It makes me crazy."

"So you're pissed at me for bringing you here?"

"Of course not, it's been a great time, it's just . . . oh, I don't know . . . Maybe it's just that you're working, you're doing your writing and I'm not, or maybe I just miss my friends at home. And then there're all these issues that come up, and you start talking, and you get that tone in your voice . . ."

"And how does that make you feel?"

"Scared . . ."

"Scared of what?"

"That I'll lose you." She was beginning to cry.

"How? How can you lose me?"

"You'll become so angry you'll go away from me. Or you'll get so involved in all this political stuff, you won't want to go back to the States, you'll just look at me as this white bourgeois woman who wants kids and wants to tie you down and . . ."

"Jesus, wait a second . . . who says I'm going anywhere?"

"Well, you keep talking about how you feel so much more at home here than in the States, how the prospect of going home seems boring."

"But what does that have to do with how much I care for you?"

"I don't know. What do you want, I'm a co-dependent."

I had moved over by then, my anger gone.

"Jesus, sometimes, Roseann Roseanna danna . . ."

"Hand me the Kleenex, would you?"

It was past three. Mrs. Hayashi was coming in a few hours.

"Set the alarm. We can't oversleep again."

"Just once I wish Mrs. Hayashi would be late."

"She can't. She's Japanese."

The futon was cool as we slipped inside. I heard steps in the alley. Images from the movie flashed through my mind.

"Susie?"

She was already asleep.

7

The leftist school where Matsuo taught was located in Jimbocho. The restaurants there were modest, the displays of food outside dusty, their color somehow off. *Donburi,* yakitori, tonkatsu—cheap fare. This area, a haunt of students, was famous for its bookshops. I'd walk down the narrow streets, made darker by awnings. Volumes were displayed in the windows. Some were used, brown with age, beside scrolls of calligraphy; the chain stores sported the bright primary colors of new volumes, color photographs of landscapes, a kimono, black-and-whites of authors. Specialty shops—for science, economics, art—the English bookshop where I spent hours, indulging my need for the anchor of words I understood. And then there were the aluminum-sided stores with no windows; inside, the row on row of pornography, in racks or spread on tables; sarariman, students milling about.

The office of the school was up a narrow flight of stairs, just above the office of a shipping company. Dingy even by Japanese standards, the two rooms had walls of institutional green. Fluorescent lights hummed overhead. Bookshelves with old magazines, pamphlets; a gray metal desk with a telephone. In one room a long, battered table with folding chairs. In the other, chairs with armrests to write on, a blackboard.

The school held classes on subjects from politics to history to poetry to critical theory. The students were in their twenties or early thirties, the same age as the group I went to the demonstration with. They dressed casually, without the hip glamour of the Tokyo young or the uniform sarariman suit. The men's hair was usually longer, like mine. Their jobs varied—schoolteacher, translator, a clerk in a music shop, an electrician, a secretary. They weren't the elite of the country, but they were all well educated. Matsuo's class was a bit of a potpourri. The readings included many areas generally not covered by Japanese universities, from Marxists like Benjamin or Lukács, to feminists like Julia Kristeva, to structuralists like Roland Barthes. Occasionally, Matsuo gave lectures on his own peculiar interests—rock and roll, jazz, the Theater for the Deaf.

I attended Matsuo's class from time to time, as well as an English class where students talked about current political issues. The students were friendly and asked me questions about America. They showed me the magazine the school produced. It contained articles on politics in Asia—the Philippine New People's Army, the Korean dissidents, Bhopal, the Japanese labor movement.

In spring, Matsuo started to talk about the two of us visiting Korea to contact the student groups in Kwangju and Seoul. We won't fly, he said. It would be safer to take the ferry from southern Honshu. The Japanese and Korean police worked in close coordination and were bent on squashing dissidents. I had no idea whether this was paranoia on Matsuo's part or not. Susie didn't want me to go. I read up on Korean politics, the massacre at Kwangju, the workings of the economy. Matsuo said I should be prepared to leave any minute.

Naturally, I felt grateful to him for the offer. And yet the trip seem so improbable, Matsuo so secretive about it, I didn't quite know what to think. As was often the case in Japan, when people were so incredibly generous and hospitable to both me and Susie, I felt uneasy, as if I were taking on some burden I couldn't possibly repay. Why, I wondered, was Matsuo interested in me?

True, we shared certain leanings to the left, but beyond that, Matsuo and his friends were intrigued by someone who looked like them and yet thought entirely differently. Because Japanese have an intense interest in anything Japanese, they found *nikkei-jin* (Japanese who have settled abroad) a curious, lost aspect of Japanese culture.

I came to understand all this a bit better one night at Matsuo's class. In preparation for this class, Matsuo had translated and handed out copies of my twelve-page poem on the relocation camps, "The Book of Relocation," as well as a shorter poem about my grandfather called "Relocation." As I looked at the students gathered around the table, my poems before them, I felt extremely grateful to Matsuo. The translations represented a great deal of work.

Matsuo first read the whole poem in Japanese, and I was pleased at being able to follow along. After this, a poet named Fujimoto, another teacher at the school, commented on the poem. He said he was surprised that instead of seeking my identity with the Japanese or with other Americans, I had looked for the basis of my identity in the Issei, in my immigrant, minority roots. He was also surprised at the attempt I made to connect the relocation with events in Europe and what had happened with the Jews and with the destruction at Hiroshima.

Another student said that, being Japanese, he had never had to question his identity, and that the poem made him think for the first time about his relationship both to the Japanese state and to the Japanese people. A woman mentioned that she had worked in Argentina as a nurse and found that while the Issei there wanted to return to Japan, the Nisei and Sansei wanted to become part of the Argentinian culture, to stay in the country. And yet, when they listened to the incredibly syrupy Japanese sentiment of the *enka* singers, all the Japanese there seemed to find some shared source of feeling, a recognizable element.

After the class, one student, who said she had been too shy to talk earlier, told me that my poem made her think of the Palestinian refugees, who also had had land taken away from them, and a book she had read about their struggle. She felt that after hearing my poem she'd understood better what these people had gone through.

Their reactions made me realize how American my themes were, how the ways in which I think about the world are so un-Japanese. I was pleased by how people seemed moved by the poem. The association between the relocation camps and the Palestinians surprised me. Though the death camps in Europe were of a completely different order than the relocation camps for the Japanese-Americans, I did sense certain parallels in the marginalization of both groups, in ways they were never considered legitimate citizens of their respective countries.

Just before the class ended, Matsuo asked me to read my poem about my grandfather. As I read, I had this feeling of a message coming back to its source. I was a tiny conduit between generations, between cultures. The images in the poem seemed at once more real and more false; these people in the class would understand certain things in the poem in a way most Americans never would. They would also sense something wrong with the image at the end of the poem of my grandfather sitting in a chair— he would have been kneeling on tatami—and with the haiku I have him writing—it lacked the proper syllabic count:

> *Bonsai tree,*
> *like me you are useless*
> *and a little sad.*

And then Matsuo began to read the poem in Japanese, and I dropped my self-conscious criticisms and felt grateful for this chance, this audience. A sense of wholeness—momentary, pleasurable, real—swept over me. I had completed another journey of sorts, had found one more fragment of my grandfather's kuni.

IV

"Reality, however one interprets it, lies beyond a screen of clichés. Every culture produces such a screen, partly to facilitate its own practices (to establish habits) and partly to consolidate its own power. Reality is inimical to those with power."

—John Berger, *And our hearts, our faces, brief as photos*

"You cannot do it," explained the Master, "because you do not breathe right. Press your breath down gently after breathing in, so that the abdominal wall is tightly stretched, and hold it there for a while. Then breathe out as slowly and evenly as possible, and after a short pause, draw a quick breath of air again—out and in continually, in a rhythm that will gradually settle itself. If it is done properly, you will feel the shooting becoming easier every day."

—Eugen Herrigel, *Zen in the Art of Archery*

1

On my way to my Noh lesson, I passed a tiny playground, its swings empty. It was early afternoon; a brisk wind was whirling through the alleys and small twisting side streets. At the corner, a washing machine sat, abandoned like a stray shoe at the curb. A man swept the front of his hardware store, but the wind kept pushing the dirt back. Before the grocery store women pecked at the tables of clogs and slippers, a rack of scarves. Here and there one had a baby strapped to her chest, a toddler tugging at her hem. *"Okaa-san, okaa-san . . ."* The woman attendant had a mole on her cheek, her makeup was overdone, caked like dust. A delivery boy on a scooter squirted past, his left hand supporting a tower of lacquered bentos, like an architectual model. With the moves of a dangerous halfback, he slipped in and out of traffic.

I hailed a taxi. The door opened automatically. Lace covered the top of the seats, the driver's white-gloved hands gripped the wheel. I glanced again at the material on Japanese radicals Matsuo had given me. The cover of one magazine, the *International Bulletin ARM of the Japan Revolutionary Communist League,* had a picture of a rally at Sanrizuka and the headlines: DOWN WITH IMPERIALISM! DOWN WITH STALINISM! WORKERS OF THE WORLD, UNITE!

The inner cover held similar tidbits: "During the last ten years we have been fighting a dual confrontation war against the state power and against counter-revolutionary civil force Kakumaru [the Japanese police], Nazis of today, and have successfully reached a stage of achieving general offensive against fascist Kakumaru and thus a stage of beginning direct confrontation with imperialist state power."

It was all somewhat hard to take.

The taxi passed the Russian embassy. A block down, the omnipresent sound truck of the rightists was blaring. They demanded the return of the northern islands, they praised the Emperor, they shouted for the Russians to go home. It was the time of the Russian foreign minister's visit, of death threats. Police in riot helmets lined the walk before the embassy walls.

In the buildings above me men were now poring over financial charts and marketing reports. They worked without individual offices, the desks lined up like cars in a parking lot. Each movement was visible, no place to rest, even if the inclination was there. Buildings that swayed when the earth cracked, towers of steel and glass. Hotels with lobbies like highways, great banquet rooms where the weddings of the elite were held.

I couldn't make sense of it—the contrast between the life of this city and the hell beneath the floorboards that Matsuo saw. Of course, I knew there were certain areas of poverty in the city, but there was nothing like in New York or Chicago or Detroit. Why a revolution amid an economic boom?

But of course, there would be no revolution. The idea was simply absurd.

Elsewhere in Asia that year, things were quite different. In my bag was a *Newsweek* with Cory Aquino on the cover, photos of the crowds storming Malacañang Palace, the shoes of Imelda. On the newsstands were photos of the student who had hurled himself from a building in Seoul. In typical Japanese tabloid fashion, the photos showed everything: the body sprawled on the street, the pool of blood and brains scattered like matting from a stuffed doll. Suddenly Chun Doo-Hwan appeared vulnerable. There were more and more reports about the Korean secret police, of U.S. aid siphoned off. The State Department argued that South Korea was not the Philippines.

In Matsuo's class, a Korean poet gave a reading. He spoke of his fellow dissidents, the kidnapping of a Korean political leader from a hotel in Tokyo, the massacre at Kwangju, the imprisonment of the poet Kim Chi Ha and others. Kept from sight until his bruises and cuts healed, one prisoner showed up in court with a handful of scabs he had saved; the evidence was disallowed. The impulsive, manic energy of faraway events, like faint jolts of electricity, charged Matsuo's discussions, gave him and his friends some small connection to something larger, grander, real.

Just a few nights before, Matsuo had called to say he had heard from radical groups in Korea. Our trip was on and would take place within the next few weeks.

The taxi halted at the beauty shop next door to Okinaka's studio. I had told Matsuo I was looking forward to going. But what was I looking forward to? Unlike Ken, I knew little about the politics in Korea. But then, did I know any more about dance? Or Noh?

"You can't believe that!"

This was Daniel's favorite expression. We were in the waiting room outside Okinaka's studio, sitting on cushions at a knee-level table, drinking tea. I had just informed Daniel that I wasn't really that interested in money, that I didn't think it had much to do with being an artist.

"You're not one of those who believe in the starving artist . . ."

"If I wanted to promote anything, I would have gone into advertising."

From the next room, through the shoji, we could hear the chanting of the doctor who had come before us. Okinaka was beating time with a stick. His pupils, like the doctor, came from all sorts of professions. Noh was a cultivated hobby for them.

"Look, if you believe in your art, why shouldn't you promote it?"

"It's just not something I'm interested in."

"And you think it's crass, bourgeois. That's crap."

"It's just not in my nature, Daniel. You grew up reading *The Wall Street Journal* with your father. You like the idea of figuring out how to make money. It's like a game to you. If you're going to play that game well, you have to be interested in it."

"So what about the other guys who are out there hustling?"

"What about them? Of course, I get jealous sometimes. But if I spent all my time worrying about that, I'd never write. Maybe I don't like self-promotion because I'm Japanese."

"That's bullshit. You're as American as I am. You've got to do both. You know, it's more egotistical to take your pot of gold and hide it in the swamp and expect people to find it than to at least put it out on the road so someone can notice it."

"I suppose that's true," I said. "But remember the other day at I-House, when we met Jack, that American businessman. You were fascinated that the division he was controlling here had a billion-dollar volume. To me, that was like saying there's a billion fish in the Sea of Japan. What's it got to do with me?"

"But you claim to call yourself a Marxist. And that's based on economics."

"I think Marxism is useful as a tool of analysis. I don't believe in it as a prescription for how to run a government."

The shoji pulled back. Okinaka poked his head out. Five minutes.

His teaching schedule was typical of Noh sensei, but it seemed strange to us. No one had an appointment. The students just showed up anytime between a certain set of hours. The first one there had the first lesson. This meant students often spent a lot of time waiting around. It didn't seem very efficient to me. It was just the way things were done.

"Have you been practicing?" I asked.

"Some. Not much."

"I haven't at all. I did go to a performance the other night. And I listen to the tapes."

"I'm interested in the movements mainly."

"But the chanting is incredible. It's like nothing I've ever heard. And the thing is—maybe this is just my ignorance—I believe I can sing it, that somehow it suits my voice in a way Western music doesn't."

Okinaka called us into the other room. We bowed to the doctor as we entered, then bowed to Okinaka. His tall, thin body reminded me of a praying mantis. He was dressed in a dark-blue kimono. His hair was short and thick, his eyes serious, intelligent.

Daniel and I sat down on mats beside a table. To our right, the small bare floor where we practiced.

Okinaka asked me about my Butoh lessons. I hadn't been going lately. I said Ono had been out of the country, which was in part the truth.

"I would very much like to meet him. I think there is a link between Noh and Butoh."

I sensed he was asking me to arrange a meeting, but I didn't feel confident about doing so. A combination of self-absorption, self-deprecation, and shyness made me a poor conduit for networking. Daniel, despite the weakness of his Japanese, would have made a better go-between.

"Well, shall we do our meditation?"

Inwardly I groaned. I think Daniel did too. We lined up near the wall and spread our legs apart. We bent slightly at the knees and held out our arms, bent like bows parallel to the floor. Okinaka pushed my back straighter, bent my legs a bit more. He then repositioned Daniel.

"You need to strengthen your *ki,*" Okinaka said. "You know what ki is? It's here"—pointing to his solar plexus—"it's where your spirit resides. When you have a strong ki, your performance will develop naturally. Of course, I practice, but the most important thing I do is meditate. That is what prepares me. You must develop keenness. Now, when you can do this for thirty minutes without a strain . . ."

I'll be Arnold Schwarzenegger, I thought.

Okinaka looked at his watch. "I'll be back in twenty minutes."

As usual, after five minutes, my knees started to shake. A few minutes later, Daniel's started to shake too. As I had at the Sanrizuka demonstration, I suddenly felt as if I were in gym class, doing squats as punishment. No, I kept telling myself. This is zen, *ritsu-zen.* You are concentrating, building your ki. You will not put down your arms, you will not straighten your back.

By the time Okinaka came back, we were both sweating and shaking like feverish patients.

"Good. Now we will dance."

Dancing, of course, was the last thing I felt like doing. Lying on the floor was more appealing. Still, I had lasted longer than I had the first time we did this.

Daniel and I went to the table and slipped our fans from their cases. Okinaka showed us again how to walk. In Noh, you do not lift your feet up when walking, but glide along, raising the front end of your foot a little at the end of each step, like a sigh. You hold the fan at your side and keep both arms slightly bowed outward from the body. He showed us a small portion of a dance, stepping forward and back, raising the fan, lowering the fan, turning, then forward, then turning again.

"Sei-yu . . . kakeru. . . ." Okinaka called out.

Though Daniel too appeared clumsy, he was much more adept than I. His body seemed to recall the movements much more quickly and accurately than mine. I felt like an Episcopalian on Soul Train.

But these are Japanese movements, I thought, and hurried my steps to keep up with Okinaka, who was turning in a slow, steady motion, the fan held out in front of him, eyes straight ahead. I glanced at Daniel. He was following just fine. I jerked the fan in front of me.

Well, I thought, at least I can practice the singing. Daniel can't do that.

"What did I get from Decroux?" Daniel repeated Okinaka's question. Decroux was Daniel's teacher in Paris, the inventor of corporeal mime. We were in the kitchen of the house, seated at a Western table, drinking tea. I'd just finished my singing lesson with Okinaka.

"Indigestion," he laughed. "You know how foie gras is made? They take a goose and they force-feed it grain with a funnel, and they do this daily to the poor goose. The liver finally gets sick from overeating. And the goose gets sicker and sicker, until finally the liver gets so big that the beast is *encrassé*—overgreased, overfatted—and they slaughter the goose and put it out of its misery, and we eat the foie gras. The same thing happened at Decroux's."

"I don't understand," said Okinaka.

"When you're at Decroux you get force-fed. And what gets sick isn't your liver but your imagination. If you get the right sickness. And that sickness no longer allows you to see a spiral staircase and a straight staircase with the same eyes."

Daniel took a sip of tea. "Decroux would look at you, and say, 'That's not the same thing, is it?' Theater is a series of choices. And if something is chosen for the wrong reason, it's the wrong choice. . . . The problem with Butoh, with all that improvisation, is somewhere you're going to make a wrong choice; just because you're going for the glitz or you're a bit lazy, you've decided to putz. I want things so tight I do the same thing every performance."

"Is that any different from Noh?" I asked Okinaka.

"It is difficult to say. Zeami, for instance, says you must adjust to the audience, their energy. And then you don't perform a play over and over on successive nights."

"But the movements, the music, the chants, that's all planned out," I said. Suddenly I thought of the demonstration at Sanrizuka. "That's why you don't have to rehearse, isn't it?"

"Yes, but each performance is unique."

"But you don't improvise, do you?" asked Daniel.

"No, you know what you are going to do. But you are constantly adjusting, changing. For instance, Zeami knew the performer would change over time. Too many young Noh actors start out with their ki too tight. Then, when they get older and their strength begins to leave them . . ."

"I'm confused," I said.

"Of course, you can't do the same performance over and over again," said Daniel. "But the choices must be thought out. There were certain guidelines Decroux never designated but always seemed to choose. For instance, he wouldn't have spread his butter on toast with a plastic knife. Given that choice, he would have eaten his toast without butter on it. Every choice can be made with those kinds of qualitative judgments."

"But what does that have to do with performance?" I said. "It's all so vague."

"No, I understand," said Okinaka. "In a way, Decroux for you was like my father for me. I've never been able to find another teacher after my father died."

I felt what Daniel and Okinaka were saying was somehow beyond me. All I was hearing was airy generalities, simple, even banal things said with an air of profundity. I could also see that Okinaka was interested in Daniel in a way that he wasn't interested in me. It wasn't just that Daniel was a performer, it was that Daniel was also a foreigner, a true foreigner in Okinaka's eyes. I was Japanese, what Okinaka already knew.

Ultimately, I didn't possess the kind of purity that Daniel or Okinaka possessed. Their art was more circumscribed, neater—they would never have paid attention to someone like Matsuo—and in their dedication and precision, they both possessed that "keenness" Okinaka talked about so often. My choices would always be murkier, less sure. I was a *bricoleur,* someone who made do with the tools at hand. I would have eaten the toast with butter on it, I would have used the plastic knife.

2

The days were growing warmer, clearer. The light in the alleys stayed longer, shadows shortened, futons appeared, drying on the balconies. In the windows of coffee shops, coats no longer hung over the backs of chairs.

In front of the Shinjuku station, rock bands belted out heavy metal or bubble-gum pop, while college kids in clusters swayed before them. Sarariman, their coats in the crooks of their arms, paged through scandal magazines, newspapers, slid coins from tiny leather purses onto the news counters, then rushed on to the ticket machines. In Roppongi, elevators lowered Toyotas, BMWs, to the ground floor of garages and spun them around. The owners slipped in, behind tinted windshields, which they kept shut. They were high-level executives, businessmen, bankers. The metal of the cars gleamed in the sunlight as they drove past shoppers, depato, billboards, and video screens thirty feet high with women in kimonos or bikinis who offered bottles of sake or beer.

Matsuo worked in this world, and yet was not part of it. He had long ago rejected the glamour of the city, the postwar miracle. He had no use for magazines like *Friday* or *Focus,* with photos of movie stars emerging from love hotels, no use for the silly game shows on TV, with contests between bikini-clad coeds or young college boys stuffing food in their mouths or, in one classic example of bad taste, a farting contest.

One night we were drinking in his apartment. The room was divided in two—one half a work desk, with various prints, cameras, rolls of film; the other half held a futon, a small low table. His record collection was immense, from Armstrong, Billie Holiday, Byrd, Davis, to sixties rock—the Doors, Janis Joplin, Hendrix—to contemporary Japanese composers like Takemitsu and Kondo Jo.

Matsuo put on Billie Holiday's "God Bless the Child," then leaned back, took a sip of bourbon. I asked him if he was a happy man.

That is not a question a Japanese would answer, he replied.

He explained that my question presumed that happiness or unhappiness was an important factor in describing the human condition. Most Japanese were descended from rice farmers. The culture was feudal in origin, from the warrior class. The qualities they valued were patience, endurance, obligation, and honor.

We got back to the question of the average Japanese. The concept of the average Japanese, he argued, encouraged conformism, the behavior of sheep. It was a dream that people were fed, so that they wouldn't see what was around them, and the world beyond Japan became unreal, a different dimension. In that way, the sufferings of those who are not Japanese don't matter or matter little compared to what happens in Japan.

So why was he so concerned with events and conditions in other parts of the world?

When he was young, he answered, he wanted to go to Egypt, to climb the pyramids, to walk inside them. He wanted to see snakes rise from woven baskets, swaying to a flute, just as he'd seen in an American cartoon. He pictured himself standing in the dry heat of the desert, riding a camel over the dunes, hearing the criers from the minarets.

He never did go to Egypt, but he had traveled to Asia. He had seen the slums there. He told me how, on the streets of Manila, on the sidewalk, on the dividers between the highway, people slap sheets of cardboard or corrugated tin together. They do this wherever they can find the space. Then they call that space home.

After the monsoons the Manila streets are flooded chest-high. When Matsuo walked through the slums there, he saw children swimming in the raw sewage, splashing as if they were in a pool. The water was a rusty gray. The people's faces were darker than Japanese faces. They stared at Matsuo as he walked by. A couple of young boys ran up to him and asked him for money. He gave them some coins.

At night when he walked the streets of the red-light district of Manila, the men shouted *"Kirei musume* [pretty sister]," and the women in the doorways of the bars came up and tried to pull him in.

He watched the crowd of sarariman blow past, enter the bar like the tide moving in.

"At that moment, I felt very ashamed," said Matsuo.

Matsuo reached up to his desk and showed me an article about another trip he and a group of Japanese leftists had made to the Philippines. On that trip Matsuo and his friends had visited an area several hours south of Manila.

In one particular village an old man told how a young tenant farmer vanished one day from the village. The next day he was found in the forest, a gash across his throat, his front teeth gone. There were wounds all over the body. Every few days the soldiers would appear, line up the villagers, march them double time up and down the roads. Then the commander selected an individual, and the soldiers forced that individual to kneel and stick his head in a bucket of water. You are a member of the NPA, the soldiers would shout. You must become an informer.

"Of course the villagers are afraid," said Matsuo. "But they will not be broken."

It was hard for me to believe this. The farmers seemed to have little actual power.

Matsuo showed me some pictures of the bloated bodies of children on Negros. Peasants there were starving in part because of the drop in sugar prices. The landowners lived like feudal barons with their own private armies. When the peasants tried to grow extra food in the ditches, the landowners' goons would plow the seedlings under.

"Many of the leftists in Japan are concerned with Negros," he said. "Everybody wants to go to Negros. But it's easy to lose sight of the larger picture. It's not just Negros, or even the poverty in Manila. We have to remember the U.S. cares only about the base at Subic. They don't give a shit about the conditions of the people or what Marcos has done. They washed their hands of him only when they were forced to."

Matsuo also showed me pictures of the great trash heap in Manila called Smoky Mountain. There, three shifts a day, men, women, and children scramble and scrounge for refuse they can sell. The pictures showed dozens of anonymous faces, gray figures tramping up and down, birds reeling above them. Smoke drifting from fires. In some of the pictures the rain made the whole mountain of trash and the bodies of the scavengers give off puffs of steam.

Looking at these photos, I wondered how he reconciled them with his advertising work, his photos of beer bottles, of a model twirling around to greet the camera, her stomach bare, her breasts bound by a thin white cloth. Did Matsuo possess the Japanese ability to live with disparity, without a center, to shuttle back and forth between roles?

Matsuo began to talk again of the trip we planned to Korea. Chun Doo-Hwan instead of Marcos. Factories instead of villages. Riot police, secret police, not government soldiers, at least not until the riots increase and there's another Kwangju. In Matsuo's next class they were going to prepare petitions for Kim Chi Ha. Some part of me wondered what good they would do.

A few days later, the police broke into Matsuo's apartment. Calls went back and forth. All his friends' apartments had been broken into also. Papers scattered about, drawers ransacked.

His phone was tapped. The police had taken phone lists. Be careful, said Matsuo. He would say nothing over the phone and his cryptic manner, added to the problems of language and culture, made our conversations strained and confused. I was to meet him at this station to go to a class where he was teaching Walter Benjamin's essay on violence. He never showed up. I had the wrong station.

Gradually, Matsuo became more and more concerned about the police surveillance. Certain his phone was tapped—perhaps they'd bugged his apartment too—he kept our phone conversations brief, vague. He canceled the class indefinitely; he began to see less and less of his friends. Of Keiko. Of anyone.

"I have to be prepared," he said. "I can't let anyone else get involved."

I didn't quite know what he meant by all this. And he wouldn't answer. He said nothing about the trip to Korea. I simply assumed that I too would have to be prepared.

Matsuo grew up in the ruins of Tokyo after the war. Burned-out streets, twisted girders, heaps of stone and brick. Brilliant temples, family houses, blackened to ash. Out of this came a miracle, which seemed to grow in prosperity as he grew. Why reject it? Why turn away and say portentously, as he always did, "Beneath the floorboards there is hell"? Why focus on the buildup of a military that seemed, to my eyes and certainly to the eyes of American congressmen, incredibly minuscule and cheap? After all, his beautiful photographs of models, clothing, cars, and whiskey were part of the fuel of Japan's economy, were as essential as the strategies produced by sarariman for the trading companies, or the products assembled by the workers for Toyota or Sony. And certainly, like the whole of his country, he too had imbibed the cultural values of the West, with his passions for rock and roll and jazz, for the writings of Sontag and Benjamin, his omnipresent jeans, baseball cap, and gym shoes. He'd even tried to copy American idioms.

Curiously, in both his attraction to Western culture and his opposition to the economic miracle, Matsuo shared something with the flamboyant figure of the right Yukio Mishima. The photographs of Mishima in a tuxedo or a three-piece suit, as well as the

range of influences on his writings, from Sade to the Greeks, belie
his criticism of Japan's Westernization. Like Matsuo, Mishima also
felt that Japan's prosperity represented a spiritual wasteland, a
chimerical victory.

     At the end of his life, Mishima organized a private army.
During an appointment with the general of one of the Self-defense
Forces, Mishima and a group of four others imprisoned the general
in his office and demanded that the Self-defense Forces gather and
listen to Mishima speak. Mishima tried to arouse the forces to take
over the government and overturn the postwar constitution. He
was greeted with hoots and laughter. He went back inside and
committed *seppuku,* along with one of his young followers, re-
ported to be his lover.

     Despite this Grand Guignol finale, Matsuo probably felt
a certain sympathy with Mishima (if not with his love of the samurai
code). After all, Matsuo too would have liked to hijack the government and, increasingly, viewed violence as a necessary response to
repression. He would have condemned Mishima's act more for its
purpose than for its terrorist tactics.

3

The Shinjuku bar was cramped, dark as a closet. Posters of Hendrix, Joplin, advertisements for leftist movies and demonstrations
hung on the rough wood walls. We were in the back, near the four
small tables. People were everywhere, lined along the walls, out to
the street, many of them from the leftist school. Saito was reading.
His friend played the flute and the guitar in accompaniment. Ken
whispered to me that the poetry was not very good. Shoozu-Ben
read his poems. His hair was long, his smile cynical. I'd read the
poems before in translation: late imitations of the Beats. The monster of Tokyo, drunken nights, lovers. He had an Australian girlfriend who dressed in leather. When he sat down, she got up and

then plopped back in his lap. Yuri Kageyama read some poems in English, then the Japanese translations. The poems were sexual, dark, contained references to her father's violence, attacked the sexual predilections of the Sansei male, the stereotypes of American films.

When it was my turn, I read a couple of poems about my grandfather, poems about hibakusha, the boat people, soldiers lost in the jungle. Saito read translations. I finished with a long poem about a man addicted to pornography, to prostitutes, to the underworld of sex. I didn't know what the Japanese made of it, I hardly had a handle on the subject myself.

As I read, I noticed that a woman poet who had read earlier was resting her head on the bar. Was I that boring? And then, when I saw she didn't move for several minutes, I realized she was drunk and had passed out. I tried to assume that she would have done the same for whoever was reading.

After the reading, Daniel took me aside. "I can't believe some of that crap. You were so much better than the rest of them."

"Thanks, Daniel. But I was reading in English."

"But some of them read English translations. Besides, I could tell. None of them was really serious, they just didn't have it."

Beer bottles and shochu glasses littered the table. Smoke hung as thick as cotton batting. Hendrix was singing "Purple Haze." My first official poetry reading in Japan. It felt a bit surreal. Daniel said he had to get going, he was traveling to Kyoto in the morning. I sat down next to Ken and Saito.

"That NHK program on the relocation camps was bullshit," said Ken. "I mean, there's this Nisei who comes over, and the first thing he does is go to Fuji-san and weep and bow. Garbage."

"But you are Japanese, like David-san."

"Listen, I'd rather be black. I mean, I never knew what shame I had about my identity until I came here. All that stuff about Japanese blood, all the prejudice against the Koreans, and no one sees it."

"Of course, it's wrong to be prejudiced against Koreans."

"Aren't you overstating things a bit?" I said to Ken. "It's not as if you or I don't have mixed feelings about being Japanese-American. I remember you telling me that in high school you felt that every white girl who paid attention to you was going to be the last one. I felt that way too. Here it's different. I feel more comfortable."

"But that's not my point. Saito-san seems to think that once you're a Jap, you're always a Jap."

"But since I've been here, I keep discovering ways I do feel Japanese, from the taking off of shoes in the doorway to the way people are introspective and shy."

"You don't see the way the Japanese make such a big thing about being Japanese."

"Maybe not . . ."

Matsuo came up, a cigarette in one hand, a beer in another. He'd taken off his cap and shoved it in his pocket, but kept on his sunglasses. In the background, I could hear Akiko talking to Setsuko and Susie. "I despise . . ." she was saying.

"Hey, man," said Matsuo, "I'm sorry I'm late."

"It's okay," I said.

"Did you read the papers today?" Matsuo asked. "Did you see what the Chukaku did?"

The Tokyo summit had been going on for the past few days, and the Chukaku had launched a missile from Shinjuku into the compound where the meetings were taking place. It landed in a cobblestone courtyard.

"Just scare tactics," said Ken, "to let the authorities know they're there."

In a way, the missiles seemed more in the spirit of a college prank than any serious attempt at political change. *Animal House* goes to the summit. We began talking about the Chukaku. Once you entered the group, said Ken, it was almost impossible to leave. Recently, members of the group had broken into a former member's home and beat him and his wife with baseball bats. It was like a cult: if you wanted to leave, you had to pay a large sum of money.

I couldn't tell how Matsuo felt about these tactics.

"The group is threatened on all sides," he said. "Have you seen all the pigs out in the streets lately? They've even brought in pigs from Kyushu. They look so lost here."

What about the Red Army? I asked. Recently, the group had been connected with the bomb planted on a Korean Airlines jet. Lacking a truly pressing issue in Japan, they had fanned out across the globe, gathering contacts with the North Koreans, with the PLO, with Islamic groups in Lebanon, with Qaddafi.

"The Chukaku are nothing like that," said Ken. "They're mainly concerned with Japanese politics."

Gradually, people began to leave. It was getting near the time of the last trains. Ken and Setsuko had to get up for work the next day, Matsuo had to get back to Keiko. He left with his familiar "Keiko's going to kill me." I had been meaning to ask him about Korea, but forgot. Susie was going on a trip the next day with Takako to a pharmaceutical factory.

Finally, only Akiko, Saito, and a couple of others were left, including the Japanese woman poet, who was still sleeping on the bar.

"That's really sad," I said.

"It's nothing," Akiko said.

"You know, in America, the first thing we'd do with someone like that is get her to Alcoholics Anonymous."

"What is that?"

I began a short explanation, but after a while it was clear that Akiko and Saito did not understand what I was saying.

"It's like when somebody works all the time, they don't have any time to feel or relate to others."

I realized that workaholism was not something the Japanese, even leftists, would understand. That a drink or addictive behavior could be used to dull feelings seemed as incomprehensible to the Japanese as the doubleness of honne and tatemae to a Westerner; nor could they connect excesses with alcohol with any imbalance or excess in the rest of their lives.

"You don't understand what it's like for women here," said Akiko. "What sort of pressure she's under."

"All I know is that when I read poems by alcoholics who

tell me how bad things are, I want to say to them, 'Go to Alcoholics Anonymous, get sober, and then come back and tell me how bad things are.' Because a lot of their problems are due to alcohol, not anything else.''

"It's too easy for you to say that. You're an American. And you're a man. You have a certain freedom. . . .''

As we talked, the owner of the bar, Kenji, slipped drinks and tiny snacks made of tofu, noodles, and dried fish in front of us. His hair was close-cropped. He wore jeans, an apron, and a food-stained T-shirt. Since we'd been to the bar several times before, I knew Kenji often got drunk quicker than his patrons, and by the end of the evening, he was constantly dancing out from behind the bar, singing to the American rock tunes.

Each time Kenji turned up the stereo, Akiko politely slipped behind the bar and lowered it. But then Kenji pulled me from my chair and began to dance with me. I wanted to be a good gaijin, so I went along.

Quickly Akiko stepped between us, saying, "No, no, no, no.'' She told the owner to get behind the bar.

Like a scolded bear, Kenji wobbled back and resumed washing glasses. When Akiko explained why she'd acted as she had, I felt a little foolish. I'd mistaken drunken sexual heat for drunken affection. Maybe I don't know how things are here, I thought. Maybe I am too naïve. Maybe I ought to loosen up.

I was drinking more than usual, or rather, more than in the States. My Japanese friends were always pushing liquor on me, and it became just too tiring to protest. At least everyone else's face was red like mine. On the stereo, Janis Joplin was wailing into "Ball and Chain.''

The bar hostess, Kumiko, sat down beside us. She was a friend of Akiko's, prettier, younger. She began telling me in Japanese about this man who was interested in her. I kept having to ask Akiko for a translation.

"Doshite? Doshite?"—Why? Why?—Kumiko kept saying, brushing her long black hair from her face as she leaned close to me. On the other side of me, Saito and Akiko were arguing. Poor Saito was trying to get a sentence out, and Akiko kept saying, *"Chigau . . . Chigau"*—Wrong, wrong.

Kumiko rose and went to the washroom.

"He thinks I'm not interested in him because I come from a good family," Akiko said to me.

"It's true," said Saito.

"No, you're just too young. Besides, I have no use for men. Especially Japanese men."

"But you have a lover," said Saito.

"Yes, but he's married."

"Well, I'm not married."

"You're just a child."

The hostess came back. On her cheeks I noticed drops of water.

And then, finally, Kenji was slumped against the back wall, snoring. Everyone was leaving. The woman poet had slipped out, I didn't recall when. I helped Akiko on with her jacket. She turned and began to hug me. I felt pleased. The Japanese show so little physical affection. And then she looked up, saying, "No, no, you don't understand," took my face in her hands, and planted her lips on mine. I could feel her tongue slip through.

I backed away gently, embarrassed. I was aware Saito was watching us.

She pretended it was all a mistake. Everyone hustled out, and she and I grabbed a cab together.

Back at our apartment, twenty minutes later, Susie awoke when I came in. I told her about the ending of the night.

"Well, so much for Japanese feminism," she said.

"Shinjirarenai," I said. "Unbelievable."

4

Daniel and I stood fifty feet apart in the middle of the highway, our umbrellas mushrooming above our heads. The pavement hugged the side of the hills just above a small coastal town. The bus taking Susie and Daniel's tea ceremony class on a trip had broken down.

Daniel and I—the only males among a group of Japanese house-wives—had gotten out and, in the drilling rain, began directing traffic around the bus.

"Is it okay?" Daniel asked.

"Okay!" I answered. "No, wait a second." A car had swerved around my outstretched hand, ignoring my best patrolman stance.

"Goddamnit," Daniel shouted. As the car passed, he smacked his hand against the hood, shouting, "Stop, mother-fucker."

After twenty feet, the car stopped, and the driver opened the door. Daniel was waving his fist. "Just try it, asshole!"

Seeing Daniel's six-foot-three frame, the driver glowered, shut the door, and sped off.

"You scared him off, you crazy gaijin."

At last the police came, and we were relieved of our duties. When we stepped back on the bus, we were greeted by spontaneous applause. I assumed it was for our efforts as traffic cops and not for Daniel's string of obscenities.

I plopped my wet and shivering body down beside Susie and resumed reading Kenzaburo Oe's *A Personal Matter,* knowing we were in for a long wait.

Oe was perhaps the literary spokesman for Matsuo's generation. Members of his generation came of age in a world without the Emperor as God, the world of Hiroshima and Nagasaki, a world with a huge gaping hole into which they stared and stared, and then began busily filling in, filling it with a rapidity that astonished themselves and the world. It did not matter what junk went into that hole, Styrofoam pieces from the West, plastic goods, commercial jingles, U.S.-style pro-wrestling, stuffed animals, doughnuts and hamburgers, Mickey Mouse watches, millions of stereos and automobiles. The hole had to be filled; that was what mattered.

In the meantime, the young scrambled for something to grasp on to. In Oe's novels, the young male characters are bursting with rage and aimlessness. They wander through the streets and alleys of Tokyo, have brief encounters with hookers, transvestites, packs of dogs or young boys, spend hours playing Pachinko or electric game machines, punching bags to try their strength, firing ray guns at spaceships. A nine-to-five job is a straitjacket, a machine of torture.

I could easily see Matsuo and his friends against this backdrop. Still, they were exceptions to the rule. Most of their generation eventually joined ordinary society, becoming sarariman or housewives, like the women on our bus.

In Oe's *A Personal Matter,* the young protagonist, Bird, is finally shaken from his rage, stupor, and dissolution by the birth of a child who is mentally defective (there are autobiographical parallels here: Oe's son Pooh is mentally handicapped). In accepting the child into his life, Bird finds a sense of purpose to anchor his world; in the process, he lets go of the aimless rage that has characterized his existence. It is hard not to see this change in traditional terms: Bird grows up.

I looked around the bus. Many of the women were the same age as Matsuo, but they never spoke of politics. They wore no denim or jeans, no leather jackets, did not hang out at night in Shinjuku bars. Their clothes were from the Japanese version of a Talbot's catalogue. They talked of their children, of tea ceremonies and the weather, of Mrs. Hosoda, whose mother was a Buddhist medium and spoke with the dead.

"Mina-san, mina-san."

At the front of the bus, Mr. Watanabe, the owner of the vehicle and the husband of one of the ladies, was apologizing profusely for the breakdown and the delay. He wore black glasses and a polyester sports coat. He rubbed his knuckles against the side of his crew cut. He had come all the way down from Tokyo. He and his wife were very embarrassed. They had let everyone down, they had lost face.

After we switched buses, I settled into my new seat, brushed the drops of rain from my forehead, and resumed reading. I was almost finished. At the novel's end, Bird looks toward the future, armed with the traditional Japanese concept of gaman— endurance, forbearance.

> *"You've changed." The professor's voice was warm*
> *with a relative's affection. "A childish nickname like*
> *Bird doesn't suit you anymore."*

Bird . . . peered down at his son in the
cradle of his wife's arms. He wanted to try reflecting
his face in the baby's pupils. The mirror of the baby's
eyes was a deep, lucid gray and it did begin to reflect
an image, but one so excessively fine that Bird couldn't
confirm his new face. As soon as he got home he would
take a look in the mirror. Then he would try the
Balkan dictionary that Mr. Delchef had presented
him before his delegation had shipped him home. On
the inside cover, Mr. Delchef had written the word for
hope. Bird intended to look up forbearance.

The family is reestablished. Bird, like a good Japanese, will buckle down and begin working.

The bus was streaming past coal-black beaches, craggy rocks where the surf smashed with spray. It was getting dark. Across the aisle, Daniel was telling Mrs. Hosoda about his wife's opera masks. Mrs. Watanabe was translating. Rain dripped down the glass.

"I don't know how I feel about this ending," I said to Susie. "It's obvious taking responsibility for his child is the only correct choice. But that choice is so laden here with other meanings. Is it really that simple? You have a child, you take care of it, you work hard and become like everyone else? I keep trying to think how Matsuo fits into all of this. Or Saito or Akiko."

"Akiko's different, she's divorced too, but she's raising her daughters, she's accepted her responsibilities. Matsuo hardly sees his daughter. Saito—well, Saito's a whole other matter."

"So is Matsuo just a remnant of the sixties who refused to grow up? That seems a pretty conservative conclusion. Maybe he needs that freedom to do what he has to do."

"But what has he actually done?"

"What about Daniel and his wife? They don't have children. If they did, they couldn't go traipsing around the world like they do. He'd have to give up his art."

"Is that what you think our having a child is going to do?"

"I don't know. It's as if this year is our last fling at being young. We're unfettered and free. We don't even have regular jobs. And I'm having a terrific time."

"So?"

"So why can't it go on like this?"

We'd arrived at the hotel, lit up like a great ship, wedged by the waves against the foot of a mountain. As we got off and entered the lobby, a photographer with a Polaroid snapped photos to sell to the guests. In the photo, I look rumpled and tired, exactly like someone who's been standing in the rain. Susie is crisp and smiling. The only other white face belongs to Daniel, towering above the Japanese housewives, their mouths curling upward in the word *Cheezu.*

We thought the purpose of the trip was to attend a series of tea ceremonies by certain masters of the sensei's school. Susie and Daniel had been going to class for several months. They had almost grown used to sitting for long periods of time on their knees, time when the circulation in their legs turned to numbness and needles, when to rise without collapsing again was a Herculean feat. They had learned the basic movements, how to use the whisk to brush the tea into a sea-green foam, how to hold the cups to the light, to turn them over and look for the signature of its maker, to clean the utensils, to wipe the lid of the tea box in eight prescribed motions. No movement was uncharted, no detail unplanned. The body, the mind, is controlled by the art. Susie found it at once restful and frustrating. There was so much to remember. To Daniel it was another dimension to add to his craft. They both were looking forward to seeing the ceremony done by the masters.

But just before dinner the first night at the hotel, we learned that the masters were not there and there would be no ceremonies. Was it because we were late? No. They had just been canceled, that was all anyone said. We never did find out why. Perhaps we had misunderstood the purpose of the trip. Miscommunications like that had happened to us before.

At dinner, no one seemed very disappointed. The women were all more excited by the activity at hand. In a huge tatami room, we were seated in two rows, one facing the other. Everyone wore yukata provided by the hotel. The food was served on tiny lacquer tables set before us. It was marvelous—sushi, sashimi, tempura— everything in abundance. The women poured each other sake and giggled.

"We don't usually drink," said Mrs. Watanabe, whose husband had gone back to Tokyo. "But Japanese women don't get to go out much. This is a very special occasion."

Susie whispered to me something about the sex trips the sarariman take to the Philippines, Thailand, Taiwan. I recalled the story of Jack, the American businessman we'd met at International House. On a trip he took with some Japanese businessmen to Taiwan, every member of the party had a woman beside him, pouring his drinks, laying out his food. After Jack retired for the night, the woman who'd been serving him showed up at his door. He said he wasn't hungry and sent her away. A few minutes later, one of the businessmen called. "You didn't like that girl?" he asked. "That's okay. We can send you another."

"Along with their shirts and socks, the Japanese wives pack condoms for their husbands when they go on these junkets," Jack had told us.

I looked around the room. The ladies were becoming quite boisterous, their faces reddened by sake. The sensei, a small woman with a salt-and-pepper bowl cut, stood up and clapped her hands, then made a speech. She said they were honored to have Daniel and Susie as guests. Everyone toasted them. Then the group sang a couple of songs, and two of the ladies near us tried to teach us the words. The sensei asked Daniel if he would perform for them. Everyone clapped. Daniel got up, bowed. The sensei giggled. He went to the front of the room, turned his back to us. A series of gestures, abstract, pointed. Without props, masks, or music, or the context of a complete piece, it was hard to make sense of his movements. That didn't matter. He had performed, the class was happy.

A few minutes later Susie tried to lead the group through "Yesterday," the Beatles song. It was a disaster, but again, it didn't matter. The women's hands flew up to their mouths, hiding their smiles. Their eyes were tiny, as if they were staring at the sun. Mrs. Watanabe asked Susie if we were going to have children. They would be so beautiful, she said. I felt embarrassed. The sensei came up and poured me more sake.

      The rest of the trip was a series of meals at various spots along the coast, roadside stops where wood carvings and porcelain were sold, where dried squid hung outside on racks. We went to a cove renowned for wild monkeys—well, by now they were pretty tame and eager for the food the tourists thrust out. We spent our last night at a hotel with a coed bath. The bath was on the roof beside a small rock garden. After our group dinner, under a sky punctuated with stars, Daniel and I sat in the vaguely sulphurous waters and got drunk on sake, still debating Butoh, politics, the need of artists to be their own agents. Behind us a shoji slid open. A couple stepped out, entered the bath. The husband asked Daniel where he was from, then nodded when I said I was a Sansei. They were from Sapporo, were on their honeymoon. The wife nursed herself into the far corner of the bath, kept avoiding our eyes. Her body was slim as a pike's, her breasts like a boy's. Daniel and I lifted ourselves up onto the pool ledge, letting our bodies cool. Steam slid from our skin in tiny rivulets. Later, Susie joined us. She said she'd tried to get some of the ladies to come with her, but they had all chickened out. They'd gotten tipsy, but not that tipsy.

      As I slipped into the bath once more, Daniel was talking about real estate in Paris. I felt my body dissolve in the heat. Who cares about real estate, I thought, I'm never going to move from here. Who cares about art. Who cares about tea. Who cares about politics. I'm having a Zen experience. I'm at one with this bath.

      The honeymoon couple left. Then Daniel. Susie and I leaned back and looked at the stars.

      A few nights after we returned to Tokyo, Susie and I spent a long session in the Shinjuku bar with Ken and Saito. Though we were drunk and tired when we got back to our apartment, I felt an urge to write. I started a poem about our honeymoon three years before and the sense of distance I felt between our room at a small inn on the island of Nantucket and the island of Japan:

> *Years away our grandchildren will come here*
> *saying,*

This room is where I began. *And returning to*
    Boston,
Paris, or Portland, they won't know how
    bewildered I was,

how alone. They'll think I felt American. I was
    always at home.

Grandchildren. God, I thought, am I getting ahead of myself?

A few days later, I sent a copy of this poem to my parents, along with a paper about my place as a Japanese-American writer (I was going to deliver the paper in June at the American Center in Kyoto). I hadn't written to my parents in a couple of months, and hadn't heard from them since. This wasn't unusual; our connections through most of my adult life had been intermittent, though with an increasing ease.

But the next week I received a letter from them. My father praised the poem, talked about showing the paper to a friend of his at work.

And then, near the end of the letter, was something I hadn't expected. After months of hesitating, of talk about the costs—protestations that I knew came from their dislike of the unfamiliar and foreign—my parents had finally decided: in a few weeks, they were coming to Japan.

V

"The nature of this sadness stands out more clearly if one asks with whom the adherents of historicism actually empathize. The answer is inevitable: with the victor."

—Walter Benjamin,
"Theses on History"

"The beauty of the Golden Temple was unsurpassed. And I knew now where my great weariness had come from."

—Yukio Mishima, *The Temple of the Golden Pavilion*

1

On sunny days, up and down the street, futons hung over the balconies, like tired, drunken bodies. Morning glories slithered up lattice fences, the sides of buildings. Women in kerchiefs swept the walks between the houses. Each day Susie and I would pass the corner shop, where in the darkness of an old wooden building a man in spectacles squatted and threaded straw for tatami mats. He wore a T-shirt, khaki pants; the shop seemed dusty, always in disarray. Sometimes he was pounding the mats into boards, sealing them at the ends, with strips of dark, silver-patterned cloth. The next shop was the candy store: gleaming white exterior, white shelves, glass counters, packages of chocolates lined up on display. Often when we visited someone we would stop at the shop for gifts. Almost any social occasion in Japan required a present, neat, hand-packaged, as a formal acknowledgment. Only our leftist friends seemed somewhat immune from these amenities, though I noticed when they came into contact with more traditional Japanese, these leftists always acted properly, bowed and spilled forth formalities as readily as anyone else.

Susie and I practiced sumie in the afternoons. The waterfalls, thrushes, gulls, bamboo, and camellias that appeared at a magical stroke surprised us, like children who have placed a coin in a machine and make the connection between the coin and the prize that arrives. Our sumie teacher was a tiny sparrow of a women, named Igawa. She had a bowl-cropped haircut and dark, leathery skin with freckles and age spots. Her movements were precise, abstract. The drawings seemed to flow from a source outside her body, as if she had plucked them from the air. She showed us pictures of her ballroom dancing. We towered over her, American giants, clumsy, prone to too many broad dark strokes. She lived alone, had never married, and seemed neither of the present nor of the past—lost in that generation old enough to remember the war, yet young enough to have gained the trappings of the West. She wore polyester suits and reminded me of my aunts. When she laughed at our drawings, the gold in her teeth seemed more profuse than the white. Like most Japanese, she cared nothing for politics. She shunned women her own age. They were too fussy, she said, too gossipy.

Susie was growing restless. The tea ceremony, sumie, her friendships with Takako, the woman doctor, were not enough. She felt her knowledge of medicine slipping day by day; at times how much she had forgotten frightened her. Matsuo bored her with his long political harangues. She liked Keiko, Matsuo's girlfriend, but Keiko seldom joined us on our barhopping. It was a man's country, a country that celebrated Boys' Day, where flags shaped and painted like carp float in the wind above houses, each proclaiming the bounty of sons in the house beneath. She was tired of being shouted at by schoolchildren, "Haro, haro," as if she were a clown in a circus. The clothes in the shops, especially the shoes, were always too small, too dark, too girlish. My leftist friends, though polite, really weren't interested in her. Some of the women talked feminism with her, but Akiko's pass at me the night of the reading had made Susie somewhat skeptical of their talk.

And then the rains of June came, the typhoon season. Every day endless streaks of gray drilled down from the sky. A note held, passing from monotone into a deeper, more permanent dirge. The air itself seemed to liquefy, like the insides of a giant invisible jellyfish. In the streets the patter grew into pools, then rushes and torrents. Umbrellas floated, black bobbing circles, close as the wings of bats in underground caves. In the empty lot across the street, the grass turned a deep, tropical green; then the earth itself seemed to bubble up in patches, foaming. In the country, square after square of rice field filled to the brim and overflowed. In the city, the city of labyrinths, the rain became another labyrinth, increased the density of inhabitants; everything seemed thicker, moving underwater.

It was time for Matsuo and me to go to Korea.

I called his house. No answer. Called again. No answer. In the morning, the evening, past midnight. Day after day. The rain continued to fall. Had he left without me? In the genkan our shoes began to curl, small spots of mold appeared. I called Keiko. She hadn't heard from Matsuo in a week, didn't know where he was. She gave me his work number. I called. Nothing. One morning, opening the closet to put our futon away, I noticed a pile of books. On the spine of Roland Barthes's *A Lover's Discourse* a huge splotch of white mold had clamped itself like a ghostly paw. I pulled the books from out of the darkness, each one sodden with mold. I brushed them off. The mold stayed.

Susie tried to calm me, said she knew Matsuo was unreliable. There was nothing I could do.

I felt betrayed. It was like when I was a kid in Chicago and the older kids had made fun of my clumsiness, and I was forced to sit in the darkness under the porch, alone, fallen from the circle. There was a riot in Korea; I read the news with envy. I called Matsuo. I felt like an American negotiator who thinks he has clinched a deal, only to discover the wily Japanese have outwitted him again. No handshake, no faith. The rain when I opened the door seemed to bar my way. My chest tightened as if a tourniquet had been pulled around my ribs. I could not breathe. Susie had gone to meet some friends in Kyoto, then to visit Korematsu, the doctor studying children in Hiroshima. I was alone, waiting to hear from Matsuo, knowing I would not. I felt drugged, slept all day. I debated whether or not to buy a plane ticket to Korea, to go on my own. What would I do there? I had no contacts. I sat down on the futon, fell asleep. Even then the rain did not stop. The smell of mildew seeped from the walls. I half expected long snakes of algae and lichen to start shimmying down from the ceiling. When I grabbed my clothes from the closet, they were damp, as if someone had been sweating inside them. I pulled them on and forced myself out the door. Snapped open the umbrella. It was hopeless. I was completely soaked.

By the time Susie returned, my skin was boiling; small creatures were eating away inside me, my blood seemed cut with acid. I slept, then woke for seconds, minutes, during which my muscles realized they had been pummeled in my sleep. The shoji opened, Susie's shadow appeared; the shoji closed behind her. When she touched me, my body was trembling like the throat of a lizard. The room was dark, hot as a bathhouse, the sheets soaked, the covers never heavy enough. I slept ten, seventeen, twenty-four hours, and the aspirin overload brought a ringing to my ears, a permanent siren. I kept asking for more. When the phone rang, I crawled to the edge of the tatami, fell back, let it ring. I missed the performance of the Suzuki group, various lessons. Korea crept through my consciousness like a cold front, a high-pressure point that would never leave. As chills rippled, erupted from my body, Susie placed the damp cloth to my forehead and kissed the wetness it had left. I recited quotations for jokes: "I am dying, Egypt." And: "His last words to mother were 'I feel awful.' " It was the Asian flu, she said. Yes, I thought, this is what Asia must feel like. Ancient, crumbling. I could not tell if the rain had stopped. I saw my father coming down the stairs; his face was puffy, his eyes thin slits, his glasses gone. His body was the body of my childhood, a bit soft, running to fat. Not the lean, muscled tightness of his later years. He was wearing as always a T-shirt. He was angry. Just as I raised my hand to defend myself, I knew he was the tatami maker, the man down the block. I heard myself whimper, kicked off the covers. My head ached, had turned viscous; my arms were heavy, numb; my eyes filled with shadows, a dark-blue light. "Matsuo hasn't called," Susie was saying. "I'll be back later." I turned to look at her. It was hours later. There was only a voice. "This rain is never going to stop."

It's difficult to say what happened to Matsuo. The train down to the tip of Honshu must have been routine, he'd traveled it often before. In Tokyo, he'd look out on the lights of the station, the buildings down the tracks; sarariman would tumble on the train, their faces already reddened by drink, their eyes slitted, bloodshot. Almost immediately he'd fall asleep, and through the night, along the great Kando plain, through the mountains, past Osaka, Kyoto, the middle-sized cities like Fukushima, then Hiroshima, the train would roar at over two hundred kilometers an hour. Just before dawn, the population would be getting thinner, the space emptier, the terrain flattening just a bit. Then he'd transfer to a smaller, slower train with many local stops across the southern tip of the island. Old obaa-san in kimonos boarded, their umbrellas resting beside them, a *furoshiki* tied around a package in their laps; school-children in blue uniforms rode briefly to the next stop, sleepy, giggling, clutching a manga comic book before them. The boys looked like little soldiers, the girls like Catholic schoolgirls. Rain shot in through one of the windows; Matsuo rose to close it.

As he boarded the ferry the next morning, it was probably still raining; the sky was gray, the sea dull and uneven like ham-mered lead. He'd have on jeans, a dark-blue windbreaker, his Puma cap. On the bow, leaning on the rail, he'd cup his hands and light a cigarette. His mouth would taste stale from the bad sleep. Around him would be a few Japanese-Koreans, a few Koreans returning home, some businessmen. In his pack would be his cam-era, rolls of film. Perhaps no one in Japan knew where he was going. Certainly not Keiko. He would have looked around at the passengers, checking again to see if he was being followed. He would try to imagine what the next few weeks would be like, remembering his last visit to Seoul, cab rides past the glimmering downtown buildings, meetings in small dim rooms penetrated by the cold, steam rising from the teacups, the mouths of the speakers, a walk through the market, a courtroom, the speech of Kim Chi Ha, which one of the students translated in whispers. He would feel the Sea of Japan moving beneath him, his stomach growling. A gull swooped down across the waves, came up with something silver flickering in its mouth. He took off his glasses, wiped away the salt spray.

One can imagine anonymous journeys like this by men and women all through this century and even before. Journeys by people with a mission, something clandestine and political, people who depended on remaining anonymous, who were anonymous, who soon would no longer be anonymous. Think of a train ride taken by Lenin or Trotsky or Rosa Luxemburg across Europe, a boat ride taken by Ho Chi Minh or Mao returning from Paris, across the Indian Ocean, still several hundred miles from their

destination. They were obscure fanatics, terrorists, flies on the walls
of rooms where history is made. Matsuo's journey would probably
not end like theirs. And yet it shared something of the same qualities of boredom and uncertainty, the will to keep on in a direction
which, according to most calculations, made no sense. This kinship
with them keeps him mysterious to me. It is part of what made me
want to accompany him, no matter how much I found fault with
him, how much I disagreed.

2

Early in the morning, the sunlight was blinding, the heat beginning
to seep up from the Tokyo streets. The long, slow simmer of
summer. On the trains, sweat poured down our necks; the shirts of
the sarariman were drenched, stuck to the spaces between their
clavicles. One by one they took out their handkerchiefs, wiped their
brows, their cheeks, their necks, as if their flesh and not the heat
were to blame. Still, all the men wore ties, carried their coats on
their arms; the women wore dresses. Casualness seemed uncon-
scionable. Shorts, a T-shirt, chinos never existed. A formal people.

The air at evening was like that in a boiler, and the dark
made the sky seem closer, heavier. The crowds still poured out of
the stations. The great square at Shibuya was still flooded with
people craning their necks, looking for their friends, fellow students, a lover. Suddenly, in the entrance to the shopping mall, a
chubby man in shirtsleeves collapsed. People stood around,
amazed, as if an angel had dropped from the sky. People moved on
as if nothing had happened. The emergency workers came, their
siren a slow drone, inching through the traffic.

We went on to the bars, to dinner in *yakitoriya,* in Indian
restaurants, to a movie. One night, after dinner with Ken, Setsuko,
and Akiko, we went to a Pachinko parlor. The boards were lit like
circuses; on twenty stools in a row, the men and a few women stared

at the bouncing steel balls, their eyes flicking up and down, their hand at the controls. The incessant clicking of the tiny balls was multiplied to the level of pistons firing.

"It used to be that you pulled a lever to send the ball up, like in pinball," Ken said. "Now there's an electronic switch that you control. It's less erratic and perhaps less a game of skill. But that doesn't seem to matter." If the ball landed in the right slot, you won more little balls, and if you won enough balls, you'd get a prize, usually cigarettes. Outside the parlor, you could trade the cigarettes for money. Neither Susie nor I could see the point of the game. It was too monotonous, there was only one move, like sumo, which ended in one quick fall. Susie, though, had a more exact touch. I wandered over to where Akiko was playing.

"Before women did not play Pachinko," she said, and dropped her cigarette to the floor and stubbed it out. Her eyes never moved from the board. She was beginning one of her harangues. Susie and I were like a pressure valve for her; we'd never cut her off, never argue.

"Sometimes you seem so bitter," I said. "Do you ever think about leaving Japan? Of going to America?"

"It's too late for me. I am too Japanese. And I have my daughters. What would I do somewhere else? Even here, they complain they don't have enough clothes, we don't have a car. They are so materialistic. They are nothing like me."

"So what do you do?"

"It cannot be helped. They are like their friends, like all young people now. I despise the way they think." She took her hand from the board, lit a cigarette, took a long drag.

I wondered if she was too scared to think of changing, though I knew what her answer would be: "You don't understand what it's like to be Japanese." Still, perhaps because of the pass she'd made that night in the bar, I felt freer to be more direct.

"Well, if things can't be helped, what good is your anger, then? You despise so many things"—did she realize the connotations of the word?—"and it's not making you any happier, and . . ."

"You don't understand . . ."

"Maybe I don't. But your anger seems to be eating you

up. What about Ouchi Sachi? That poet who got drunk at the reading. I know you told me I didn't understand her either. But still, that's hardly . . ."

"Yeah, yeah, yeah," she said, her hand with the cigarette brushing the air beside her.

It was nearing time for the last train. Ken had won some cigarettes, so had Akiko. We emerged into the neon-lit mall that flows to the Shibuya station. Young boys tottered down the mall. Their faces were red, their eyes clenched by drink, by uproarious laughter. Young women in crisp cotton dresses and heels pulled their bodies away from them, giggled, frowned, kept walking ahead. I suddenly felt much older, undignified, bewildered, as if I should have been spending my time more seriously than playing Pachinko. I wondered if Akiko had understood anything I'd been saying.

By the time we were on the platform waiting for the train, the feeling had passed. All I wanted was to get home and soak in the bath. On the train home, I told Susie about my conversation with Akiko.

"She's such a mass of contradictions," Susie said. "It's not just the pass she made at you, she was, as they say, *yoparatta.* Like that night at Haruki's, that time he said he was jealous of you. Still, here's this avowed feminist who talks about dismantling the roles of mother and grandmother, and she divorced her husband because she didn't love him and didn't want to serve him, and yet every night she goes over to her father's house and makes him dinner. This traditional Japanese gentleman, who sits there wearing a kimono, waiting for his daughter to serve him."

"And when you confront her about things, all she says is, 'You don't understand what it's like to be Japanese.'"

"Maybe we don't. But I don't think they understand what it means to be an American either."

"In a way, I was trying to tell her about the serenity prayer, about deciding what you can and cannot change. I don't know why I keep talking about these things to her. It just doesn't seem to register. There's just not a corresponding slot in the Japanese mind for these concepts."

"Jaa, sho ga nai."

"So desu ne," I agreed, and leaned my head on Susie's shoulder. *"Tsukaretta desu yo."*

"Watashi mo," she said, slumping into me. *"Watashi mo."*

A few nights later, in the theater of a suburban department store, Daniel gave a performance. We were almost late, since we lost our way in the huge shopping mall where the store was located. It seemed an odd place to have a theater, Susie remarked on the escalator, as we passed the china department. But then that was Japan.

At the beginning of the piece, Daniel came out in a mask with two faces that covered his head like a hood. Wielding a long pole, he changed his movements with each turn of the mask. The masks were cruel, empty, the gray of death masks. The music was electronic, sparse, with hints of dissonance. The mask came off. He twirled two chairs in front of him. A drama, a courtship, anger, reconciliation, the course of a love affair through the tiltings and rockings of furniture. The performance moved like a dance, like a book unfolding, a series of fairy tales.

The audience was young, dressed in dark colors and jeans. They applauded loudly. In the lobby afterward, Okinaka, our Noh sensei, told Daniel he had unfolded a new sort of language from his limbs. "You are in very good shape," he added, "you have sharpened your skills." A young man with a beard came up and, in halting English, asked Daniel about Decroux, about studying perhaps with Daniel in Paris. Mrs. Hayashi, who was also Daniel's language teacher, came up with her daughter, Michiko.

"Joozu desu ne," Mrs. Hayashi said.

Michiko wore glasses and was smaller than her mother. In a gray skirt and a white blouse with a Peter Pan collar, she seemed overpowered by her mother's teacherly manner, her lacquered coiffure and bright-red wool suit. Daniel asked Michiko in English where she was going to study. Her face froze. Her mother leaned forward, laughed nervously.

"She's going to study international law at Todai University," she said proudly. "Speak English," she instructed.

Susie started complimenting Daniel, filling in the gap. I tried to think of something to say in Japanese. Michiko continued looking down, said nothing, and did not smile. Her muteness began to disturb me. Her mother had told us about how bright her daughter was, how studious, how serious, how unlike the frivolous young of Roppongi or Harajuku.

Susie talked about a reading I was giving in Kyoto the next week, and Mrs. Hayashi began listing all the things we should see there. Michiko drifted to the edge of our circle. Just as we all began to leave, she looked up. Her eyes were small, her nose and mouth delicate, tiny. I felt if I reached out to touch her face, it would cave in like papier-mâché.

3

In Kyoto, the attaché at the consulate, Zimmer, came to meet me at the train, but missed me in the crowds. I was wearing a suit and looked like any other sarariman. He'd expected something scruffier, angrier, some *enfant terrible* in denim or beachwear. The last poet, a Pulitzer Prize winner, had refused to read when the time was changed by half an hour. She hated her hotel, Japanese food, the lighting in the auditorium, the mike. She sat in the corner smoking furiously, her fingertips yellowed, her face pulled back tight, unyielding, steeling itself against wrinkles. She talked to no one. In contrast, I had no demands, was calm, unfocused, looked younger than the others. My credentials were small, somewhere in the future.

The carpeted auditorium at the American Center held an audience of expatriates and Japanese who were interested in American literature. I wondered if any of the older expatriates were missionaries. One older woman, with white hair and skin like rice paper, wore a peach pillbox hat and white gloves. Her husband was tall and balding, and sported a rumpled seersucker suit that seemed too large for his body. He brushed the sweat from his shining red pate with a handkerchief. I felt nervous, I didn't know what to expect. Susie winked at me and smiled. Sitting beside her, Zimmer kept craning his neck around to look at the crowd. Finally, he got up and introduced the translator, Nakayama Yo, and then introduced me, trying to make me sound as impressive as possible. It was not very convincing.

Before I read, I talked about being a Japanese-American writer. One advantage of my position, I said, was that I could not pretend that literature has nothing to do with politics, or economics, or that literature is not intimately connected with power and, as Walter Benjamin points out, with acts of barbarism. Quoting Frantz Fanon, I spoke of how black children in the Antilles read books which praised "our ancestors, the Gauls," and learned to identify with the white explorers who conquered the dark savages of Africa. Fanon knew the source of psychic sickness might lie not always solely in the individual or that individual's family but in the greater sickness of a society, in the relationships and ideas that society has produced. He also taught me the liberating power of anger.

I looked at the woman with the pillbox hat. Her face seemed dour as a Puritan deacon's.

I ended by explaining my changed sense of the tradition:

Finally, I come to this year, this time I have spent in Japan, and the healing that has taken place here. What I write in the future will almost certainly carry an even greater sense of Asia as a continent; I want to delve even deeper into the problems of crossing cultures, and to find more and more inspiration from Japanese sources, from the theories and plays of Zeami to the novels of Mishima, Enchi, and Sei Shonogan, to encounters I've had with the culture and people here. In doing this, I find myself feeling a sense of rightness, a claim to a body of material that other white writers do not have. A compensation arrives, and if I feel other American writers come to European or English culture before me, I come to Japanese culture before them, and not just because of the color of my skin, but because of the traces of the culture that were handed down to me

from my parents, despite their efforts and mine, to deny
it; such traces have made me feel here a sense of ease
that has surprised and gladdened me. If my poems and
personality seem a bit distant, a bit quiet, a bit imper-
sonal to other Americans, it is that distance, that
quietness, that impersonality that gives me an intuitive
feel and pleasure in Japanese culture that white Amer-
icans sometimes lack.

I looked up from the page, and felt that what I'd said was somehow false and wrapped things up much too neatly.

Nakayama asked if there were any questions.

The woman with the pillbox hat raised her hand. "Why are you so angry? Don't you feel American?"

I tried to explain how, in Japan, I had come to understand how left out of American culture I felt, how there was a certain comfort I found in Japan that I had not experienced in the States.

"But you grew up in America. Do your parents feel the way you do?"

It was hopeless. As I went over the history of the camps, of my parents' sense of identity, I suddenly recalled the scene in *Annie Hall* where Woody Allen is listening to a pompous professor in a movie line theorizing on Marshall McLuhan. From behind a billboard, Allen brings out McLuhan, who proceeds to dismiss the professor. I could see this woman bringing out my father, who would look at me and say, "My son knows nothing about Japanese-Americans. How he got to lecture on anything is beyond me."

The reading afterward wasn't a disaster, but it wasn't a command performance either. Most of my poems seemed too racially charged and political for the expatriates, too filled with an anger the Japanese did not feel. Perhaps they would have preferred the Pulitzer Prize winner's poems about nature. Or a mime like Daniel, who seemed to win praise wherever he performed. I felt I had let Zimmer down.

A few hours later, I stopped writing in my journal and looked out the hotel window. The far mountains held the haze of evening, and the grids of Kyoto spread out on the plain below in orderly fashion, unlike the labyrinthine streets of Tokyo. There was no large center of skyscrapers, no huge highways running through the city. The boulevards were wide, the traffic flowing and even.

The ancient capital of Japan, Kyoto had been spared by American bombers because of the temples and treasures it held. In contrast to the neon and chaos, the crowds and the up-to-this-second fashions of Tokyo, Kyoto is the quiet city, the city of the "Philosophers' Walk," tied more to the culture of the past than any other city in a nation which has embraced newness, achieving economic miracle after economic miracle, technological innovation after innovation, sweeping away the past like the rubble and ash heaps left by the B-52s. A perfect place, it would seem, for a tourist jaunt, a respite from Tokyo life. And yet, perhaps because Kyoto lacks many of the modern touches that make Tokyo seem like a wacky, Japanese *Doppelgänger* to New York, I didn't warm to it as I had expected to.

The hotel didn't help. I plopped myself down on the Western-style bed, feeling as if it were still a bit foreign. The room was the Japanese version of a Holiday Inn double: twin beds, a lamp in the middle, a bureau. Susie was soaking in the bath. I turned on the lamp. It was dim, reflecting what I thought of as Japanese frugality. I started writing again. The talk and reading that afternoon at the center had made me wonder who my real audience was, or if that audience even existed. And what *was* I writing about? My poems, the woman in the pillbox hat, Kyoto, my father, my mother, my grandparents, all the traces and rubble of history . . .

What is it to write a "history" of a people? Is it to gather up individual stories and fit them together into a logical, coherent structural whole? But what if the stories are all lost, if those who tell them have been silenced? And no one actually lives a story; a story is a sequence of events which can be arranged as a romance, a tragedy, a comedy, depending upon the viewpoint of the teller, who is constricted and guided by a number of biases.

Is the story of the Japanese-Americans a comedy? A triumph? Does the reconciliation of the Nisei with America represent a romance? Or is it a tragedy, followed by a satire, where each identity is tinged with irony, the false fit? . . .

Susie came out wrapped in a towel, her hair dripping.

"Shall we christen these decadent beds from the West?"
I asked.

She smiled. "They are ugly, aren't they?"

She sat down beside me and, as she kissed me, reached to
the stand to turn out the lamp. I leaned back, beneath her weight,
felt my journal at my shoulder blades.

"Wait a second."

I tossed it on the floor. The last light shimmered through
the window, pale as a moth's wing. I could hear the soft whoosh
of the traffic below. Just before my mind began to go blank, I
decided, at least at that moment, it was going to be a comedy. To
hell with irony. To hell with history. This was enough.

That night, in Gion, we watched the geisha stepping into
taxis, their painted faces standing out starkly in the neon lights,
apparitions of another lost world. Of course, it is endlessly pointed
out to tourists that the geisha are not prostitutes. Wrapped around
their bodies, their kimonos flowed with colors, as if the silk were
pouring from inside them. They seemed sexless, almost robotlike.
On clogs with two flat boards raising the sole, they moved in tiny,
mincing steps. In Mishima's *The Temple of the Golden Pavilion,* a
monk has an affair with a geisha, and I suddenly remembered that
the dirtiest sex shows are always placed near the temples; it is an
old tradition. Susie told me about an American woman who had
become a geisha and wrote a book about it. For some reason I was
annoyed at this. It seemed another Western fetish for the mysterious East. Perhaps I was still upset by the response at the American
Center. Or perhaps it was the way people talked about Kyoto. What
did it mean when they said, "This, this Kyoto, is the true Japan;
forget about Tokyo"? As we passed the clerks, repeating *"Irasshaimase"*—welcome—amid geisha postcards, geisha wooden dolls,
geisha scarves, geisha prints, geisha combs and purses, I felt the city
clinging to an aristocratic past that no longer existed. It all seemed
leaden, a museum culture.

Soon we came to the Gion Corner, where in an hour one
may see Bunraku, *Kyomai, Gagaku,* a tea ceremony, koto music,
ikebana, and *kyogen,* instant Japanese culture, the tourist's exotic,

quaint, Madame Butterfly Japan. That was too much. We decided on the Kamagawa Odori, where the performance is less of a TV-dinner version of Japanese culture. Unlike in the "official" Kabuki in Tokyo, the performers were women. This seemed like a small triumph, especially since they appeared quite skilled. Still, I felt put off at the institution of the geisha and the screen of beauty. "Since its first performance in 1872, the Kamogawa Odori has won popularity both in Japan as well as abroab [*sic*], and has earned great admiration of such celebrities as Jean Cocteau and Charlie Chaplin," said the flyer. The audience was mainly middle-aged Japanese, many of them probably tourists, most of them women. A few had cameras, the straps looped around their necks like bridles. Here and there was a Caucasian face, rare and unsettling as an albino. And yet, I thought, whom are you sitting with?

After the performance we walked along the concrete banks of the river. The current was slow, almost motionless. The paper lanterns just outside the theater glowed like jellyfish in the dark waters.

"You know I've got to be going back soon," Susie said.

"Why?" Despite my blank response, I suppose I knew this was coming.

"My program starts up again in July. You've known that for months."

"But do you really have to go? I'm going back in September, that's just two months."

We passed a small *ramen* noodle stand; the owner was cranking down the awning, closing up for the night. A pair of young girls passed us. One of them giggled, cupped her hands to her mouth.

"Do you think my work's not important? You're so infuriating."

"No, of course not. But the residency's been so hard on you, why wouldn't you want to take a vacation?"

"I have. But I'm ready to go back to work now. I miss it. Just going to Takako's clinic once in a while is hardly enough. You've been able to do your work here. I can't."

"Back at home, we always do things according to your schedule. But when things are changed . . ."

"You know that's not the issue."

"All this year you've been resentful of my work. I had to fight at the beginning to get time to write."

I looked down the river. Beyond the city, the mountains were black bulks just visible, like the hulls of huge ghostly ships. Moths fluttered above us, battering the streetlight.

"Look, I've had a great time this year. And I'm grateful to you."

"That's not my point."

"Listen to me. Jesus, sometimes you're so impossible."

"I'm impossible?"

"I've got to go back. It's my work. Besides, we've still got a month left."

"I know. It seems as if we've been here forever, and yet as if we've just arrived."

We took a cab back to our hotel and, on the way, decided to check into a *minshuku* the next day. Susie talked about whether or not she was going to take on a specialty after her residency and what that might be. Maybe cancer, she said. She spoke of Korematsu and his work in Hiroshima, the medical center there, Reiko's breast cancer, the freedom of being away from the States. She felt older now, more rooted in her body, her life, her career. She knew she needed to practice medicine, that she had to get back.

I didn't say how I felt. It was her time to speak.

As we walked the streets of the city the next day, the sunlight seemed everywhere, glaring with brightness. Shadows were absent, we were no longer in the canyons of Tokyo. When we entered the museum, its indoor dark, I almost put my hands in front of me, groping my way. Footsteps echoed from the cement floors. The air was damp, cool. Hall after hall of treasures presented themselves—the lavender paper with flecks of gold on which the Kokin Waka-shuu poetic anthology was written in the early twelfth century; the famous painting by Korin, flowering plants of summer and autumn, done during the Edo period: luminous green reeds, hiding a few pink buds, and larger, brighter white bells, while above them, set in the flat expanse of silver, a wavy blue stream wandered, etched with swirls, flowing in abstract pattern. We passed the formal wear for a lady of the fourteenth century, white pants flowering with chrysanthemum crests, small grass shoots and lilies by a stream; and the Genji *emaki:* painted images unfurling through the centuries, the world's first novel, a diary of elegance and lust, intrigue and wit; a woman's insight and dreams on pale-gold panels, some fading, some retaining their aristocratic sheen.

Later, at a nearby temple, walking in silence before the immense bulkiness of a brass Buddha, cast in shadows by the heavy, overhanging roof, the drift of incense, I felt like a barbarian, an intruder amid such immeasurable beauty. It was too much. It made me feel silly.

Suddenly I understood something of the young monk who, in 1950, burned down the priceless and immortal Golden Temple, a national shrine, whose present-day replacement is described in the guide pamphlet as "rebuilt"—no mention of the arson, the unbeautiful deed. The monk was diagnosed by psychologists as a psychopath. He had intended to commit suicide, but did not have the courage. At his trial, he admitted it all, asked for whatever punishment he might deserve. Mishima fictionalized him a few years after in *The Temple of the Golden Pavilion.* Where is that monk now, I wondered.

But perhaps it was merely the clichés of tourism that I disliked, the feeling of seeing what everyone has seen before. Every object of art, every shrine and temple, every famous vista told me my experience, and thus my self, was not unique. How I hated being made one of the crowd. How I hated sitting on the wooden steps before the garden of Ryoanji, with a view of its precisely placed islands of stones, its sand etched by the rake's teeth into furrows of silence, the stroke of a master's brush, the endless abstraction of waves. Though the garden was as I'd seen in pictures, I hadn't anticipated the hundreds of schoolchildren marching behind me, giggling, pushing each other, or the lecturer in his tacky yellow blazer trying to shout his lecture over their mumblings, inculcating certain chunks of canned culture but trampling over whatever Zen meditation and emptiness the garden might have provided. Even for Americans this garden is not new; thirty years before, the poet Gary Snyder, one of the first white West Coast Buddhists, came here to study.

And then, beside the schoolchildren, there were the bloated American tourists, in nylons and jeans, snapping pictures. They reminded me of the America I wanted to leave behind, even the Nisei and Sansei. I winced at the nasal tone of their voices, the calls of "Herb, come here, look at this," the loud laughter, and the cornball jokes: "Well, I just sat on my brain and a great idea came out." I remained silent, provided no hint that I understood their words, and pretended I was Japanese.

We returned to the minshuku, with its slate roof and wooden beams, with the tiny garden scrunched into the back, with its *tsukubai* (small stone fountain), its stones and gravel, its small twisting bamboo. Here was another beauty, something simpler, less elegant, less refined. As I read Tanizaki on the futon, the beauty was lessened by the glare of the neon light:

> *A Japanese room might be likened to an inkwash painting, the paper-paneled* shoji *being the expanse where the ink is thinnest, and the alcove where it is darkest. Whenever I see the alcove of a tastefully built Japanese room, I marvel at our comprehension of the secrets of shadows, our sensitive use of shadow and light. For the beauty of the alcove is not the work of some clever device. An empty space is marked off with plain wood and plain walls, so that the light drawn into it forms dim shadows within emptiness. There is nothing more. And yet, when we gaze into the darkness that gathers behind the crossbeam, around the flower vase, beneath the shelves, though we know perfectly well it is mere shadow, we are overcome with the feelings that in this small corner of the atmosphere there reigns complete and utter silence; that here in the darkness immutable tranquility holds sway.*

I looked around the room: in one alcove, on a scroll, a watercolored carp arched its back, its blue scales curved so quietly that the arching possessed no strain, was immersed in stillness; beneath the scroll was a thin emerald-green vase, with a single white camellia. In the next alcove, shelves, a small shrine, a brass cup for incense, and yes, the delicacy of shadows, the softness of the paper shoji. Suddenly I felt this magical overlapping between the setting and the gauze-like transparency of Tanizaki's signifiers, as if, in the silence, his spirit had entered the room.

But then Tanizaki moved to the beauties of shadows on the gold panels of the castles, an effect I'd seen that day wandering again through the corridors of Nijo Castle—tigers leaping out of the dark gold, or the huge, twisting cypresses, or the wide, pure panels of gold leaf, in front of which life-size models of the shogun and his vassals, the ladies of the court, bow and cavort. Both Tanizaki's words and the objects themselves began to rankle me. They seemed like a lie. Not a direct lie, but a lie of omission. I felt distracted, impatient, pledged to a moral impulse that seemed extraneous to the pleasures of a tourist. The very intensity of my response reminded me how part of the purpose of beauty is always to make both the poor and any revolution they attempt appear to be crude and in bad taste, to be a breach of manners. There is simply no way, when power has acquired the trappings of beauty, to avoid the spiritual wonder and humility such beauty provides. Any opposition somehow acquires a stridency, leaves itself open to charges that the world it seeks to destroy will always be more uplifting, more miraculous, than whatever replaces it, whatever you propose. The better choice, the wiser choice, is to remain allied with the beauty, to support what it upholds, since they cannot be separated.

But was that what I so disliked about the geisha? In the woodblock prints by Utamaro, in the indolent postures, the deep-dyed colors, in the picture book or teacup on a tray held delicately in the geisha's hands, in the combs piercing the elaborate chignons, the pure black strokes of abstraction, so abundantly thick; in the flat perspective that turns the faces into part of the design, melding with the patterns of maple leafs or chrysanthemums on the kimonos, yes, in these masterful prints I could see a beauty which impelled me, which I wanted to keep.

Yet when the geisha walked down the street of wooden houses into the bright neon of Gion, and stood at the stoplight, starkly white, they seemed to be elaborate fakes, a guise for misogyny, and the trappings of culture that surrounded them merely a cover for their abasement by men. It was the use of sophistication, the elaborateness of the lie, that bothered me. That, and the attraction such a lie held for Westerners.

No, I'd made the right decision to live in Tokyo. Or did my reaction to Kyoto mean I was finally getting tired of Japan, that I was ready to go home? Very quickly, I tried to bury that thought.

4

Near the end of any stay in a foreign country, there arrives a point where friendships don't seem worth the effort, where the attractions you feel for people can't outweigh the lack of time, and you see them as if across some fenced border that neither of you may cross. At the same time, perhaps even earlier, you begin to reevaluate your friendships. At the beginning you were delighted simply to be talking to people, exchanging certain set commonplaces about each other's culture, breaching the barriers set up by language and history. Everything seems then like entering a magical kingdom, and it is magic, isn't it, meeting these people you feel in some way you have no right to meet, that you meet against odds that seem impossible? But then you begin to tire of the routine of newness; faces and facts blur together, like a text you memorized long ago, the color of paint on your door, the smell of a season that has passed its summit. Harder questions rise up. What kinship is there here? Who is this person really? Will I be friends with this person after I leave? Could I be friends with this person in the States? When I began to see how many friendships failed these questions, I was startled. Near the end of my stay, there were friends I hadn't called in weeks.

Nakayama Yo was the last Japanese friend I made. An English professor at a women's college, he had translated all of Studs Terkel's works. Nakayama's speciality was Japanese-American writing, John Okada's *No-No Boy,* Toshio Mori's *Yokohama, California,* poems from an anthology of Asian-American poets, *Breaking Silence,* including some of mine. Like many Japanese, he smoked incessantly, rapping the cigarettes against the counter or table. He had the small body common among the prewar Japanese. His teeth were yellow, his hair salt-and-pepper. His Adam's apple bobbed up and down as talked. His English was fluent, slow; here and there in the pauses he placed a *"da kedo"*—yes, but—one of those meaningless Japanese qualifiers, signifying nothing, softening everything, backing away from the thrusting American assertion.

He was fifty-three and had first been to America twenty-five years ago. Unlike some older Japanese men, he had few pretensions, wasn't impressed with himself simply because he had passed fifty.

Nakayama was more interested in Japanese-American literature than I was, more than anyone I've ever met, in fact. Despite my experience in Kyoto, I had met a few other Japanese with this interest, and this both pleased and saddened me. They were my best audience, but they lived halfway around the world, were not my compatriots. Would my displacement continue even into my readership?

After we had met briefly in Kyoto, Nakayama came down to Tokyo a few times. We'd meet in coffee shops for long talks about literature, about Japanese-Americans. He was nearly my father's age. He was the older brother I had never had, the one who left home before I grew up, who had studied, lived his life abroad. We were casual, distant. He told me about his first trip to America on a fellowship. I pictured him as even thinner then, hunching down with the others to listen to the wireless on the ship. To ease the boredom, they had placed bets on horse races; the results came through the static, angry, faint. He didn't lose much, but the yen was so weak then that when he arrived in America he discovered he could barely live on what he had left. The hotels were immense, gleaming, forbidding. Their lobbies were like highways. He managed a small room in an abandoned warehouse. Rats scurried through the walls at night. There was a leak from the roof. He went up there mornings and read, looking out on the hills of San Francisco. The Golden Gate rose up through the fog, the mountains in the distance. In his hands was a copy of *Howl, A Coney Island of the Mind,* or *On the Road.* He understood little of it. He saved his money, went one night to a jazz club. Without knowing it, he had arrived at the start of an era; unknown masterpieces were being pulled from the air. He felt lonely, afraid. On the bus one morning, he was reading Mishima's new novel. A Nisei sat down next to him, looked at the kanji, got up, and left. It was as if his foreignness were a virus, something you could catch. The hakujin, the whites, were more friendly. People were discovering Japan and Zen. Gary Snyder went to Kyoto and returned. Ginsberg, Rexroth, Ferlinghetti read in bookstores and coffeehouses. Nakayama would meet them all. It would be several years, a second trip, before he discovered Okada's *No-No Boy,* before the Nisei began to talk to him. By then the war had faded far back enough in memory; their place was safe.

Listening to Nakayama, I glimpsed what it must have been like for my grandparents to sail to America a half century before him. The things he found strange they would have found strange too: the size of the people, the buildings, the food, the space. The fields of white faces in the stores, on the streets, ghostlike in the clear California sun. The impatience of shop clerks, the alternating sense of being invisible, of standing out. I was a third of the way into my novel, could see its shape gathering. The faces of my grandparents seemed to pop into my head as he talked. I returned from the coffeehouse with my mind on fire. I wrote through the night. The next day. The pages piled up.

And what was I to him? He had married late, his children were young. Perhaps I was the older son he should have had. He preferred the work of the Nisei over the Sansei. "The Nisei have struggled to become part of America," he said. "Their work may be less sophisticated, less skilled. *Da kedo.* They seem to have more emotional content." He found my poem on a hibakusha startling. "No Japanese would have written that." I thought he meant it was false. "No, we are still too inhibited. *Da kedo.* You show us something of ourselves we can't express."

One day in early June, Nakayama and I met in the Renoir

in Shinjuku. The coffeehouse was huge, with several levels; the walls were white, the decor stark and metallic, all Bauhaus without a hint of Japanese. In the booths, the young patrons smoked, talked, and read. The coffee before them was thick and strong. A young waitress in fishnet stockings took our orders. The scones in the Renoir were served hot, with whipped cream and preserves, and were better than those I had had at high tea at the Pavilion Hotel in Hong Kong.

Nakayama lit his cigarette and announced that he had a request. He wanted me to give him some poems and a prose piece based on my talk in Kyoto for his magazine, *The Kyoto Review.* I was flattered. The magazine had published work by Snyder, Rexroth, and Corso, not necessarily my favorite writers, but writers whom I'd known about since college, who were among the first poets I had read. And Nakayama's request meant my performance in Kyoto wasn't as bad as I'd thought, or at least he hadn't thought so.

I told him I wanted to concentrate on the dilemma of the Sansei. I understood his point that the Nisei had had to fight to figure out who they were, that the Sansei seemed more at ease and perhaps more complacent. I had never had to sign or refuse to sign a loyalty oath, had never been in a relocation camp. My questions about identity were less urgent. Still, the very fact that they were less immediate and more abstract made them in some ways more difficult to grasp, much less answer.

He nodded, took a sip of coffee. Had I read John Okada's *No-No Boy?* he asked.

No, I answered, and felt embarrassed, called on the carpet, though I knew this was not his purpose.

Read him, he instructed. He told me the story of how Okada's book about a Nisei who had refused to sign the loyalty oath was rejected not just by the general public but by Japanese-Americans. The main character, Ichiro, expressed too much doubt about his identity as an American, was too bitter. It was not an image an organization like the Japanese American Citizens League wanted to spread.

A few months after Okada died, some young Asian-American writers came to visit his widow and asked if he had written any other works. She told them that in a fit of grief she'd burned his second novel in the back yard. She hadn't thought anyone was interested.

"There are passages in *No-No Boy* that have so much passion," said Nakayama. "There's no Sansei who writes like that."

I didn't say what I was thinking. I knew that much of the way I looked at the earlier Asian-American writers was colored by the prejudices of my grad school training and by my own need to stake some ground. Instead, I asked him about Japanese writers.

He preferred writers like Tanizaki over the present ones. "It used to be that writers built up a life's work, book after book. Now the young authors just write pages. They're more concerned about sales than a life's work." A favorite pejorative of the young today was *kurai,* or dark. It was used to label anything serious. Nakayama said that when he came back from America, it was the time of the student political movements and riots; students spent hours in the coffee shops, reading and arguing politics, philosophy, literature; listening to jazz, Mozart, and rock and roll.

"Da kedo. Now the young people just shop and go to restaurants."

"Yes," I said. "I have the feeling that Mishima killed himself just at the time when it was no longer possible for Japanese culture to produce and include a figure like Mishima. His seriousness was like that of the student radicals. Even he saw that they were alike. Now he's dead, and the radicals are sarariman, and the next generation wants to be pop singers, movie stars, and lady wrestlers."

We both looked around the room. Nakayama nodded. *"Da kedo . . ."*

Later, as I came back from the washroom, Nakayama was reading a book. He put his index finger to his lip and used the moisture to turn the page. The gesture reminded me of my father. I could see him turning the pages of his reports, sitting beneath a pool of light at the kitchen table in Morton Grove. Nakayama was about my father's age, but I could never have talked to my father like this. Next week, my parents would be here. I felt something sink inside me, as if I'd suddenly remembered an appointment I'd already missed. I sat down and asked Nakayama what he was reading.

"Oe Kanzaburo," he said. *"Teach Us to Outgrow Our Madness."*

VI

"If the Japanese had been paranoiac about the injustices inflicted upon them . . . they would merely have reinforced the prejudices against them. But because they accepted with quiet dignity, prejudice against them has all but disappeared. . . . The radical left, like the radical right, is unwilling or unable to understand that paranoia is a mental illness, not a program of social action."

—S. I. Hayakawa

"Old prisoners who identified themselves with the SS did so not only in respect to aggressive behavior. They would try to acquire old pieces of SS uniforms. . . . When asked why they did it, the old prisoners admitted that they loved to look like the guards."

—Bruno Bettelheim

1

In Tokyo, I often joked that given the choice between a trip to Japan and to Hilton Head, my parents would rather go to Hilton Head. They were interested in golf and tennis, not rummaging around for their cultural past. But of course, when I first found out about my grant, I would have taken France over Japan. In that way, I was still their son.

When I was growing up, my parents simply did not call attention to themselves as Japanese. Neither my mother nor my father ever said to us, "We take off our shoes at the door because we're Japanese." They never told us that the reason we ate rice almost every meal—even with roast beef or meat loaf—was that we were Japanese. They never taught us that the Japanese words for rice and for meal are the same: *gohan.*

Only rarely, such as the Labor Day when I was eight, did the subject of race even make a brief appearance. During the afternoon the men and boys watched the baseball game in our paneled rec room. Uncle Byron would comment on the game, on the Cubs' chances next year. My father nodded. They both wore T-shirts, khaki pants, glasses. My uncle had the lean whip-like body of Ernie Banks, my favorite Cub player, and had played semi-pro for a Nisei team. His son, my cousin Steve, was a Little League All-Star. Uncle Byron worked for the post office. My father wrote press releases for the AMA.

We sat on the floor. I could smell shoyu, chicken frying. Upstairs, my baby sister started to bawl.

Uncle Elbert came down. He was broader than my uncle Byron and my father, had started to take on the weight of middle age. His hair was beginning to gray.

"Well, how are the Bears doing?"

His inability to tell the football Bears from the baseball Cubs seemed appalling to my eight-year-old mind. And yet I knew that he'd received a Purple Heart during World War II for the scar around his belly. It almost made up for his ignorance of sports.

Supper was laid out on the dining-room table, before the picture windows at the front of the house. Except for the fried chicken, everything was Japanese: teriyaki chicken, futomaki (vegetable sushi), maze-gohan (vegetables with rice), Japanese pickles and roots—which I never ate—sometimes tempura. Dessert would be ice cream, cake, and mochi, a gooey rice dumpling which I also never ate. I loaded my plate with fried chicken.

We all sat in the living room; the grownups talked.

"I just feel comfortable going to a nihonjin," said Uncle Elbert. "I've known Tosh a long time."

"But why?" said my father. "You just said there's something still wrong with your bridge. You should go to the best dentist."

"So you go to a hakujin?"

"No, I go to see Joe Takehara. But that's not the point. Besides, Tosh has got this chip on his shoulder. He's always showing me these clippings from the JACL [the Japanese American Citizens League]. He's always complaining about how the Japanese-Americans get a rotten deal."

"Tosh had a hard time renting office space when he came to Chicago," said Elbert. "I had the same thing happen to me after the war."

"But this isn't after the war. And he did find an office. If you look for prejudice, you'll find it. And Tosh is always looking."

At this point, my aunt Miwako interrupted to tell Aunt Satchi how good the futomaki was. Aunt Yukimi commented on the weather. And the debate about identity drifted into the background, which was probably where my father wanted it to be.

My battles with my father came early, over my behavior and grades in school, over his decree that in second grade I do two pages of a fifth-grade math book before I could go outside to play, over the fact that I always went to bed an hour before everyone else in the neighborhood. Was this simply Japanese strictness, Japanese stress on education, or was it something in my father's own makeup? I don't know. I do know that I always took my father's dictums more seriously than my brother, who, when forced to do the same math books, found the answer sheet in my father's drawer and breezed through what he thought of as a ridiculous burden. Ironically, even as he dreams of being a rock and roll artist, it is my brother who makes his living now with numbers, doing financial analysis for banks and film studios.

A Republican who maintains that the only good Democrat was Mayor Daley, my father possesses the practical energies of a self-made man. Beginning at the end of the war, he worked himself through college, through jobs at the International News Service and the American Medical Association, then to a vice-president's slot at the national Blue Shield. "I loved being a reporter, but it didn't pay the bills," he said once. Later, he would tell me over and over, "When Joe Stetler and I were at AMA, we used to work long after everyone went home. That's the only way you'll get ahead. You've got to buckle down and work." In grade school, he wrote on my report card: "I have talked to David and he has promised his deportment will improve." The promises were often elicited through the back of his hand. In high school, he'd complain about the single B that sometimes appeared on my report card. By the time I was in college, the B's had disappeared. I used to believe I'd get an A on every test, since I'd studied twice as much as everyone else in the room. But even with those grades, it was clear I wasn't driven like my father by the desire to succeed. I was driven by the fear of failure, by my proximity to loss rather than gain.

When he was twenty-three, my father went to a Nisei dance on the south side of Chicago. I find it hard to picture that segregated world. (He noted in his diary that one of his friends, Mas, had gone out with a white girl, and it wasn't that bad.) But even harder for me to picture is my father's certainty. Spying across the room a pretty eighteen-year-old Nisei with an aquiline nose and sharp cheekbones that gave her an aristocratic air among the softer, rounder faces, my father turned to his companion and said, "That's the girl I'm going to marry."

I asked my mother about this dance years later. "This isn't the place to talk about it," she said. We were walking down Michigan Avenue, Christmas-shopping. She is the quiet one, for whom the past means nothing. Now that the children have left, her house is always immaculate and white: white walls, white carpets, white furniture. The light leaps from the purity of the surfaces, the quiet, immaculate tones. Not a trace of standard Nisei middle-class tastes, the Montgomery Ward furniture, with plaids and browns, ruffles and lace. My worst argument with her, at least in terms of theatrics, came after my typewriter had left an ink stain on her kitchen floor. Her life is the air-conditioned mall and tennis courts, the golf course just out back of the family-room picture window.

Theirs was an American storybook rise—from the lower-class neighborhood on the South Side of Chicago to the working-class area near Wrigley Field to the middle-class suburb of Morton Grove and then to the upper-middle-class suburbs of Northbrook and Vernon Hills. Looking back, I don't see how our being Japanese fit in with all this; perhaps it never did.

There *were* tensions, ripostes of anger. After my freshman year of college, my father drove me home from Grinnell, Iowa. About the time we hit Joliet, Illinois, he decreed that I had to get a haircut even before I stepped in the front door. As we argued back and forth, weaving down the Kennedy Expressway, my brother, who was ten, sat riveted between us. He recalls my father reaching across and grabbing me by the collar, shouting, "You kids have been this chain around my neck for years."

Neither my father nor I remember these words.

After the haircut, I stood shouting in the living room: "I don't want to be depressed the way I was all through high school."

"I didn't know you were depressed," my father replied.

"Oh, Tom, you knew," said my mother.

For years this incident epitomized my parents for me: my father blind to anything emotionally difficult; my mother seeing everything, saying nothing.

When I was in the throes of depression during grad school and sleeping sixteen hours a day, Susie became so frightened she called my parents. She told them she was worried that I might commit suicide; she said that the reasons for my depression seemed connected with them. Could they please call back in a few minutes? She was phoning in secret from the bathroom.

My parents never called.

Four years later, my parents came in for a session with my two therapists from group therapy. I had been working for three years on dredging up the past. But I was stuck. I kept calling my parents, shouting in anger, demanding that they acknowledge what they'd done—my father's physical abuse, my mother's put-downs ("David, you think too much of yourself").

"Either you terminate now," said my therapists, "or you bring them in."

The session with my parents took place in a small well-lit room. My parents sat on a couch together; my therapists and I sat in front of them on chairs. My father wore a dark-blue suit, my mother a green dress. They were obviously nervous. Dick, whom I'd begun therapy with, was intense, serious, his gaze unblinking and sure; his body was wiry and angular, his hair receding. He was the son of a Montana rancher, had fled early to the city. Rick wore a workshirt and jeans. His hair was long and blond; he had a mustache and the jocular manner of an ex-bar hound, which he was. The session started slowly, my therapists assuring my parents that the purpose was to foster communication, not to hurl accusations.

I was aware that nothing like this had ever occurred in my family.

After a stammering start, I brought up the time Susie had called them. My mother said that they thought the situation couldn't be as serious as Susie had described. I then brought up the incident where I stood in the living room and shouted about my depression. My father said he didn't remember.

Dick got my father to talk about how hard he had worked as a young man to support his family, to become a success. Slowly, my father's voice started to tighten, a small quiver began moving up his neck to his cheeks, a sliver of red started to show in his eyes. And then, as if an alarm had gone off, he pulled his head back, away from some unseen fire, shrugged, and said, "No, no, that was just what you were supposed to do. It wasn't anything at all."

When I saw this, I realized I could let go, I didn't have to convince my parents of what had happened. It was impossible. I could shout from the rooftops about my childhood and they were never going to believe it.

But even as Dick was talking to my father, Rick was whispering that I should tell my mother how much I needed her.

"I can't," I hissed, "I can't."

But he kept at me. Finally, I blurted out, "I need you, I love you, I need you so much," and burst out in tears.

My mother sat there, stunned. And then, to my surprise, she rose and hugged me. It was not a typical gesture. I was rippling with sobs.

In Japan when I thought of that session, it seemed like a dream. Part of me wanted to pretend it had never happened, that I couldn't have been so vulnerable. Four thousand miles seemed like a more appropriate distance.

2

Alone on a hill near a highway, the Akasaka Prince Hotel sends up its white brick stories, large windows that glare in the sun. From certain windows you can glimpse the empty center of the city, the Imperial grounds: the moat and huge stone wall, gardens, walks, great empty buildings kept immaculate by servants. Across from the hotel, at a station entrance, crowds pour forth from beneath the earth, headed toward hotels, shops, banks, office buildings.

The day my parents arrived, my father, Susie, and I went to dinner near the hotel. My mother was resting to get over the jet lag. At the sushi restaurant, all of us ordered in Japanese. My father's Japanese was even clumsier than mine. He exclaimed over the unagi (the eel) and we ordered a couple more servings. The chef behind the counter muttered *"Hai,"* his hands already placing the eel on the grill, then cupping the rice firmly with his fingers against his palm. The end of his *hachimaki* (headband) brushed his ear. His back was bent like a jeweler's. He had the body of a high jumper, lean, tense, young.

"The trains are so clean," my father said. "It's amazing. And cushioned seats. In Chicago they'd be slashed by the end of the first day, and graffiti would be splattered everywhere."

Susie told him how safe she felt in the city; she could take the last train home alone and her only worry was to avoid the sarariman who looked as if he was about to spew up his evening's drink. Her manner with my father was easy, convivial. She had known him so long, she was almost a daughter. My parents have always liked her, have felt she was solid, dependable in a way I wasn't. They seemed relieved when we finally got married, especially my mother. I was now Susie's responsibility.

If Susie felt at ease with my father, I did not. I was trying to hold back my anger. I had sent my parents two letters since November and they had never written back. I had also asked them repeatedly to bring some computer paper with them. The Japanese computer paper was not the proper size; this meant I had to print only one page at a time, then hand-crank the paper to the next perforated line. My parents had decided I didn't need the paper, I could probably get it in Japan. Besides, they said, they had enough baggage.

I felt as if they had refused to acknowledge what I needed to do my work. And somehow that seemed tied to their refusal to acknowledge being Japanese, to speak about the past. If my work was obsessed with the past, their silence had left me with an incompleteness, huge gaps I could never fill in. And yet those gaps fueled my obsession, gave it a reason to exist.

The letters, the paper were not the only reasons that I was angry. There were all the old grievances.

"I work out at the club three nights a week," said my father. "Weights, aerobics. I'm usually the only male in your mother's class."

His body was solid, leaner than when he was thirty, leaner than mine. His hair was jet black, brushed to the side and back. I'd only recently discovered that he and my mother used coloring.

Rummaging for hair spray on a Christmas visit, Susie had discovered two bottles, one labeled *Tom's Mix,* the other *Terry's Mix.* Even without their pure black hair, my parents possess the movements, the style of a younger couple. "They're so beautiful," my friends said at our wedding, "especially your mother." I nodded, embarrassed, pleased, annoyed, thinking, Why make such a fuss, it's only physical appearance.

"Here, feel this." My father had taken off his suit coat, rolled up his sleeves.

"Jesus, Dad."

"No, feel this."

"Watashimasu." The chef bent over the counter and placed the sushi before us. Thank God, I thought. My father passed the sushi over to Susie, then rolled down his sleeves.

"So do you and Terry play much tennis now?"

"She plays two or three times a week. I don't play that much anymore. She's gotten so she can give me a pretty good game. Sometimes she even beats me. She plays at the club with women ten years younger. They can't believe she has a son David's age."

We began discussing where they would go on this trip—Ise, Kyoto, then back to Tokyo. They weren't planning to visit Shingu, his father's hometown.

"Maybe next time," my father said. Then, turning to the chef: *"Benjo wa, doko desu ka?"*

The chef looked puzzled, then pointed to the back.

"Dad, benjo is slang, nobody uses it."

"Sure they do. What's wrong with it?"

"Dad, trust me."

"Well, what do they use, then?"

"Otearai or *toire,* though I seem to have trouble with both. Benjo is easier to pronounce."

When the check came, my father picked it up. I didn't want him to pay. It always made me feel like a child. But we were nearing the end of the month.

"You don't have to tip," said Susie.

"I know. That's terrific. It's a whole different attitude toward service." My father put on his suit coat. His body was broader, more beefy than the sarariman around us. I wondered if they could tell we were an American father and son. Ken had told me that after a while he could pick out the Japanese-Americans at tourist spots. But I didn't want to believe him. I still wanted to blend in.

Out in the street, we passed a Pachinko parlor. Inside, men sat on stools before the upright flashing boards, sending steel ball after ball up in an arc, then down through numbered slots. Cigarettes hung from their mouths.

"Have you played?"

"Just once. I thought it was boring. You have to be Japanese, I think, to appreciate it."

We left my father at the corner, near the station entrance. I hugged him stiffly goodbye, thinking it was not a very Japanese gesture. Susie kissed his cheek. We walked off, waving. Looking back at his figure against the other sarariman and young couples walking past, I thought, No, he doesn't look like them. It's not just the Hart Shaffner suit or his body, it's the way he holds himself, the solid, casual confidence of his smile, of the arm waving. It emanated from him as if his body were Broadway neon. My father—American.

3

As a child, I worshipped the standard American sports heroes, Mickey Mantle, Ernie Banks, Paul Hornung, Bob Cousy. Later, I listened to the Beatles, the Beach Boys, the Animals, Marvin Gaye. Growing up in a Jewish suburb, I learned more about Jewish culture than about the Japanese, and my favorite author as a teenager was Philip Roth. Until I was seven, we lived in the same building as my relatives. The family of my father's brother-in-law owned the building. Amid the Uyemuras, Hirakawas, Ogatas, Fujiis, Fukiyamas, there was only one white family. Most of us went to a Japanese-

American Congregationalist church, a couple of the boys took judo classes, I was a member of the Nisei Drum and Bugle Corps.

But after we moved out, more and more of my friends were white. I began to shun the stereotype of the quiet, unobtrusive, studious Asian student. Sometimes I played the part of an extroverted clown, wanting to stand out, not be part of a group. I ran for class president. I certainly didn't want to be thought of as Japanese-American. I was an American, pure and simple. I was proud I didn't know Japanese, that English was my sole tongue. I didn't want to be classified as one of the typical Asian science geeks, even though math was my best subject in high school. When I left for college, I was going to be a lawyer and planned to work in civil rights or poverty law.

Still, by the summer before my senior year, things have changed. At the kitchen table in our house, I argue with my father. He wants me to go to law school, I want to go to graduate school in English. We've argued so much in the past couple years—about the Vietnam War, about my draft application as a conscientious objector, about my hair, my clothes. He's in his T-shirt, and his black glasses make him look studious; his face is stern. My hair's at my shoulders, I'm wearing a work shirt and blue jeans.

"I talked to Bernie Hirsch, and he thinks you ought to go to law school."

"Dad, he's a lawyer. Of course he'd say that."

"It's just more practical. There's so much you can do with a law degree."

My father is getting nowhere, and he sees this. "Well, I'm paying for these applications. Let's just say you'll apply to both and we'll see what happens."

Later, back at college, I write him a long letter, filled with quotations from William Carlos Williams, Keats, James Wright. I tell him I fear working in a law office will somehow destroy something vital in me; that it will decrease, not increase, my freedom. I tell him how, when I worked in the Blue Shield office last summer, I kept hiding poetry books in my desk. If I become a lawyer, I'll have to do that all my life. I want to do something that will let me keep those books on top of my desk.

He writes back: "Well, wouldn't it be something if you got accepted to Harvard English grad school and Harvard Law School? Wouldn't we have a choice then?"

I don't get accepted at either, and though I do get accepted at Stanford Law School, I decide to go to grad school in English at Minnesota. A year later, home for the summer, I'm rummaging through some things in the basement. I come upon an old briefcase. In it I find stories, poems, a diary, rejection slips from *The New Yorker* and *The Atlantic*. I've known my father wanted to be a writer, but never how much. He's even typed out a passage on writing from Hemingway's *Green Hills of Africa.* One poem has him playing with a young white girl, the daughter of a neighbor of Professor Bigelow. At the end of the poem, he takes her hand, and the contrast in their colors marks a tension I hadn't thought my father was ever aware of. As I look at the pieces, I wonder about his opposition to my writing. Perhaps he felt he had given up his dream, had started a family and been forced to seek other work, and he wanted to save me the same disappointment. He could not conceive that my life or my talents might be different.

But that's not the whole story. Two years later, I'm in grad school, writing poems, taking courses on the Romantics, Elizabethan and Tudor drama. Sitting in my small apartment in the Native American section of town, my father leans back in a battered secondhand chair and says, "You know, when I die or when I retire, they're just going to get someone else to take my place at Blue Shield. In a way, it will be as if I was never there."

He pauses, sits up a bit, and looks at me. "But only you can write your poems."

He had given me his blessing, a parental gift many writers never receive. Why wasn't I more grateful? In Tokyo I was aware that the man with whom I had eaten dinner, with his talk of Nautilus and aerobics, was not the driven father of my childhood. The man in the Tokyo restaurant was more relaxed. He had made it, he no longer had to keep up the rectitude of Episcopalian airs, he no longer had to drive himself or his children. Perhaps I wanted to keep dealing with the old father. This new one did not fit in with my *Sturm und Drang* version of father and son.

4

I thought Susie and I had left my father standing near the stoplight, but the next day I learned I was wrong.

"Tell them what happened," my mother said in their room.

"I was walking along, and this man came up to me and said something about having a *kirei musume*" [pretty daughter]. He wanted me to follow him."

"Oh, God, you didn't?"

"I know," said my mother, grinning in exasperation, "can you believe that?"

"So we got in this elevator, and at the sixth floor the door opened and I walked into this dark bar. There were booths with women in them, and this middle-aged woman in a kimono came up to me. I told her, I'm just looking, and smiled, and began to turn around. She grabbed my arm and said, You can trust me, I am a good old woman, you can trust me, and I kept saying, I'm just looking, *mite dake, mite dake.*"

"With his Japanese, who knows what trouble he could have gotten into?" said my mother.

"Finally, I got back to the elevator, but when it opened and I got in, the woman pressed the button and the doors wouldn't close . . ."

"It serves you right," my mother said. "I told Tom that's just how things happen. I can see the headlines now, NORTH-BROOK MAN FOUND IN TOKYO ALLEY . . ."

"Well, I'm here, aren't I?" said my father.

"We can't leave you anywhere," I said. "From now on, we're not letting you out of sight. You're like a little kid."

My father just grinned and repeated, *"Kirei musume ga imasu yo."*

* * *

"Come here, Tom. Take a picture of this."

We were passing a tennis court, down the block from the house of Susie's tea ceremony teacher. My parents had just watched Daniel and Susie go through the ceremony.

"It's just a tennis court, Mom."

"I want to have a picture of it."

My father pointed the lens through a small hole in the tarpaulin strapped against the chain-link fence.

My parents, I thought, they come all the way to Japan and what do they take a picture of?

"I really enjoyed that," said my mother, referring to the tea ceremony class. "It reminded me of my mother's ikebana club. Just a bunch of middle-aged Japanese housewives sitting around and gossiping. I used to go with her all the time. I guess it was because I was the youngest."

I can almost count on my hands the times my mother has spoken about her mother.

"It's strange. I haven't thought of that club in years. I just remember sitting on the floor, playing with my doll, and all these ladies sitting around a table, drinking tea and laughing. It was like a memory machine . . . Tom, take a picture of us here, in front of this sign." It was the sign for the tennis club.

As we lined up, Susie, my mother, and I, my mother added, "But I never had to sit the way I did today, on my knees for an hour. When I got up, my legs were numb."

"Even the Japanese have a hard time with that now. We saw this movie recently, *Ososhiki,* about a family attending a funeral. The whole family had to sit formally like that, but then the camera panned behind them, and you could see everyone twitching their legs and trying to shift their weight. When the phone rang, one of the men got up and collapsed because his legs fell out from under him."

"Wait, I've got to let the battery recharge," said my father. "Okay, everybody. *Cheezu!*"

* * *

We're at Mrs. Hayashi's house for lunch, a lavish spread of tempura, of Japanese chicken balls, sushi, vinegared rice with pickled vegetables. Mrs. Hayashi's house is huge for a Japanese house. It's got three bedrooms, an upstairs and a downstairs, a living room, a dining room, and a large kitchen. The furniture is mainly Western. We sit at a table rather than kneeling on the floor. We're all speaking in Japanese. My father talks of going to Ise Shrine, of standing before the gates and realizing that they've been rebuilding the shrine for seven hundred years, long before the United States was founded. In the week and a half they've been here, his Japanese has shot past mine like the bullet train. It's quite discouraging. He talks of how surprised he was, surprised and proud. My mother doesn't say much, but I can tell that when Mrs. Hayashi speaks, my mother understands. Mrs. Hayashi tells us about her neighbors, who have joined us for lunch. Mrs. Harada looks a bit like Mrs. Hoshizaki, our neighbor from Morton Grove. Her husband has his own cleaning service. Mrs. Imada is young, pretty, and her four-year-old daughter is a darling. I wonder what it would be like to raise our child here, among faces that look like him or her. But then I think: No, they would look like both Susie and me, they would be caught between.

Mrs. Hayashi is explaining how it's sometimes easier for young people to make money by going into business by themselves. There's more prestige in working for a company like Mitsubishi, her husband's company, but there's not as much money. Out the window, there's a par-three golf course. My father asks Mrs. Hayashi if the balls ever come onto her lawn. He tells her about their house in Northbrook, where the back yard looks out on a golf course. Mrs. Hayashi remarks how expensive it is to play golf in Japan.

Later, I talk about the Hatto bus tour we took yesterday around Tokyo. My father comments how efficient and organized the tour was. He was disappointed we couldn't go into the Imperial grounds. I realize I am seeing my parents for the first time in an all-Japanese environment, seeing a side of them I have never seen before. This must be more like what their dinner table was like when they were growing up. Of course, the kids spoke English to each other, but they had to speak Japanese to their parents. I suppose, since my mother was the youngest, she didn't speak much, exactly as she's doing here. She just listened. For a second, I have a vision, no, a ghost of a vision, of the child she was, like the brief wisp of steam that rises when you take off the top of the rice pot. In an instant, it passes. She was never a girl, she is ageless, always a grownup, always older, alien from me.

For some reason, my father is talking about the racial mixture in Chicago. I hear the word *kurambo.* Mrs. Hayashi puts on her best teacherly manner and explains to my father that the word *kurambo* isn't used as a word for blacks. It's like an insult. "Like nigger?" I ask. *"Hai, soo desu ne."* My father looks bewildered, begins to protest, as he did when he used *benjo* for washroom in the sushi restaurant. I ask Mrs. Hayashi about my parents' Japanese. She says my father's is pretty good, but some of the language he uses is more a child's. After all, he last spoke fluent Japanese when he was about fourteen. The Japanese-American Japanese is like a time-capsule object and sounds a bit strange to modern Japanese. It's filled with Meiji era expressions and lacks current slang terms (for instance, *pinku,* a replacement for the traditional Japanese word for pink).

My father's bewilderment lets me sense how difficult the question of identity must have been for him, how the Japanese he spoke at home must have clashed with the language of his classmates in the L.A. schools, how he must have felt it was a choice of either/or, and not both.

As we walk home, my mother remarks on how friendly Mrs. Hayashi was, how she seemed so familiar, like a Northbrook housewife. "I can't remember when I've spoken that much Japanese," she says.

My father tells us more about their trip. One night my father had put on this white cotton robe that was on the futon in their hotel room, and went down to the lobby on his way to the hot baths. He was halfway through the lobby when a hotel employee came up to him. "You can't wear that in the lobby," said the man, who looked at my father as if he were a bit off.

"Why?" my father asked in Japanese, "it was there in my room, I'm going to the bath."

"It's underwear," said the man.

"Underwear?"

"Underwear."

My mom was laughing. "What a man. First he gets stuck in a bar with a mama-san and a bunch of bar girls, and then he wears underwear in public. It's lucky you didn't get arrested."

5

The house I grew up in, the one in Morton Grove, was a cookie-cutter bi-level of the fifties. As it was being built, we would drive out from the North Side to look at the progress, stopping at Mc-Donald's along the way. I recall the burgers and shakes better than the building of that house, but my father still talks of standing in front of the brick façade and large picture windows and thinking, This is my house. I can't believe it. He had mowed lawns as a boy in L.A., his father was a gardener there. He had spent his teen years behind a fence near the swamps of Arkansas. And now he would soon buy a Buick Le Sabre, then a Wildcat, and, a few years down the line, a beige Coupe de Ville.

There were still open spaces near our house, great un-tamed fields where we used to hunt rabbits with bats. We'd line up in a row and move through the knee-high grass like reapers, and when something moved we'd hurl our weapons. We rarely hit anything but more grass or a stray stone. It was the idea of hunting that excited us.

My friends then were Terry Hoffberg, Herb Bartlett, the Hoshizaki boys, Bob and Doug. I was closet to Bob. He was the smartest, the oldest, the best baseball player. It mattered little that he was Japanese.

Sometimes my father would take me out to the park near

our house and hit me ground balls and looping flies. "Two hands, two hands," he'd say. I was the unusual case of someone who could hit but couldn't field. These were better times than later, when I played football in high school. Every Saturday, after the game, he'd recount to me the tackles I'd missed, how I had failed to hustle. Even worse were the times he went over my English papers. I see us at the kitchen table, lit in the cone of light. My paper on Hester in *The Scarlet Letter* is before him. He's marking almost every line, muttering in disgust. He writes speeches for a living, press releases on medical coverage, on public health. At one point he shouts, "Where did you learn to write, you stupid idiot?"

In college, English, which had been my worst subject all through grade school and high school, suddenly became my best. I got nothing but A's. I was out of my father's house. I was learning to speak.

Still, even now, I have the sense of being a slow learner, of the language not coming to me naturally. There's a passage in Joyce's *Portrait of the Artist* where Stephen Dedalus is talking to an English priest. Dedalus, the Irishman, the colonized, listens to the priest speak and wonders why the words *chalice* and *ale* sound more at home coming from the priest than from him. Occasionally, when confronted with an articulate white writer, I too feel this way. Is it that I am also an interloper, someone who has lost touch with my ancestor's speech and so must take up that of a more powerful force? Or am I simply recalling those moments with my father, at our kitchen table, the smell of *bara-bara* hamburger—ground beef and soy sauce—still lingering in the air?

A year before I went to Japan, I sent him a copy of my play on Mishima. A week later, my father called from his hotel in Indianapolis, where he had just given a speech to the Indiana Blue Cross/Blue Shield Plan. He said he had finished the play with tears in his eyes. After reading a portion of it he had told a co-worker, "My son's the real writer in the family. I'm just a hack."

I didn't know what to say. I had already decided the play was a failure.

6

The lobby of the Akasaka Prince Hotel was immaculate and white, like a mausoleum. Near an open staircase, on a white piano set on a dais, the piano player glided through "Yesterday," "The Shadow of Your Smile," "My Way." Along a railing, beside a wall of jade plants, we sat in low, plush chairs, my parents and Susie with glasses of wine, me with a glass of Coke, and Saito with a Sapporo.

Saito looked rumpled as always. He wore a blue windbreaker, jeans, a white shirt; his hair kept falling in his eyes. His glasses made his eyes smaller, distant, as if seen through sea water. His skin and teeth were bad. He spoke slowly, the words jerked from his mouth in odd rhythms. The tape recorder lay like a wallet on the glass table.

"What do you do in America?"

"I don't work, so I guess you could just say I'm a housewife."

"I'm in advertising and I'm a writer and I'm in public relations."

Saito was interested in nikkei-jin, Japanese who lived in other countries. He'd translated their literature; they were like odd, distant cousins, exotic and familiar. He was going to write an article on them, perhaps a book.

My father leaned forward and spread his hands out as he talked, his palms face up. My mother was less relaxed, her back upright. My father told Saito they knew more "American families than Japanese families"—I noted the adjectives—then launched into a JACL civic speech about how the Japanese-Americans were quiet, hard-working people who never made any trouble. Even Susie had heard this speech several times before.

When Saito asked him about the war, my father repeated

the story about playing baseball in the camps. Saito was unsettled; he seemed to want some other response.

"The government doesn't regard you as an American citizen. It is very baffling to me."

"Well, that was during the hysteria of the war. And today, many Americans feel it was wrong. I'm not bitter. It was unfortunate for many people, but for our family it wasn't so bad." Of course, his father took financial losses, he said, but the camps opened up opportunities for the Nisei in other parts of the country. It seemed easier to move into more professional jobs away from the West Coast.

Saito saw an opening here. "You experience some discrimination?"

"I personally don't feel it. And I travel a great deal in the United States. In reality, everybody faces a little discrimination, no matter if you're white, black, or yellow, but if you're very sensitive to it all the time, you may feel you're discriminated against when you're not. If you think you'll be treated equally, you'll be treated equally."

The ostrich approach, I thought. Saito turned to my mother.

"Oh, I'm sure prejudice exists," my mother said. "But we don't go out of our way to keep on looking out for it. You could become so obsessed with it, you can't do anything else. We're not stupid, we're not blind to it." She had read what I was thinking. "There're certain people who will always react that way."

Saito decided to take another tack. "Do you read David's poems?"

"Certainly."

"What do you think about 'Nisei Picnic.' "

Silence. I thought of the line in that poem "He beat his son." Or did they simply not remember?

"What do you think about Sansei writing about camps?"

"I think they see things through their eyes and their feelings, based on what we have told them. It may not be the way I remember it or feel it, but it's the way David sees it or feels it."

"I think it's good for you to talk to my father," I said to Saito. "He sees things very differently than I do."

"My feelings probably aren't typical," said my father. "You can't judge the Nisei by what I say."

"But there are people who feel like you," I added.

Why was I defending my father?

Saito kept pressing the question of race.

"When we raised our children, we didn't think so much that we were Japanese," my mother said. "We were raising our children to be good human beings . . ."

"I felt American before I was Japanese," my father added.

"I don't have an image of an identity of American," said Saito. "I have an image of African-American, Japanese-American, Wasp, yuppie, et cetera."

"A lot of my father's generation thought that way," I said, trying to translate for Saito. "That they were Americans first."

"When we were seated at the table yesterday at Mrs. Hayashi's house," said my mother, "I thought it was so great. There were the two neighbor ladies with their kids, and you could transport us to Northbrook, Illinois, and find their counterparts in America. That's what I thought, the universal love of mothers for children. And you could tell they were very good people. And that's the way we tried to raise you as children."

Here my mother paused. "Maybe in a way we went so much one way we forgot. Maybe we should have included more of Japanese culture."

I was astonished. Japan had changed my mother, if only briefly. Suddenly I saw she was a different woman from the one who raised me. She'd admitted she might have been wrong.

"For Japanese the image of America is of white culture," remarked Saito.

"Because most of the people are white," said my father.

I couldn't help myself. "But if you're taking pure percentages, one out of twenty Americans on TV should be Asian. And three out of twenty would be black. Asian-Americans are never in the leading roles."

"Well, did you see *The Karate Kid* . . . Besides, you can't have a commercial success with two percent of the population."

"But there's an overwhelming percentage of blondes on TV . . ."

"And why couldn't you have a commercial success?" said Susie. "If we're all Americans, why can't the main characters just happen to be Japanese-Americans?"

"Because I don't think they're at ease with themselves as actors," said my mother. "It's not that they're Japanese."

"They need to be sure enough of themselves that they could make you forget," said my father. "I haven't seen a Japanese-American actor who can do that."

"Oh, come on. Cheryl Ladd. Morgan Fairchild. Are they good actors?"

"It's not that it's not there. I'm not naïve," said my mother. Her voice was more terse, as if she were holding something back. "At one point we just decided we had to deal with it, and if we make it more important than it should be . . . I know it's there, I'm not stupid."

"Are there times TV programs offend you?" I asked, backing down a bit.

"Oh yes . . ."

"If they would portray a Japanese-American in an unrealistic way or in a caricature that is negative, then we would feel that it wasn't right," said my father.

In the end, though, my father was more concerned with the ways other races were changing America. "My image of America is mixed," he said a bit later, "but I know that the basic population is white. But America is changing so rapidly, because of all the different races. Sometimes I think it's not for the better. That the good law-abiding citizen is going to be outnumbered by the citizens who are not as well educated . . ." Here my father went into a long digression about *Escape from New York,* a futuristic movie where black and Hispanic gangs take over New York City and take the president hostage.

"Would you say that was a racist movie?" I was baiting him.

"There are sections of Los Angeles where if you're white and driving a good car it's dangerous. It's the same in Chicago; there are many sections where if you're white or Oriental it's very dangerous to be there."

It's no use arguing, I thought. We've gone over this before. My parents wouldn't fit into Saito's neat definition of Japanese-Americans, nor would they fit into mine. Their fears were not my fears; their desires were foreign, born of another time.

The interview ended with Saito asking them about their visit.

"When my father retired," said my father, "he returned to Japan and he said to me that I should come back to Japan and see the kind of culture that I came from. He told me that whatever success I achieved in America, I shouldn't think I'd done it on my own. I was a part of him and his culture, and my culture was in Japan, which had a written language for centuries before America was even discovered. I was benefiting from something many centuries old."

My mother, surprisingly, wanted to come back again. "We really enjoyed ourselves. Now when we go back to America, I would like to study more about Japan. One of the things that impressed me is that it's such a safe country. In the United States you don't feel safe wherever you go. And everything here is so clean and well organized. When we went on this tour the other day we were both very impressed by how smoothly things went. We felt very proud about being Japanese."

7

"I don't quite believe this newfound pride in Japan will last very long. But it was nice," I said to Susie. We were walking down

Mejiro Avenue, past the 7-Eleven near our house. My parents were going back the next day. "Of course, who knows what we'll be like once we get back to the States. We'll probably forget everything we learned here."

"I think they enjoyed themselves here. You gave them a gift. They wouldn't have come if you hadn't been here."

"It's so strange. I dreaded their coming. I was still so angry at them. And now . . ."

"Now what?"

"I look at the way they took the culture in, and it all seemed more natural to them and at the same time more foreign. I could see how much came back, how much they'd buried. They didn't have the same eagerness I had just after we arrived. It was as if they were reliving something . . ."

A taxi whisked by, a sarariman in the back seat, his head slogged to the side, his mouth open. We turned the corner at the candy store.

"Maybe it was because we were guiding them, helping them around at first, but I could see this vulnerability there. They probably weren't even aware it was showing, but I saw it. And I felt I was seeing them outside of my own memories of them."

"It must have been strange for them too, seeing you here."

"I think my whole life must be strange to them, *ne?*"

"But I think they were proud of you, of your being here. Of your grant."

"Of course, but they never said anything about it."

"That's very Japanese."

"I suppose so. But you can hardly pin all the things they did on being Japanese. And no matter why they acted the way they did, I *was* depressed in high school. I was an unhappy child."

"And now?"

"Now I'm happy, but it's hardly because of them. My dad still kept telling me I should write a novel, something that will sell. And the thing is, it didn't bother me. I just let it pass. It's as if he's no longer my father anymore, he's just this person I keep referring to as my father."

"Did you read that letter Mary sent the other day?" Our friend Mary had just gone through a trying time back in Minnesota. A couple of days after her second child was born, her father died, and she had to make the trip with her newborn to New York for the funeral. She had written us about how confusing that time was, filled with joy and sadness, hope and regret. She had suggested that however difficult things were with my parents, they were at least alive. My struggles were with real people, not with ghosts.

"Of course she's right," I said. "It's infinitely better that they're alive. And I do have a chance to make connections with them now. And yet I feel sometimes that the anger I have toward them is like this sinkhole, and the only way I can keep from not going down into it is to distance myself, to think of them as little as possible."

"And yet they're so much there in the things you're writing now. And in your poems."

"Well, that's different. There, they're not just my parents, and I'm not just me. They're larger, more symptomatic and symbolic; they stand for a whole generation."

"But they're still your parents."

"I know, I know. But the more I think about it, the more I see that my anger toward them is really a substitute, a cover for a larger political anger. It's not just the camps or the loyalty oath or any of the historical events that made them what they are, what they reacted against. It's the way they look at themselves as Americans, as separate from other races, from the rest of the world. And I find myself feeling that less and less."

"I don't understand."

"Well, for one thing, I don't look at myself that way, I can't just write like a white American writer; I'm not John Updike, I can't write about four white people talking about their divorce at the table, as if the rest of the world didn't exist. That sort of despair doesn't interest me." We had reached our door. "Let's keep on walking, it's such a nice night." We passed the playground with its swings and slide, the light of the all-night laundromat, a small travel agent's office with posters of Iwo Jima, Bali, Hawaii, Thailand. The alley-sized street wound back and forth like a snake, led into other

snakelike passages. Smells from the sewer, sweet and rotting, drifting past us. A young girl passed on a bicycle.

"I think sometimes it's easier to get angry at my parents
than to get angry at anything political. At least I think I have some
connection to them, some control. But so many feelings I have
about them are colored by political issues. Despite whatever they
taught me, I always knew I was somehow different from the whites
around me. And now I'm so much more conscious of myself as a
colored person. It's as if I've discovered not only Japan, or even
Asia this year, but a whole new way of looking at the world. Maybe
the fact that I don't fit in back home or even here is an advantage.
You know, when we went to see *Out of Africa,* I found it harder and
harder to identify with Meryl Streep and Robert Redford. I was
more interested in what was going through the minds of the blacks
around them, what the natives were feeling, how the energy must
have been there, waiting for something like the Mau-Maus to
begin. I saw that I couldn't focus on the whites and blacks at the
same time, and I felt like I had to decide whose vision I was going
to side with."

"That's not something your parents understand."

"No. And yet when I write about them, I'm actually going
against everything they said to Saito the other day about American
culture, about who should always be at the center, who should
always be the star, the hero, the lover." Here I paused. "I just
realized that's probably why they're both proud of my work and
never really want to talk about it directly. Secretly some part of
them is pleased, but another part is terrified of it and wants to
ignore it."

"Something's changing for you here."

"Yes, I can feel it. It's as if my life in America, my sense
of it, is drifting away. I won't ever be able to go back to it. But I
can't quite see what's going to replace it."

"That scares me. I want to go back, I can't live here."

"That's not the point. Even if we go back, it won't be the
same."

"But your parents will."

"No, not even them. Even though they stayed only two

weeks, they're not the same. Even if they never come back. Which they probably won't."

We turned and started back to our house.

"No," Susie said, "they probably won't."

VII

"Yes, we withdraw into ourselves, we deepen and aggravate our awareness of everything that separates or isolates or differentiates us. And we increase our solitude by refusing to seek out our compatriots, perhaps because we fear we will see ourselves in them, perhaps because of a painful, defensive unwillingness to share our intimate feelings."

—Octavio Paz, *The Labyrinth of Solitude*

"They are cowardly and immoral. They are different from Americans in every conceivable way, and no Japanese . . . should have the right to claim American citizenship. . . . A Jap is a Jap anywhere you find him, and his taking the oath of allegiance to this country would not help, even if he should be permitted to do so. They do not believe in God and have no respect for an oath."

—Senator Tim Stewart, Tennessee (1942)

1

One day a Mexican named Ricardo moved into our apartment complex. I thought of him as one of the displaced like me, but perhaps that was wrong. His parents had emigrated from Turkey, and if you looked closely you could see the Turk in him—the mustache helped—but his blond hair and neutral complexion made him seem neither Mexican nor Turkish but French. He spoke Spanish, French, Turkish, and English. A composer, he was writing an opera with Octavio Paz, the great Mexican poet. When he was young, Ricardo had studied all over Europe. Later, he had had his pieces performed in London and Paris, had taught at Princeton. He preferred the States to Europe. There was something about the people in Europe's capital cities, the rich there: everything was too excessive, money too necessary. His wife had left him when he refused to become a banker. "She knew what I was when she married me," he said bitterly. But except for the separations from his children, the divorce came to seem like a gift for him. "I will never marry again," he said. He wanted no obligations. Women fell in love with him anyway, but they knew what they could expect. Nothing. He did this without malice. His seductions were irrepressible, part of his nature. He was a challenge to me in more ways than one.

Physically, he was as tall as my friend Daniel, but wider, with the bulk of a tackle, a professional wrestler. His manner never reminded you of his size. I see him always with this smile, spreading wider and wider, his mustache curving just slightly at the end. It is a boy's smile, the smile of someone who has raided the candy jar, who knows that even if he is caught, he will charm his way out. His charm is a gift. Why refuse it?

Susie too thought Ricardo was charming. Charming and despicable.

Ricardo was studying Gagaku, a court music which had been imported from China more than five centuries ago. The music had disappeared from China but was still performed in Japan, as it had been when it crossed the Sea of Japan. Typical of the Japanese, this masterful preservation. High-pitched pipes, piercing, mysterious, unsettling, hypnotic. Music to charm snakes and demons, to thread through courts of intrigue, the affairs of power. The melodies wavered, went off in unknown, unpredictable directions, like an alien object in the sky. Ricardo took them down, dreamed about them, wove them through his score, tore them out. Waited. Wrote again. At night, we argued about Foucault's *Madness and Civilization,* the dissolution of the universal. Opinions poured forth from him. Foucault and Paz were his fathers and, of course, Stravinsky; Fuentes was lugubrious, Cuba a disaster; in many ways, Vargos Llosa, the conservative Peruvian, was right. At Princeton those who wrote computer music were now programmers, doubling their salaries. In *The Labyrinth of Solitude,* Paz had created in an instant the Mexican intellect, a history of a nation.

"If you're Mexican, you know it's not enough to know Mexican culture. You're just this shitty little country," Ricardo said. "With you Americans, it's different. You can ignore everybody." He knew a son of García Márquez, had been to his wedding. The great author leaned against the bar like a bear, bursting from his tux. His books, Ricardo thought, were slight, amusing. Ricardo read me poem after poem by Ruben Dario, trying to get me to hear the music. I knew no Spanish, my ears were numb.

Ricardo lived in a small village far outside Mexico City. An Indian village, pre-Columbian, another world. He had a lover in the city, Gabriela. He cherished his students at the university. "It's so difficult to do anything in Mexico City," he said. "When they show up at your class, you know they want to learn. If they disappear, you know there's a reason. One woman, who wasn't registered, came for several weeks. She returned a year later, a baby in her arms. It wasn't like that at Princeton. The students were like poodles, primped and ready for show. They had no fight. She was like one of those cocks they breed for fighting. She had this instinct. She was ready to kill."

There were ways our Americas met. "When some Latin American poets, friends of mine, went to the States, they found they couldn't talk to the white poets. They had nothing in common. Then one day they went to a university where there were some Black writers, then to another with Chicanos. They talked about politics, the heart of the beast. They lived in the same world."

Would the Asian-American poets have reacted the same? I hoped so.

He played tapes of his other operas. The music was neo-classical, with tinges of Debussy. Airy, dreamy, like breezes and light through an orchard in Provence, the shallows in the bay of a small Greek island. I liked it, it soothed me; I felt disappointed. It moved nothing forward.

"My friend Carlos, the poet, tells this joke. It's about his trip to America. You should meet him when you come to Mexico. Anyway, there's this American archaeologist who's digging in some ruins in Mexico. It's in the desert; the sky is clear, not a cloud in sight. A old peasant walks by. 'You're going to have to stop,' he says, 'it's going to rain soon.' The archaeologist looks at the blue sky and goes on digging. In an hour the sky is pouring . . ." Ricardo got up, poured me some sake. "A few days later, the peasant walks by again, says the same thing. The archaeologist thinks the first day was a fluke. But the rains come down. The third time the peasant comes by, the archaeologist asks, 'How can you tell it's going to rain? Do you use a divining rod? Do you sense it in the wind? Where do you get this sixth sense?' The peasant looks puzzled. 'I heard it on the radio,' he says."

Every time he told this joke, Ricardo chuckled. It was infinitely amusing. Our arguments never rose to cacophonous heights, unlike those I had with Daniel. Our friendship was lighter, less personal, less American, would have fewer strains. We were two artists, not quite young, not quite old. Our future was elsewhere. We were passing through.

2

From the first time I met Saito, and he brought Akiko along, Saito enjoyed introducing me to people—from Japanese poets, like Shoozu Ben, to other Japanese-Americans, like Ken, to people interested in Japanese-Americans or Japanese-American literature. His impulse was part hospitality, part a natural facility for making contacts, and part may have been a certain amount of status, however small, he gained from showing me around. I was an oddity, possessing the glamour of an American and the familiarity of a Japanese face. I was a writer on a fellowship sponsored by the Bunkacho. Whatever Saito's motives, I did want to meet people, and I was grateful for his efforts. Still, not all the meetings went well.

Through Saito's arrangements, Susie and I visited a study group on Japanese-American literature one Sunday just before she was to leave for the States. The group met in a new four-story apartment building in Roppongi, where Misao, one of the women in the group, lived with her mother. She and her mother owned the land, a small corner of the richest real estate in the world. The rooms were small, modern, with no tatami and large windows, an upright Yamaha against one wall. The mother's watercolors were hung in a row like cabin windows, small glimpses into marshes, seas, a bright, airy sky, like the music of a flute. Misao served us cookies and tea. She was young and pretty, with hair that swept down like a waterfall when she bent to the table. Small teeth like pebbles, a button nose. She translated novelizations of American movies, wrote articles for a fashion magazine. The other women in the group were plain, spoke in high, childish voices; they looked like librarians, church secretaries, nothing like the fashionable young drifting three stories below through the streets of Roppongi. Along the avenue, the shop windows displayed clothes of rich, dark fabrics, silk blouses glimmering like light on a lake. The sound of traffic, even at our height, was still intense.

The leader of the group was Nozawa. Bearded, with scruffy black hair, he was the Japanese version of an artist, the perpetual graduate student, someone who shows up at avant-garde theater, at performances of Butoh, jazz clubs, foreign movies. When he spoke he seemed to spit the words forward, as if their force couldn't be controlled. He was an ethnographic filmmaker and had recently spent a year and a half around Santa Fe, filming a documentary about Native Americans. Just above his beard, on his right cheek, there were two moles. He asked about my favorite authors.

My answers—Faulkner, Márquez, Woolf, Barthes, Benjamin, Milosz, Kundera, Sontag—met with occasional blank looks. Was it my pronunciation? With a shake of his head, Nozawa dismissed Barthes as a semiotician, Sontag as a mere critic. His words held a small twist of tension.

Misao asked Susie a question about her stay in Japan. It was polite, concerned. Susie answered briefly, was quickly forgotten. Nozawa began to pass out Xeroxed sheets of Japanese-American poems, the stories of a Nisei writer. I said nothing, resorted to tatemae, keeping up appearances. The poems were flat, like a base coat of paint, meant to be covered over by whatever art or brilliant colors would come afterward. The life behind them, the years of the camps, the shifting sensibilities of the postwar years were reduced to clichés of sociology. Nozawa spoke of meeting Japanese-Americans and feeling ashamed he knew nothing about them. I was an artifact, the message from a probe sent out into space years ago.

How could I tell them what it had been like? I sensed they wanted a list of name-calling, of blackballing, refusals to rent an apartment. They wanted the racism in America to be more blatant, more clear-cut, than it often was. I told them about seeing the NHK drama on the relocation camps that showed Nisei who were merely Japanese who spoke English, who were nothing like my father or mother, my aunts or uncles. Of course the actors were Japanese, but that was beside the point.

I was in an exam, I was failing. I tried again explaining the effects of living in an all-white culture.

Nozawa observed that I had married a hakujin.

I glanced at Susie, paused. Had he said this with a snarl, or was that merely his manner?

I could feel myself sinking in quicksand. It was impossible. How could I explain how the love I have for Susie was somehow mixed with a sense of inferiority and rage around my race and color?

I simplified; I evaded, tried to make it understandable. I felt that I, like Susie, had suddenly become some sort of pet, some stereotype, a "young Sansei poet." Tell us about the Japanese-American experience, but don't confound our expectations, lay it out in the neat, clean lines we've provided.

Susie looked at her watch. "Oh, God, it's four o'clock."

I felt myself being ushered out the door by some urgency concocted without me.

"What was that all about?" I said on the street. "I felt so embarrassed. It was clear you didn't give a rat's ass about Nozawa's feelings."

She apologized, she paused, she continued: "You never think about how I feel in those situations."

We were under the highway that rested on stilts above the street. The tiers of traffic were a solution to density. The air was sticky with the promise of rain. The sky was darkening with gray.

"Oh, excuse me, I don't always put you at the center of my life. God forbid I should do anything else."

She was rushing up the street, sputtering in rage and tears. "I can't stand it when you're like this. You just make me furious. You're such an asshole."

Suddenly I sensed this wasn't entirely about me.

"I get tired of feeling out of place," she said, "tired of being the only hakujin in a group, of trying to smile and be sociable and put on my best front, as if I'm some foreign-service official and I've got to make a good impression. I get tired of feeling as if I'm on display." She turned to me. "And then Nozawa just asks that question as if I wasn't even there."

We were walking down a small alley, trying to get away from the crowd at Hobson's Ice Cream Parlor, seeking a quiet refuge from the Tokyo traffic. For the Japanese, confrontation is anathema, especially in public. I kept pressing her: there was something else.

"It's just that I'm aware I'm going to leave soon," she said. "And I think, who do I really know? Who am I really friends with? With most Japanese, I'm still just a pet. If my relationships are going to get any deeper, I'm going to have to go to a new level. I'll have to learn the language better, but I'm not going to, I'm going home. So what did I do with this year? What did I accomplish?"

I didn't know what to say. It was true that as a gaijin, she was often regarded as a novelty, treated graciously, even generously, but valued more for her foreignness than for who she was. And problems of language made relationships so much more difficult. She knew, as an American, she placed more value on intimate personal revelations as a sign of friendship. Many Japanese, like Reiko and Haruki, can have a perfectly fine friendship over the years and never know even the most basic things about the other person's private life. And the friendship is not less valued because of this. But knowing all this wasn't enough.

Yet in certain friendships Susie had broken through, had achieved a sort of intimacy I had not. People sensed they could trust her. They could open up to her, as when Reiko told her about her cancer. Susie was a passionate listener, a probing questioner. She was also a gaijin. People felt freer with her; she wasn't going to judge them like a Japanese. Intimacy came precisely because she started out as a curious outsider. Takako had recognized this difference. She was now filing for a divorce, in part because of Susie's encouragement, and for a long time, Susie was the only one besides the family members who knew about the separation.

"I think of going back home, and going back to work, and getting caught up in my life, and it will be as if nothing's changed. And there's all sorts of things I want to and have to do before I leave. . . ."

I started to list all the changes that were coming. "And now you're going through this period of despising certain things about Japan, letting yourself be critical. . . . At the same time, you're going through a grief period for all you're going to miss."

Her face relaxed for a second. "Oh, God, cognitive dissonance. Psych 101." She sighed. "But really, what do I have to show
for this year? Did I waste my time? Do you think I used my time
wisely?"

"You know more about the world, you're larger. You're
going to understand the Vietnamese and Hmong refugees who
come to see you at the hospital in ways you couldn't before. You're
going to have a sense that the world is larger than Minnesota or the
United States, and you're going to give our kids that sense, a sense
of possibilities I know I didn't grow up with." I put my arms around
her. "Jesus, give yourself a break. . . ."

And so we stumbled on, in that alley in Roppongi, giving
each other hugs, asking for reassurances, evaluations, reassurances,
doing the kind of patchwork job, that comforting, that lies at the
heart of marriage when it works, when it is good. I realized again
how quickly we understood in the other where the pain, the fear,
the insecurities are buried, and thought how much we would miss
each other in the few months we'd be separated. I felt, for the first
time, a real anticipation of that short loss, and her sadness became,
awakened, my own. We were hugging each other, next to the
chain-link fence and the bushes behind it, closed off for a moment
from the traffic and crowds of Tokyo. We were leaving Japan.

VIII

"Sometimes spectators of the Noh say that the moments of 'no action' are the most enjoyable. . . . The actions before and after an interval of 'no action' must be linked by entering the state of mindlessness in which the actor conceals even from himself his own intent."
—Zeami

". . . either I can be like some traveler of the olden days, who was faced with a stupendous spectacle, all, or almost all, of which eluded him, or worse still, filled him with scorn and disgust; or I can be a modern traveler, chasing after the vestiges of a vanished reality. . . . A few hundred years hence, in this same place, another traveler, as despairing as myself, will mourn the disappearance of what I might have seen, but failed to see."

—Claude Lévi-Strauss,
Tristes Tropiques

1

After Susie returned to the States, I spent much of my time working on my novel about my grandparents and the relocation camps. I realized that only now, after spending time in Japan, could I write this novel: if my factual knowledge was still lacking, I felt I now possessed some sense of where they had been before they came to America, of what America must have looked like to their Japanese eyes. I could hope research and imagination would take me the rest of the way.

Involved in this novel, I saw fewer and fewer people. I felt I needed to live within this dream I was creating. The novel opens after my grandmother's death, with my grandfather having returned to Tokyo, amazed at the changes that had already begun taking place in the late fifties and yet still enjoying some of the privileges of being the rich American uncle to distant relatives. He buys meat, refrigerators, and other appliances for them, smokes huge Cuban cigars after meals all paid for by himself. He is contemplating a new marriage. I felt that living alone in Tokyo now gave me the perspective I needed to write this section. Still, I missed Susie.

With Ken and Akiko, I took a trip to Osore-zan, a mountain in the north of Honshu where blind women shamans meet every year for a festival. The mountain is volcanic, and on a clear, hot summer day, after the taxi left us off, we climbed past hissing sulphur springs up to a shallow, clear blue lake. Near the shore were tiny stone mounds, with little *jizo,* miniature Buddhas, on top. At their feet pilgrims had placed an odd assortment of food, from rice crackers to potato chips and koala bear cookies. On a plateau just above the lake, dozens of tents were set up. Outside each tent were lines of people, mostly women and a few old men, all waiting to meet the shamans.

"The shamans speak to the dead," said Ken. "These old people come here to talk to their dead relatives."

We plopped ourselves down outside a tent and waited. Around noon, the heat had hit ninety. Akiko said she couldn't quite understand the dialect of the shamans. I kept speaking to a tape recorder, making a tape to send back to Susie. Ken and I joked about how beautiful the shamanesses were. Akiko frowned. *"Nan da yo."*

As had happened so often before in Japan, I wondered what I was doing, especially when I was told the visit with the shaman would cost ten thousand yen (about sixty dollars). I had wanted to try to talk to my grandparents. "My grandmother used to have prophetic dreams," I explained to Ken.

Finally, we moved up the line to the edge of the tent. As the shamaness rattled her amber beads, chanting in a six-beat rhythm, nodding and weaving back and forth, I suddenly recalled the service we had each year for my grandparents. With my aunt Ruby's family, we'd go to the apartment of a Buddhist priest on the North Side, and he would sit in front of his small altar and chant, rattling his prayer beads. They sounded like paper crackling. His voice and language were so strange that all the children would begin to giggle. We'd try to hold ourselves in, but often by the end of the service we were practically rolling in the aisles. The priest seemed to pay no attention. He simply droned on.

The shamaness was about seventy. Her skin was weathered, white, wrinkled as a dusty riverbed. Her kimono fell loosely about her, and her body seemed large, though in the darkness of the tent I couldn't tell where her body left off and the kimono began. The tent was hot as a sauna. As my eyes adjusted, Akiko explained that I was from America and that I was seeking my grandparents. I didn't feel quite like laughing, just chuckling. It seemed so absurd. *"Nikkei-jin . . . Sansei . . ."* I picked out certain words. The shamaness began to chant, each line punctuated by the syllables *"Soreba . . ."* Her body moved forward and back, her lip quivered.

And then, after a few brief minutes, she stopped and

dropped the beads into her lap, as if they were red-hot stones. The séance was over.

It was a good thing I had my tape recorder, because afterward both Akiko and Ken said they didn't understand much of what she had said. They told me my grandmother had thanked me for coming and said *"Gambatte kudasai"* (the Japanese phrase for good luck, which literally means, work hard), but even I had gotten that. When we listened to the tape back at the inn, we discovered most of the shamaness's other phrases were stock lines. She did say, Watch out for July 15, but she didn't say why. There was also an allusion to a relative, an uncle or a great-uncle, who had hung himself, and something about a stillborn child.

"What a ripoff," I said. "Ten thousand for that?"

Ken nodded. *"Sho ga nai. Sho ga nai."*

"Well, at least it wasn't a tourist trap I fell for. I didn't see anyone else on that mountain who was a year under fifty."

"How can you say such things," Akiko said. "You don't know for sure."

"But that's the way all these people work, the same in America. They tell you all sorts of general things and then they make a few cryptic comments, which, if you're inclined to believe, can be interpreted to mean anything you want."

"Don't tell me you believe in these things?" Ken asked Akiko.

"You don't believe in them because they're women."

"It has nothing to do with their being women," I said.

"It's true. Women can see things men can't. There's a long tradition of shamans."

"But I thought you didn't believe in tradition, in the family," I replied.

"This is different. They're like, they're like"—she was searching for something—"that writer from Denmark, Isak Dinesen. She wrote this essay where she said that women who live without men, who don't need men, are always called witches. Men believe they have magical evil powers."

"But we don't believe that. That's just the point," I said. "You're always so angry, Akiko. Sometimes you ought to take it easy."

Akiko lit a cigarette. "Yeah, yeah, yeah . . ."

"Did I tell you about this dissertation a friend of mine is writing on the shamans?" asked Ken. I knew we were in for another long disquisition.

Two weeks later, as I set out for a Noh performance, about fifteen yards from my door, I came upon a dead dog, raucous with flies. The stench moved toward me like a claw, and I suddenly recalled the date. July 15. So what the hell does this mean, I thought.

I walked past the dog, giving it a wide berth. By the time I hit the main avenue to the station, I was telling myself I should buy a sports coat before I left. Something by Kenzo, I thought. If I have the money.

2

In the theater of Seibu, the city's largest department store, two American musicians stood ten feet apart, dressed all in black. Suddenly they began tapping their heads, their chest, their hands, their stomachs, clicking their mouths, whistling in a version of the Afro-American music "The Bones." It was as strange to the Japanese as Gagaku or Noh was to us. They did some pieces with their voices, not singing, but exploring the range of sounds they could create, like Meredith Monk. It was like a child playing with language, an experiment in sound performed on the body. Then they did pieces with instruments they'd created out of rubber and brass tubes, pails, synthesizers.

"Amusing," said Ricardo. I couldn't tell whether he liked it or not.

We were sitting with Daniel and some Noh musicians, including an American, Rick Emmert. As we rose to leave, I noticed Mieko sitting a few rows back. Ever since she had broken up with Haruki, she seemed less a part of our circle. We hadn't seen her in weeks. I introduced her to everyone, mentioned to Ricardo that Mieko was a composer. We headed off to a yakitoriya. Behind me I could see Mieko and Ricardo talking, Ricardo bending down to hear her voice above the traffic. He must have seemed like a giant to her. The lights of Parco depato sprayed above us like fireworks, neon shooting back and forth. We passed two theaters with marquees advertising soft porn. The sidewalk was narrow, crowded with students. Rick Emmert was demonstrating the calls Noh drummers use to keep time, a combination of yodel, groan, and shout, like the sound a cowboy would make spurring on his horse, only drawn out in slow motion, as if a record were being played at half speed. I loved the sound almost more than I loved the sound of Noh chanting or the wails of the Noh flute, a herky-jerky running up and down the scales that should have sounded manic but instead drew you inward, like a trance. I was so involved with our discussion I didn't even give a second thought to Mieko and Ricardo.

I often compared Ricardo with Daniel. They were two hakujin artists living in Japan. Daniel would never have been attracted to Mieko. His wife was older, European. Mieko would have been too young, too slight. I'd have thought Ricardo would feel the same. Perhaps it was because I was not attracted to Mieko.

At the time he met Mieko, Ricardo was already seeing two other Japanese women. One worked at the Mexican consul, the second was a flight attendant. He had met them at cocktail parties held at the Mexican embassy. I think there were others. It was hard to keep track. I met one of them: she was older, more worldly than Mieko, had a desperation Mieko lacked. This woman saw Ricardo as her ticket out of Japan, a way to escape the box-like existence of a sarariman's wife. But underneath I think she knew he was no ticket at all. Perhaps that explains why she was so quiet sitting beside him at this party. Any word more and the spell might have been broken. "These women are inexhaustible," Ricardo complained to me in mock fatigue. "They're wearing me out." I gave him little sympathy, though I couldn't quite make myself come down on him with all of Susie's moral approbation. I was like the good Christian friend of a Mormon in the days of polygamy. I watched intently for signs of damnation. I was certain it couldn't be all that much fun.

"Why Mieko?" I once asked. He said that I underestimated her, her quiet.

The same age as Haruki, Ricardo was even more distant from Mieko culturally. Their relationship seemed doomed from the start. Perhaps that was why it became so quickly physical. He cajoled her, questioned and mocked her, criticized her compositions. They went to concerts, listened to recordings of Takemitsu and Kondo Jo. He met her parents, stood like an aberration before them, barely fitting in their doorway. His whiteness was astonishing, so pale, so broad. It must have seemed inconceivable to them that Mieko and this man could be together. They would have dismissed the thought from their minds. Later, when they were forced to entertain it, they saw it was impossible, knew if they ignored it it would go away. Somehow Ricardo seemed better than Haruki, though if you asked them, they probably could not have told you why.

Mieko blossomed, began talking about going to Europe to study, lost some of her virginal shyness. She seemed unperturbed at the prospect of Ricardo's leaving Japan. She would never ride a huge Honda like Reiko, but she would find her own way.

3

My dubious dealings with the underworld and my grandmother's spirit at Osore-zan reminded me I had not yet gone to my grandparents' hometown. It was something I needed to do for the novel, something I had been planning on ever since I had come to Japan. But I had somehow put it off. In part, I had been waiting to go with Reiko, who had talked of the trip several months before. But she hadn't mentioned it since. I could have gone on my own. Perhaps I was afraid of being disappointed, as I had been with my trip to Osore-zan.

And then, a few weeks before I was to leave, Reiko called one day out of the blue and said we were going. I felt relieved. And, for some reason, a little sad.

I am going to Ise, to Koyasan, to Yoshino, to Nara, to all those places the poet Bashō visited on his journeys. Sad, funny pilgrim, ascetic spirit, indelible, wise and witty artist of nature, he spoke of days and months as travelers of eternity, of those pilgrims who have died on the road. I, on the other hand, do not truly fear my own death, I can hardly imagine it. I am one of those unwise grasshopper spirits who must be reincarnated and suffer again. Time, for me, seems merely in endless supply, freely offered, as much a birthright as the American fat on my bones, the greater stature of my cartilage, what sets my body apart in this land of my ancestors.

But that's not it. I am also going to Shingu, the home of my grandfather and grandmother, the home of my ancestors. Who were all Japanese. Who are all dead. Whose home I could never have visited, or imagined visiting, when they were alive. When I announce this trip to others here, I receive friendly laughter and a mispronounced "Rootsu."

Several times at keiko, following my Butoh sensei's instructions to keep my eyes open and communicate with the world of the dead, I have looked for them, my grandparents. I probably couldn't have spoken to them more than a couple of dozen times in my life. They seemed to me, even when they were alive, like ghosts, like beings transported from another world, lacking the profound, everyday, corporeal sense of my aunts and uncles, my cousins and siblings, my parents. All that's left of them in me is perhaps a taste for something sweet and salty, a sandy Buddhist incense (and perhaps not even that).

On the way to my grandparents' village, we passed through Toba, home of the Ise Shrine. It was late afternoon and the mountain above the shrine was already deep in shadows. The parking lot in front was surprisingly empty, a pleasant change from my trip to Kyoto. We walked through the famous first torii and across the first bridge. The torii was unpainted, a soft gray wood, like a dove's feathers, not the more common red or orange lacquer finish.

After walking down a stone path through a wide lawn, we entered a grove of trees, and then a clearing. I washed my hands

in a small tsukubai, and walked down the stone steps to the river
to wash my hands again, performing the ablutions of the pilgrim.
The steps were about forty feet wide, and the river was the shallow,
stone-bottomed river you find everywhere in Japan, with patches of
rock rising here and there above the surface, and farther down,
great stretches of gravel. During the dry season of fall, these rivers
appear to have never been filled, becoming streams or a series of
small puddles and ponds.

There were carp right next to the steps, waiting to be fed.
I stared at them, trying to figure out which was the most mutant-
looking. Years before, I'd written a poem which ends with a woman
comparing herself to a mutant carp (well, the image in my poem
was a little more poetically put than that). It had been so much
easier to choose what images I needed when I was totally ignorant
of how ignorant I was of this country. Now things were harder. I
was conscious of the inaccuracy of certain images or statements in
my poems concerning Japan. Of course, I'd been taught that you
put in a poem whatever the poem needs. The problem was, now
I had a choice I'd never had, and prompted by my new knowledge
of the country, I felt a much stronger obligation to accuracy.

Suddenly some men from a tour group, dressed in cardi-
gans and V-necks, gray-and-black-checked pants, loafers, sarariman
on a *ryoko* (vacation) came jogging down the steps. They jostled
one another, laughed, attempted to push their friends into the
water; they yelled *"Tsumetai"* (it's cold), splashed, washed their
hands, dried themselves with handkerchiefs. I was struck by the
boyishness, the playfulness, the immaturity of their behavior.

As they left, I looked upriver; the trees were *kunugi* (oak),
momiji, ginkgo, bamboo, and above them, the evenness of the firs
and pines gave the slopes of the mountain a gentle roundedness,
darkening with shadows. Downstream, a man with a wheelbarrow
appeared, then another, and both began dumping small piles of
stones in the riverbed. As usual in Japan, the landscape was not
nature *au naturel* but nature shaped by human labor, by men in
straw hats with kerchiefs, the unnoticed wielders of wheelbarrows,
the dumpers of stones, figures in black boots and soiled gloves, blue
canvas coats, faces reddened by the wind and sun, beards tough-

ened, steely eyes without expression. Slowly, bearing the calm of the *kurokata,* the hooded black stagehands of Kabuki and Bunraku, invisible to the audience, they waded through the current as the evening swept on.

My family does not even know where my grandfather's ashes are. They were supposedly moved from one graveyard to a mountain temple, where there was more room, where there are thousands of little markers, each marking for someone a death. My aunt Ruby, who had paid the money for the upkeep and blessings of the ashes, went to look for the urn site about ten years ago. She couldn't find it and, frustrated, broke down in tears. She felt she had been a bad daughter. But the forces she was fighting were larger than she. She was American, this was not her home, and her father was not a Japanese who had clung to his kuni. He had sent his genes, if not his soul, across the seas, to the barbarian land.

I think ahead, and I think there will be no story. There is nothing to tell. I know no one in the town. My closest relatives are in America. My grandfather's sister and brother have died. His widow, the one he married on his return to Japan after my grandmother died, is also dead (it was, I am told, a marriage of convenience, of companionship in old age, a financial arrangement, nothing of importance—so says my aunt, my father). Even the paper on which my aunt Ruth wrote down in characters the names of my grandfather and grandmother, names which I never knew as a child or even through much of my adult life (at this writing I cannot remember my grandmother's name), even that paper I will bring along on the slim chance that it might be of some use in finding some shard, some filament, some sign of my past, is water-stained, crumpled, the characters fading into each other, blurring their lines. How many myriad fadings have taken place since they first left that village? I will not even receive the faint remnants of a disaster, a few smoldering ashes and ruins. It will all be rebuilt. It will all be new. Everything has vanished. No one has survived to tell the story.

I carry their names in my wallet, names I cannot read.

Ise Shrine is one of the many places where Bashō wrote a poem and thus left his mark. The wooden shrine is taken down every twenty years and reconstructed in an adjacent site, using the exact same design and traditional methods of carpentry. When I tell Americans this, they always want to know why, a question that automatically underscores their distance from Japanese tradition. Although surface and structure, as opposed to substance, are important in Japanese aesthetics; although the Japanese have a penchant for new things—they throw out year-old appliances and have, through tax laws, literally banned old cars from their roads—I suspect that the fact of tradition best explains this tearing down and rebuilding. In face of a centuries-old tradition, you do not question why or talk about practicalities of cost. Certain questions which seem automatic to a Westerner simply do not exist here, have no place in the structures of thought.

The wood of the shrine, which is like that of the entrance torii—unpainted, a deep-grained, rough-hewn gray—supports a thatched roof, whose strands are visible yet so closely packed together as to seem welded solid. The effect is one of a startling calm and simplicity, which makes the largeness of the structure seem merely the impression gained by looking at it from a closer distance, rather than the force of imperial and lofty imposition, which you sense at many other shrines. Standing before it, I felt the peasant origins of the architecture, the source of Shintoism in the ancient gods and rites, in the primeval forests and mountains, in the worries and backbending labor of the rice fields.

I threw a coin in the offering box and stared at the white banner cloth hung in the entrance gate, behind which, when the wind moved, I could see the stone courtyard and the shrine inside. I clapped my hands twice and thanked, as I had done so many times in this country, my ojii-san and obaa-san, from my father's side, from my mother's side. I stared at the white cloth. A breeze flared; the flap flew up, then fell back down again. As I turned, I saw a priest walking across the stones, in a white, loose-fitting gown, light-green khaki trousers, a black cap tied to his head. I was struck by the fact that he wore glasses. I knew my grandparents had been Buddhist, but I didn't know if they were Shinto, though most Japanese consider themselves both. It didn't really matter. I had made my pilgrimage. I had said my prayer.

Several times during my stay here in Japan, I have been reminded of a passage in Wordsworth's "Prelude," where he is traveling up the Alps to see Mont Blanc; at a certain point, feeling that he is lost, he asks a local person where he is and how far it is to the mountain, and the person tells Wordsworth that he has already passed that mountain, that it is farther back through the gorges and roads by which he has just come. I don't remember what point he makes of this moment, or what point we made of it in graduate school, but it seems its significance rests in its anticlimactic character, as well as the dream-like, uncanny cast to the narrative: the traveler both feels he knows where he is going and at the same time knows that he is lost and that the significance of what he is seeing and experiencing is more mysterious and unreadable than it appears. He knows a message is being given, but does not know what the message means.

Japan for me has been the land of lost connections, of wanderings from the path of the guidebooks, missing what I was supposed to see, and yet always knowing that I am seeing something which strikes me, which I will always remember, which I have never seen except in dreams. So often, though, the significance remains occluded, lost, the connection to the past impossible and inpenetrable.

After Toba, to get to my grandparents' hometown, we drove through range after range of mountain, valley after valley. And then we reached the coast, getting small glimpses of beaches, then going back into the mountains or through them by long, dimly lit tunnels. We stopped for lunch at an inn for fishermen and there had a huge miniature boat of sashimi: maguro, large *ebi* (prawns), and a whole fish, its entire body laid out, carved in tiny pieces, ending with the head, still intact, curled upward, as if leaping one last time. Sometimes the fish served like this are still alive and, through the whole meal, quiver and flick back and forth, gills shuddering for breath. Reiko's friend Moko told me that Shingu was famous for the log rafts they used to float downriver. It was a logging and fishing town, and a center for trade for the surrounding area on the peninsula. She didn't know how large a population it has.

A travel writer, Moko took pictures of the meal during its various stages: first the tempura, then small broiled fishes, and then soup. Like the previous night's dinner, it was another in a series of huge meals at various places on the trip, so that finally, despite my love of sashimi and tofu, I was thoroughly glad to reach Tokyo and reward my taste buds and stomach with something less healthy and far more greasy. (As it turned out, I wasn't even able to make it back to Tokyo; waiting for the train in Nara, I went to the McDonald's for a quick American fix.)

Seven miles before Shingu, we hit a magnificent stone beach. I asked that we stop in front of the shops along the highway so I could take a picture, a good Japanese reason to stop. On the beach were a couple of small fishermen's huts, with nets hanging on poles outside. The fishermen, cigarettes held like permanent fixtures in their jaws, were tending the lines. They looked at us, and went back to work. Down the beach, the peninsula thrust out into the ocean, carrying with it a series of mountains, slope after slope rolling into the distance. Beneath the violent orange of the sunset, the slopes of the mountains were slowly turning to soft shades of blue and the stones of the beach to a faint, pale purple. Small waves rushed up to the shore, sputtering little pockets of foam, and I had the urge to wet my shoes, in a sort of ablution, like a pilgrim at a shrine. When I scrambled down the greater slope that led to the water, a large wave rushed to greet me. I scrambled back up, the rocks slipped beneath me, I stumbled and was bathed up to my thighs in foam, the seawater drenching my new, Harajuku-bought Kenzo pants. My shoes were completely filled with water. After finally scrambling back up, I emptied them on the beach, picked up a few pebbles, and used my socks to carry them, souvenirs of sorts.

While my companions continued to look for stones and to take pictures, I went back to the car, walked between one of the buildings, and, for the first time here, availed myself of the Japanese custom of pissing in public, the relief a slight compensation for being wet and cold. This was my other, unmentioned reason for asking to stop the car. (Ken once told me a story of walking through a narrow street in Tokyo one night, around one o'clock, and finding two women, their skirts pulled up, squatting by the side of the street and pissing; he found this so startling that he stood and watched them, and continued to do so even when one of the women asked, "What do you think you're looking at? Go away." Finally, one of the women asked him if he had a cigarette, and he said sure, gave it to her, lit it, and she took two or three puffs before finishing and pulling up her panties and letting down her skirt.)

A half hour later, as I sat uncomfortably wet in the back

seat, we turned a bend and there was Shingu, just across the Shingu River. I could see factories on the side of town near the sea, the stacks sending up gray snakes of smoke—not quite the quaint, picturesque village I had envisioned. Still, I asked Reiko to stop the car, and in the failing light I took a couple of pictures of a castle-like structure that loomed on a hill above the river, right above the bridge you cross to enter the town. As with many of the pictures I took in Japan, I failed to judge the light. In the pictures the white of the castle merges with the landscape into one indistinguishable gray, as if to reinforce my sense of how mundane the place looked, my slight disappointment.

What my grandparents experienced, what kind of people gave birth to and raised my father, all this represents an impossible knowledge. Does culture ordinarily form a net of remembrance, a safety guard against forgetting? Does it provide the individual with at least some clues, some vague outlines, from which to discern his family history? All I have are these doubts and feelings of loss, these questions which pull me on, step after step, a dance of folly. Over and over, knowing it is futile, I try to create my own myth of history.

Like other towns along the coast, Shingu seemed narrow, scrunched between the sea and the mountains. As we crossed the bridge and hit the main street, we turned to go to the one large temple in town. It seemed a typical Buddhist temple, but I was pleased to be at a place where my grandparents might have walked and prayed. For some reason, I bought a rather tacky wooden placard of the Shingu Hi Matsuri, or Fire Festival, and four sets of chopsticks for the members of my family. Only later on in my trip did I learn from Reiko that four was considered an unlucky number by the Japanese, because the word for the number four, *shi,* puns with the *shi* which means death.

It was dark by now, and in the early-evening light, under the glow of the lanterns lit by electric bulbs, I again said prayers for my grandparents in front of the shrine. It didn't feel much different from similar prayers I'd performed elsewhere in Japan. As we left, Reiko said that the temple was new, had been built in 1959, although the grounds had been a place of worship for hundreds of years. So, I thought, my grandparents never saw these buildings when they were young. The buildings aren't the link I'd hoped for. Everything is new; the connections are lost.

As we left, my last sight was of a lighted soft-drink machine, with red dots which seemed to connect little streams of light and a display case where you could see cans of Coke, Fanta, Kirin Orange, and Kirin Lemon. For some reason, I wanted to and now wish I had taken a picture of this. It is what I remember most vividly about the place, what I see most clearly now in my mind's eye. And it is there that I think I glimpse the ghosts of my grandparents: if I close my eyes I seem to see my grandfather's face more clearly, since his portrait did hang for a while in our living room when I was a child, though I can see that my grandmother is dressed in a black dress, a black veil, funereal. They are lit on one side, the side where my grandfather is standing and waving, by the soft fluorescent light of the machine. The other side, where my grandmother stands soberly, quietly, not waving, is the darkness of evening, the darker shadows of the temple pines. As we turn a corner, I am, according to Japanese custom, still waving, till they are out of sight.

IX

"We will gather images and images of images up till the last, which is blank. This one we will agree on."
—Edmond Jabes, *The Book of Yukel*

"What happens to children—yes, that's what one longs to know."

—James Salter, *Light Years*

1

When I think back to that year in Japan, what comes to mind isn't the nights drinking with friends in tiny bars in Tokyo, or the Noh performances, or my dance lessons in Butoh, or even going back to my grandfather's hometown. What comes to mind is the image from my trip to the Philippines, of me riding a jeepney in the mountainous region of northern Luzon. Although the jeepney—a used army jeep with an extended back end and a canvas cover on top—is the public transportation of the Philippines, I'm riding alone with the driver and his friend. As they jabber in Ilacano, wind and rain slash through the sides of the jeepney. I peer out at valleys that fall away in mist down the mountainsides, at the dense underbrush of vines, man-sized plants, and palm trees with wide, wet green leaves. From time to time, we pass a shack with no windows, a corrugated iron roof, a pig tied to a post in the yard, bits of board and nameless metal junk scattered about, everything dark and gray, the color of cinders. When a woman with a bundle runs out of the hut, flagging down the jeepney, we rush past. I feel guilty: only by hiring a jeepney which doesn't stop can I get to the famous terraced rice fields and return to Manila in time for my plane the next day. I watch the back of the woman, her drab print dress popping with rain, as she slogs through the mud back to her hut. The jeepney smashes a bump, rattles, and storms on, winding around mountain curve after mountain curve, hugging the edges. I want us to slow down. I say nothing.

There was no real reason why I needed to see the ancient rice fields of Banaue. They are listed as one of the few tourist attractions of this region, which is a stronghold of the New People's Army, the Communist insurgents. Perhaps I had some wacky notion I might run into some mountain guerrillas. I'd learned in Japan that the final destination always ends up being less significant than what happens on the way.

The air was damp and cool that high up in the mountains. My face was dripping, my clothes soaked, my body hungry and cold and constipated (the last born of a puritan's fear of unclean facilities or, rather, in this sparsely populated region of poverty, no facilities). I felt at times as if I were in the Andes rather than the Philippines, some scene from Herzog's *Aguirre: The Wrath of God,* the camera descending down the slopes of green and mist, focusing on some indistinguishable, ant-like figures in the valley below. But suddenly, on the edge of the road, there was a series of shacks, and then, on a ridge just below us, the long tan tourist hotels of Banaue, stucco roofs and balconies, smoke rising from chimneys. A muddy, tarred main street.

As we reached the turnoff to the town, the driver asked if I wanted to keep going to the top of the mountain to a point where you can look down on the rice fields. Just as I said yes, a figure appeared on the road waving an umbrella. He had on a terry-cloth golf cap, a blue windbreaker, and white shorts, tennis shoes. A Nikon was strung around his neck. When we reached him, the driver, recognizing a tourist, did not rush on as he had when the local citizens flagged him down, but stopped. The man in the road leaned into the jeepney, revealing a Japanese face: *"Biupointo?"* he asked.

I burst out laughing, recognizing the tones of Japlish, English words pronounced according to the rules of Japanese pronunciation (*v* becomes *b;* no consonants can stand without a vowel attached). Immediately the Japanese man and I began talking in Japanese, asking where each other was from, how long we'd been in the Philippines, and a circle formed between us, as there had been a circle between the driver and his friend. I was now grouped with the Japanese man, a compatriot of a sort. It was probably as close as I came that year to being Japanese.

2

A few weeks after I returned from the Philippines, Ricardo had a going-away party for me. He cooked a chicken molé, Daniel somehow managed a cassoulet. Akiko, accompanied by the bar maid from the Shinjuku bar, brought two platters of sushi. Ken and Setsuko brought a bucket of Kentucky Fried Chicken, since Susie had always joked about how I was the only one of my friends who actually ate the stuff.

"To prepare you for the States," Ken said. He talked about going back for graduate school in Asian studies. Setsuko worried about what she'd do there.

"I have my brother, and my father, and *yari, yari, yari* . . ." *Yari, yari, yari* was an expression they'd cooked up together. Ken had thought it was Japanese, and Setsuko had thought it was a synonym for et cetera. Neither of them could determine who first thought up the term.

Ricardo's apartment was a bit bigger than mine, but the place was soon crammed. Reiko showed up on her motorcycle. Saito came, bearing a copy of the anthology of Japanese-American poets he'd translated. He gave it to me as a goodbye gift.

"Doomo arrigato gozaimasu," I said. "Thanks for all the things you've done for me."

Saito talked of editing an anthology of Japanese-American fiction.

"It's strange," I said. "The Nisei seemed to be mainly prose writers. They wrote memoirs about the camps, a few novels. Now most of the Sansei are poets."

"Maybe that's because nothing's happened to us," said Ken, "and the Nisei never talk about the past."

Ricardo put on a Gagaku tape. I asked him if Mieko was coming. He nodded.

"There's also this woman I want you to meet, who's coming later. She's from the embassy . . ." He smiled sheepishly.

"You're incorrigible," I said.

"No, I just want to be realistic. Nothing's going to come of me and Mieko. She knows it. I know it." Later, I saw him approach Kumiko, the bar maid.

Leaning against the door, Daniel was telling Akiko about studying Noh. He said he was going to try to bring our teacher, Okinaka, to Paris. Next month Daniel was supposed to perform in Berlin. His wife was going to meet him there. I introduced Reiko to Daniel. They began talking about Pina Bausch. Sometimes Akiko had to translate. I had the sense that for Daniel Japan had been an interesting excursion, a sidelight. His real trip had taken place when he went to Paris at twenty-two. Now he traveled all over the world—East Germany, Egypt, Thailand, Bali.

"I keep thinking about my next play," he said to me later. "I've got this idea of using windows as the center. There's the American window that works like a guillotine, the French window that goes from the floor almost to the ceiling and opens inward, and the Japanese window, which isn't a window at all, and which slides open. And each of them embodies a different psyche, a different culture . . ."

I thought about Haruki and Mieko, about Ono and Okinaka. I had hoped Okinaka would be able to make it to the party, but he was performing in Kyoto. I thought of Gisela, whom I'd seen a couple of days ago in the local post office. She was dressed in a white T-shirt and white shorts. She looked oddly American, and almost dowdy. We said hello. I felt inordinately awkward, as if we'd never met.

". . . with the exchange rate, I actually made a profit with my deposit," I told Daniel. "Maybe I'm learning something about business after all."

Ricardo told me to have some more mole. "This is great stuff," he said, "only it sits in your gut for days. Sometimes I think that's why Mexico is in such an economic mess. We eat this food that puts you in a permanent stupor. You don't want to do anything but sit around and groan."

He then proceeded to tell us about his friend Maria, who was an opera singer and who had had an affair with a Russian singer at a music festival in Tokyo. At the end of the festival the Russian decided to defect, and Maria asked Ricardo to help get the Russian to the American embassy. "We had a wild time trying to lose the KGB, or whoever it was that was after him. We kept on changing taxis, all over Tokyo. I had him stay the night at the apartment of this girl I know."

"Ricardo knows women all over the city," I told Daniel.

"The thing is," he continued, "the affair between these two opera singers is never going to last. I know that. She knows that. But he, poor chap . . ."

Just then, Keiko, Matsuo's girlfriend, walked in the door with a bottle of sake.

"It's from Matsuo," she said. I hadn't heard from him since he disappeared and went to Korea.

"I kept trying to call him."

"He said he would have liked to come, but he has to be away on business."

I didn't know what to think. Was he avoiding me? Was he, for some reason, angry at me? Had we ever planned to go to Korea? I knew it was useless to ask Keiko, he never told her anything. I thanked her for the sake and asked her to give my best to Matsuo.

A while later, I found Akiko sipping a Kirin on the steps outside. She started telling me about this married man she was seeing. He wasn't like the men she knew at the leftist school. They were like boys; they believed the right things, but they were boys.

"But he's married, Akiko."

"You don't understand what it's like for a woman like me. I don't have a choice."

"Maybe you should try moving to America."

"I can't. I'm too old, I'm too Japanese. I'm trapped." She paused. "Like you. You like it here, but you can't live here."

"No, I suppose not."

"You're not like us."

"I just know that after a while I'd feel too cramped here.

It's not just the physical space. You're always supposed to act a certain way, and for a while it's okay . . . It's amazing, Tokyo is this gigantic city, but you get the feeling that it's actually quite small, that the whole society is like a small town. Okinaka knows this Noh performer who went to America and stayed there too long. After a while, everybody began to talk about him. He had lost his ki, he had the hots for American women. Some even said he was gay. You can't step out of line. . . ."

"But you've just been here a year."

"I know. And I can do all the right things for a while. But I can feel it now, perhaps it's just because I'm leaving. After a while, I'd go crazy here . . ."

"See," she laughed. "That's just what I've been telling you. I despise Japan." But she was smiling, her voice was softer than usual.

"But I've learned something from you," she said. I looked up, puzzled. "You've taught me not to be so angry. I want to thank you for it."

I felt embarrassed. "Well, you've taught me things—"

"Yeah, yeah, yeah," she said, grinning at me with her head slightly atilt.

I laughed. I looked down the steps at the jade plant set in a small garden of stones between the buildings. The air was hot and muggy, no hint yet of the coming coolness, the season of rains. Suddenly I felt relieved, as if a year-long performance were coming to a close. Was that all it was? A performance? Maybe it was just that I missed Susie. I heard laughter and clapping behind us. Reiko was performing a traditional Japanese song, dancing Buyo. Her hands flipped back and forth, her palms open, her large, barreled body swaying from side to side, up and back, turning in a circle. Even with her bulk, her movements flowed with grace. Beside me, Akiko picked up the song Reiko was singing; the syllables, despite all my efforts, still unintelligible. The melody was sad, wistful, and yet, like Akiko, a little drunk. I could hear beneath it the crickets in the empty lot across the street. I began to clap in time to the song, to hum along. It wasn't rock and roll, but it was easy to keep the beat.

3

It's been three years since I left Japan. Often, as Ricardo remarked in a letter, it feels like a dream kingdom, some Brigadoon that keeps recurring in my mind, fainter and fainter. But I have only to look at the day's headlines to see this is not so. Japan's economic power continues to expand, and those American measures which seem designed to restrain that expansion seem only to underscore its power. When I first came to Japan, the yen was 248 to the dollar; when I left, it was 155; now it is 127. This lowering was supposed to begin balancing the trade deficit between the two countries, but has hardly made a dent.

Across the country, politicians and business people ask, How can we control our future if our businesses and properties are owned by foreigners? There are calls for a level economic playing field, as if a change in trade rules would suddenly solve America's economic problems and hold back the Asians, as if the economic playing field has ever been level. I find myself increasingly angry and frustrated at the rhetoric of the Japan-bashers, their ignorance of history—the way America has used its military power in Latin America, for instance, to maintain control of local industries, to tilt the playing field. I think of the worker in Korea or Taiwan who does the same work for less pay than an American worker, and I do not see this as obvious evidence of how American workers and businesses are cheated; I think instead of how that worker in Korea or Taiwan might also feel cheated.

Japan allowed me to see myself, America, and the world from a perspective that was not white American. I do not feel as bound now by my national identity, do not feel that being an American somehow separates me from the rest of the world. This is not easy to explain to many Americans, especially white Americans. They take their sense of identity for granted, they have no questions about it. As I've uncovered complexities concerning race, feeling at once more clear-headed and more baffled, as I speak of the issue of race and let my emotions show through, I find myself met more and more by blank stares, resentment, even anger.

In Japan, I saw how much I am not reflected in American culture, how much it is not my culture. This made me more aware of how much of the resentment Americans have toward the rising Asian economic powers is based on racism: there's no way the slant eyes could beat us if everyone played fair; there's no way they could ever be better than America, than a nation of whites. American racism is revealed by America's ignorance of how Japanese culture has fit into the Japanese postwar surge, in the inability to distinguish differences within Japanese society, either between particular groups or between individuals. Nor do Americans have much sense of how the Japanese look at them. They seem unable to think of the Japanese as a completely human Other, with all the complexities that Americans grant themselves.

As an American, even after my time in Japan, I share some of these limitations. And yet I also know that when white Americans look at Japanese-Americans today, they still see us through the gauze of stereotypes they possess about the Japanese; we too are still somehow Other.

Because of this position, I find it impossible to share the picture of Japan presented by Lee Iacocca or Richard Gephardt. They fear Japan's success. For me, Japan's changed status became part of its attraction, part of my desire to identify with the Japanese.

I realize that my feelings about my Japanese background would be less positive if I had returned to a less prosperous land of origin. Japan also possesses an incredibly well-preserved and complex indigenous culture. This makes it very different from a country like the Philippines; there the combined colonialism of the Spanish and the Americans has served to obliterate much of the native culture. When I went to the Philippines, there were no equivalents of Noh, Kabuki, Bashō, or Lady Murasaki, no museum filled with scrolls and ink-block prints. What would have resisted or modified the influx of culture from the West had disappeared. Half the television programs were broadcast in English.

All this reinforces a point which those who are conscious of a dual cultural heritage should know well: identity is a political and economic matter, not just a personal matter.

Japan helped me balance a conversation which had been taking place before I was born, a conversation in my grandparents' heads, in my parents' heads, which, by my generation, had become very one-sided, so that the Japanese side was virtually silenced. My stay helped me realize that a balance, which probably never existed in the first place, could no longer be maintained. In the end, I did not speak the language well enough; I did not have enough attraction to the culture. In the end, the society felt to my American psyche too cramped, too well defined, too rule-oriented, too polite, too circumscribed. I could have lived there a few more years if I had had the money and time, but eventually I would have left. I would not have become one of those Americans who find in Japan a surrounding society which nourishes and confirms their own sense of identity. Either I was American or I was one of the homeless, one of the searchers for what John Berger calls a world culture. But I was not Japanese.

In coming to this realization, I gained more sympathy for the position of my parents, the second generation. Part of this came from a deeper understanding of how far they had to travel in their childhood, from the mainly Japanese world of their Issei parents to the America of their schools, the streets of L.A. and Seattle. For Americans unacquainted with Japanese culture, as I had been, it is difficult to comprehend the enormous differences between the two cultures, how their concepts of what constitutes both a human being and a society are so fundamentally unlike.

I came back with a sense of Asia as a continent, of which Japan was just one part, and in that there was another balancing, both politically and culturally. For years, writers on the West Coast have been turning to Asian cultures for sustenance. But I grew up in the Midwest, in Chicago, that inland city beside that inland sea, surrounded by miles and miles of fields and prairie. That was our ocean, and beyond it lay neither Paris nor Beijing but New York and Los Angeles.

Aside from these layers of interpretation, I'm left with a welter of images, the clear outlines of certain moments that possess

an irreducible resonance. There was the first time I saw Ono on the
video in Reiko's office, crammed with papers piled on desks, bookshelves overflowing, the precise opposite of the spareness of traditional Japanese space. What I saw on the screen was also not
traditional, that man in whiteface, wearing a dress, falling on the
floor in slow swoons, as if tripped, as if fainting, as if his nerves did
not quite work right. There was the first time Susie opened the door
to Mrs. Hayashi, who walked into our genkan and announced that
we should have slippers laid out for guests, that our shoes should
not be on the floor but in the cupboard next to the door. There was
that moment in Ono's studio when I exchanged looks with a German woman I did not know and did not get to know; there was the
fire festival with the men in loincloths and headbands carrying
torches the size of tree trunks and shouting *"Sei-rei, sei-yo,"* the
moment when I knew what I had come to Japan for was not an
escape. There were those moments riding the subway, when I
looked up to see all those faces, the young Japanese schoolboys and
girls in their blue uniforms, the women carrying bags from Seibu,
the men in their suits holding up the *Asahi Shimbun,* the still mysterious characters running up and down the pages; moments when I
thought I might actually become part of that country, when I felt
at home in ways I have never felt in America. There was the mud
and crowd and speeches of that day at Narita, the moment when
I looked up and saw the helicopters above the clearing and tiny
puffs of tear gas bursting above us, and I turned to see a line of
marchers carrying poles and Molotov cocktails. There was the first
time I heard the drum cries of the Noh drummers and knew I
would want to hear them over and over; the time I cradled, in
Okinaka's studio, a Noh mask handed down through generations.
There was that moment on a mountain road, near the terraced rice
fields of Banaue, in the Philippines, when my jeepney picked up a
Japanese tourist, and as we talked Japanese, I felt an identification
with him I could never have felt in Japan, an identification which,
in the three years since, has slowly slipped away. There was my trip
to Shingu, the home of my grandparents, and the vision of them
waving outside a temple, underneath a cedar, beside a pop machine
glowing in the dark.

This last image seems tied to two other images, one from

Japan, one from my life. The first is a photo of an old man, in tears, on his knees, rising from a bow, getting set to bow again. He is dressed in a suit, a V-necked sweater, a shirt without a tie. He looks vaguely like my grandfather in the pictures, the same fine silver hair, the long, sad face, not quite stern, but more resigned. Small age spots are noticeable on his cheeks. His hands are thrust halfway out in front of him. The man is praying for and mourning the Emperor Hirohito, who, as I write this, is slowly dying. Hirohito's death will bring the end of the Showa era and is for this man and for all of Japan a symbol of enormous complexity, enormous change. What we see on the man's face is an image of Japan we will not see again. The mourning for Hirohito's son will not be as desperate, as filled with regret, will not be tinged with the same sort of imperial worship, a worship which helped fuel a war that ravaged a continent and killed millions. Such destruction may come again, but the postwar era, with its guilt and enormous growth, has ended. Hirohito's son, the Japan of the eighties and nineties, the product of that growth, are something else.

The next image is not of death but of birth. Each night, in our apartment in St. Paul, before we go to bed, I lay my head on Susie's stomach and feel the kicks of our daughter. Only one pound, she kicks with a sound that has come from nothing, from everything in our past, from my Japanese genes to the genes of my wife, English and Hungarian Jew. Susie remarks that although our daughter lives in her belly, she will look more like me than like her mother, but that, of course, is a matter of viewpoint, a product of cultural sight. Our daughter has made me feel much older than I was in Japan, much more tied to my grandparents, my parents, and to the future. This split I have felt between America and Japan, this fusion of two histories, will reside in her, in a different, more visible way. I would like to think she is part of a movement taking place everywhere throughout the globe, our small planet spinning along in blue-black space. I would like to think that the questions of identity she faces will be easier than mine, less fierce, less filled with self-neglect and rage. That she will love herself more and therefore be more eager for the world, for moving beyond herself. And I know how little control I have over these wishes and their outcome.

What I have is a tiny thump bumping my cheek, a note from the future, and this enormous love for her, for her mother, a love I feared I would not feel. A grandchild, a great-grandchild. Our child. In the darkness, a tiny thump.

Tokyo; St. Paul; Little Marais, Minnesota—October 18, 1988

Acknowledgments

Portions of this book appeared in earlier versions in *The Graywolf Annual V: Multi-Cultural Literacy, Partisan Review, Threepenny Review,* and *The Kyoto Review.* My thanks to the editors of these publications.

I wish to thank the National Endowment for the Arts and the U.S./Japan Friendship Commission for the Creative Artist Exchange Fellowship, which allowed me to travel to Japan. A Bush Foundation Fellowship provided me time to work on this book.

Several people in Japan were very helpful to me, some of whom appear in this book under different names. I am deeply indebted to them for their generosity and hospitality. I also want to thank Rick Emmert, Tatsuro Ishii, Daniel Stein, and Francois Van der Wansem for their companionship and guidance.

I owe considerable thanks to my writing group, who read earlier drafts with care, intelligence, and critical acumen: Sue Halloran, Jill Breckenridge, Julie Landsman, Ellen Hawley, Shannon King, and Bart Schneider. Wes Uemura was extremely helpful in checking both the Japanese and various facts, and he has provided me with much useful information. James Fenton and Susan Mitchell also provided valuable readings. Jay White, Jim Moore, Deborah Keenan, Mary Rockcastle, Patricia Weaver Francisco, and Sheila Murphy gave me useful literary advice, as well as moral support.

My Aunt Ruth and Aunt Baye deserve special mention for the stories they provided me and for the example of their lives.

I want to thank Amanda Urban, my agent, for helping to make this book possible. My editor, Anne Rumsey, was all I could ask for and more. The book has improved greatly under her guidance, and I feel enormously lucky and grateful for her help.

Finally, I wish to thank my wife, Susan Sencer, for the innumerable ways she's added to my life, in particular for the reading of countless drafts and for giving birth to our daughter, Samantha, whose presence ends this book.